CW00832075

DETAIL Practice

Insulating Materials

Principles
Materials
Applications

Margit Pfundstein
Roland Gellert
Martin H. Spitzner
Alexander Rudolphi

Birkhäuser
Edition Detail

Authors:
Margit Pfundstein, Dipl.-Ing. (FH)
Roland Gellert, Dr. rer. nat.
Martin H. Spitzner, Dr.-Ing.
Christoph Sprengard
Wolfgang Albrecht
Alexander Rudolphi, Prof.-Ing.

Project manager:
Nicola Kollmann, Dipl.-Ing. (FH)

Editor:
Christina Schulz, Dipl.-Ing. architect

Drawings:
Nicola Kollmann, Daniel Hajduk

Translators (German/English):
Gerd H. Söffker, Philip Thrift, Hannover

An Edition DETAIL book

ISBN: 978-3-7643-8654-2
Printed on acid-free paper made from cellulose bleached without the use of chlorine.

Typesetting & production:
Peter Gensmantel, Cornelia Kohn, Andrea Linke, Roswitha Siegler, Simone Soesters
Printed by:
Aumüller Druck, Regensburg
1st edition, 2008

This book is also available in a German language edition (ISBN 978-3-920034-18-8).

A CIP catalogue record for this book is available from the Library of Congress, Washington D.C., USA.

Bibliographic information published by
Die Deutsche Bibliothek
Die Deutsche Bibliothek lists this publication in the Deutsche Nationalbibliographie; detailed
bibliographic data is available on the internet at http://dnb.ddb.de.

Institut für internationale
Architektur-Dokumentation GmbH & Co. KG
Sonnenstraße 17, D-80331 München
Telefon: +49/89/38 16 20-0
Telefax: +49/89/39 86 70
www.detail.de

Distribution Partner:
Birkhäuser – Publishers for Architecture
PO Box 133, 4010 Basel, Switzerland
Tel.: +41 61 2050707
Fax: +41 61 2050792
e-mail: sales@birkhauser.ch
www.birkhauser.ch

DETAIL Practice
Insulating Materials

Margit Pfundstein
Roland Gellert
Martin H. Spitzner
Alexander Rudolphi

Contents

Introduction

Margit Pfundstein

Insulating materials play a major role in energy-efficient building measures. Thanks to their heat-insulating effect, they save heating and cooling energy and hence contribute to reducing carbon dioxide emissions.

The importance of insulating materials has continued to grow in recent decades, and, subsequently, the range of insulating materials on offer with their different applications and properties profiles.

Accordingly, many questions arise when insulating materials are to be used in buildings: Which standards apply? Are there special requirements for installation or use? Which raw materials do they contain? How are the insulating materials produced and what are their characteristic properties? What should be done with waste and offcuts?

This book attempts to answer these questions with a systematic presentation so that suitable insulating materials can be selected to suit the respective requirements.
The varying selection criteria result from the applications themselves, but also from the multitude of different properties of the insulating materials, specific to particular products or particular applications. This book reviews conventional and also less conventional insulating materials for buildings plus new developments. As a direct price comparison has only limited validity owing to the different processing and installation costs plus the constructional boundary conditions, and prices are subject to local and market economics fluctuations anyway, this book does not attempt to deal with this issue.

Depending on raw materials and methods of production, the insulating materials exhibit characteristic properties that in some cases are not relevant for other materials, which means that a direct comparison is impossible in many instances. Nevertheless, in order to guarantee a defined quality for users and to comply with construction legislation, thermal insulation materials for buildings are covered by standards or national technical approvals. The construction legislation aspects regarding the Construction Products List, insulating materials standards, approvals, etc. are explained in a separate chapter.

This book also describes the requirements placed on insulating materials resulting from the various applications, and takes into account special cases such as thermal bridges, summertime thermal performance and applications in other climate zones.

Apart from the functional issues, the use of thermal insulation and the choice of the respective insulating material is affected by ecological aspects. Questions regarding the consumption of resources, the energy content, the availability and the environmental compatibility during the production, use and disposal of insulating materials are discussed in the final chapter.

The appendix contains references to associations, institutes, manufacturers and suggestions for further reading plus an index to help readers access the information in this book quickly.

Properties of insulating materials

Margit Pfundstein

A low thermal conductivity is without doubt the most important property of any thermal insulating material. However, additional criteria such as compressive strength or reaction to fire can also be critical when choosing an insulating material, depending on the particular application.
The insulating materials available these days cover almost all requirements in the most diverse areas. But there is no insulating material that fulfils all – including ecological – requirements perfectly, even among the more expensive products. As a rule, certain criteria, e.g. high compressive strength and good impact sound insulation properties, or low diffusion resistance and moisture resistance, cancel each other out.

The following sections provide an overview of the most important characteristic properties of insulating materials, their definitions and the associated data of relevant insulating materials in a number of tables. Besides density, any assessment of an insulating material must consider the material's behaviour when exposed to heat, water and moisture, the mechanical and acoustic properties, and its reaction to fire. The ecological aspects of insulating materials are dealt with in a separate chapter (pp. 93–105).

Density
Density is defined as the quotient of the mass of a material and the volume occupied by that mass, and is measured in kg/m^3.
The density is critical for the thermal performance properties of an insulating material. A low density generally also implies a high porosity or a high volume of voids, which leads to a decrease in the thermal conductivity, i.e. to a better thermal insulating effect for that material.
The density of thermal insulating materials is measured according to DIN EN 1602.

Thermal conductivity
The capacity to conduct heat is a material-specific property of all substances, irrespective of whether they are in solid, liquid or gas form. The thermal conductivity is the capacity of a substance to transport thermal energy.
Insulating materials are supposed to conduct heat badly in order to prevent large heat losses. The lower the heat conduction in a material, the less heat flows through it. Thermal conductivity λ is therefore an important factor.
The thermal conductivity is measured specifically for a material in W/mK, a unit which specifies the quantity of heat passing through a 1 x 1 x 1 m cube of material for a temperature difference of 1 K between one side and the other.

According to the definition in DIN 4108 "Thermal insulation and energy economy in buildings", materials with a thermal conductivity $\leq$ 0.10 W/mK may be classed as thermal insulating materials. Most insulating materials have thermal conductivities in the range 0.030 to 0.050 W/mK, and such values can be regarded as good. Materials with thermal conductivities $<$ 0.030 W/mK can be regarded as very good, whereas values around 0.060 W/mK are only moderate, and values $>$ 0.070 W/mK are relatively high.
The heat conduction of an insulating material is heavily influenced by the following factors:
- raw material used
- density of insulating material
- nature and microstructure of solid component
- moisture content and temperature of insulating material
- cell gases

Density (values of customary products, tested to DIN EN 1602)

Thermal insulating material	Density [kg/m^3]
Aerogel	60–80
Cotton	20–60
Pumice	150–230
Foamed glass	150–230
Expanded perlite (EPB)	90–490
Expanded clay	260–500
Flax	20–80
Cereal granulate	105–115
Hemp	20–68
Urea-formaldehyde resin in situ foam (UF)	10
Wood fibres (WF)	30–270
Wood-wool boards (WW)	350–600
Calcium silicate foam	115–300
Coconut fibres	70–120
Ceramic fibres, ceramic foams	120–560
Insulation cork board (ICB)	100–220
Melamine foam (MF)	8–11
Mineral wool (MW)	20–200
Phenolic foam (PF)	40
Polyester fibres	15–20
Polyethylene foam (PE)	50–110
Polystyrene, expanded (EPS)	15–30
Polystyrene foam, extruded (XPS)	25–45
Polyurethane rigid foam (PUR)	30–100
Pyrogenic silicic acid	300
Sheep's wool	25–30
Cellular glass (CG)	115–220
Reeds	120–225
Sea grass	75
Vacuum insulation panel (VIP)	150–300
Exfoliated vermiculite (EV), expanded mica	70–160
Insulating clay bricks	500–750
Cellulose fibres	30–80

1

Thermal conductivity (typical nominal values)

Thermal insulating material	**Thermal conductivity λ [W/(mK)]**	**Standard or approval**
Aerogel	0.017–0.021	individual approval
Cotton	0.040	according to approval
Pumice	0.060–0.080	according to approval
Foamed glass	0.070–0.093	according to approval
Expanded perlite (EPB)	0.045–0.070	DIN EN 13169
Expanded clay	0.085–0.10	according to approval
Flax	0.037–0.045	according to approval
Cereal granulate	0.050	according to approval
Gypsum foam	0.045	according to approval
Hemp	0.040–0.050	according to approval
Urea-formaldehyde resin in situ foam (UF)	0.035–0.040	DIN 18159
Wood fibres (WF)	0.040–0.090	DIN EN 13171
Wood-wool boards (WW)	0.090	DIN EN 13168
Calcium silicate foam	0.045–0.065	according to approval
Ceramic fibres, ceramic foams	0.030–0.070	according to approval
Coconut fibres	0.040–0.050	according to approval
Insulation cork board (ICB)	0.045–0.060	DIN EN 13170
Melamine foam (MF)	0.035	approval not applied for
Mineral wool (MW)	0.035–0.045	DIN EN 13162
Phenolic foam (PF)	0.022–0.040	DIN EN 13166
Polyester fibres	0.035–0.045	according to approval
Polyethylene foam (PE)	0.033	according to approval
Polystyrene, expanded (EPS)	0.035–0.040	DIN EN 13163
Polystyrene foam, extruded (XPS)	0.030–0.040	DIN EN 13164
Polyurethane rigid foam (PUR)	0,024–0,030	DIN EN 13165
Pyrogenic silicic acid	0,021	–
Sheep's wool	0.040–0.045	according to approval
Cellular glass (CG)	0.040–0.060	DIN EN 13167
Reeds	0.055–0.090	according to approval
Sea grass	0.043–0.050	according to approval
Straw bales	0.038–0.072	according to approval
Vacuum insulation panel	0.002–0.008	individual approval
Exfoliated vermiculite (EV), expanded mica	0.046–0.070	according to approval
Insulating clay bricks	0.080–0.140	according to approval
Cellulose fibres	0.040–0.045	according to approval

2

Several methods can be used to measure the thermal conductivity which take into account the specific material properties. Thermal insulating materials covered by standards are usually tested according to DIN EN 12664, 12667 and 12939, and those materials not covered by standards are tested according to DIN 52612.

In fibrous insulating materials, the fineness of the fibres and their orientation play a major role. In foam insulating materials, on the other hand, the thermal conductivity is determined by the fineness and distribution of the cells and particularly by the gases in those cells, also possibly by any blowing agent trapped in the cells. And in insulating materials made from wood fibres or wood wool, it tends to be the density that is critical for the insulating capacity.

Generally, the most favourable densities are in the range between 20 and 100 kg/m^3. At lower densities the heat transmitted by radiation increases, and at higher densities the heat transmitted by conduction increases.
Furthermore, the moisture content of an insulating material affects its conductivity. The thermal conductivity of fibrous insulating materials rises more steeply than that for closed-cell foam materials for the same increase in moisture content.

As the thermal conductivity of a material or product is subjected to certain fluctuations depending on the quality of the raw materials and the methods of manufacture, values must be measured and checked continually.
In order to give designers some degree of assurance when calculating the thermal performance of a building, standards and building legislation stipulations have therefore been introduced that specify the "thermal conductivity design value"

1 Constituents of cellulose fibres

(see also p. 69). It is these values that should be used when carrying out analyses according to Germany's Energy Conservation Act (EnEV).

Thermal resistance, total thermal resistance, thermal transmittance
The thermal resistance, total thermal resistance and thermal transmittance are not values specific to a material, but instead variables for determining the thermal performance parameters for building components. For the sake of completeness, however, they will be explained here with the other material properties. To calculate the thermal resistance R, the specific thermal conductivity λ of a building material is placed in relation to its thickness d:

$$R = d/\lambda \ [m^2K/W]$$

The higher the thermal resistance of a building component, the greater is its heat-insulating effect.

By adding up the thermal resistances of all the building component layers, including the surface resistances between the air and the component surfaces internally (R_{si}) and externally (R_{se}), we can calculate the total thermal resistance R_T:

$$R_T = \lambda \, (d_n/\lambda_n) + R_{si} + R_{se} \ [m^2K/W]$$

The total thermal resistance specifies the component's resistance to the flow of heat taking into account all the different layers in that component.

The thermal transmittance, known as the U-value, is the reciprocal of the total thermal resistance:

$$U = 1/R_T \ [W/m^2K]$$

This value specifies the quantity of heat exchanged per second between a surface of 1 m^2 and the surrounding air during constant heating with a temperature difference of 1 K between the surface and the air.

Specific heat capacity
The specific heat capacity c describes the specific ability of a material to absorb heat depending on its mass.
It specifies the quantity of heat Q required to raise the temperature of the mass m of a substance by 1 K (temperature difference ΔT).

$$c = Q/(m\Delta T) \ [J/kgK]$$

The specific heat capacity of an insulating material is measured using a special technique known as calorimetry. Just how much heat can be stored depends very much on the microstructure and density of the material. Heavy components take longer to heat up, and if their specific heat capacity is higher, such materials can store more heat.

Although the specific heat capacity of thermal insulating materials is not so significant, in summer, good values can have a positive effect on the interior climate in lightweight structures (which includes the majority of roof spaces) (see also pp. 90–91)

Temperature stability
In practice, resistance to extreme temperatures is primarily relevant for insulating materials where they come into contact with hot bitumen or other hot adhesives, or when they are used to insulate hot vessels and pipes. In the case of plant and systems, the lower limiting value can be important.

Furthermore, the duration of the thermal effect is often critical for the temperature stability. Many insulating materials can withstand brief temperature excursions beyond their specified temperature limits. But if extreme temperatures continue for longer periods or indeed are a permanent feature, then dimensional changes plus loss of form and strength, even thermal decomposition, may be the result.

Specific heat capacity (to DIN EN 12524)

Thermal insulating material	**Specific heat capacity c [J/(kgK)]**
Cotton	840–1300
Pumice	1000
Foamed glass	800–1000
Expanded perlite (EPB)	1000
Expanded clay	1100
Flax	1300–1640
Cereal granulate	1950
Gypsum foam	1000
Hemp	1500–2200
Urea-formaldehyde resin in situ foam (UF)	1500
Wood fibres (WF)	1600–2100
Wood-wool boards (WW)	2100
Calcium silicate foam	1000
Ceramic fibres, ceramic foams	1040
Coconut fibres	1300–1600
Insulation cork board (ICB)	1700–2100
Mineral wool (MW)	[illegible]–1000
Polystyrene, expanded (EPS)	1500
Polystyrene foam, extruded (XPS)	1300–1700
Polyurethane rigid foam (PUR)	1400–1500
Sheep's wool	960–1300
Cellular glass (CG)	800–1100
Reeds	1200
Exfoliated vermiculite (EV), expanded mica	800–1000
Cellulose fibres	1700–2150

2

Most manufacturers therefore specify maximum values for their products in use (maximum service temperature). Insulating materials can react very differently to heat or cold and there is no uniform test method that enables a direct comparison between all insulating materials. Easiest to compare are the strength properties of the materials according to the test criteria for dimensional stability.

Maximum service temperatures (based on manufacturers' information)

Thermal insulating material	Maximum service temperature, short-term [°C]	Maximum service temperature, long-ter [°C]
Cotton	< 400	100
Foamed glass	no details	600–700
Expanded perlite (EPB)	250	110–800
Hemp	120	100
Urea-formaldehyde resin in situ foam (UF)	no details	110
Wood fibres (WF)	no details	110
Wood-wool boards (WW)	180	110
Insulation cork board (ICB), not bitumenised	180–200	110–120
Mineral wool (MW) with binder Glass wool without binder Rock wool without binder	250 600 1000	100–200 500 600–750
Phenolic foam (PF)	250	150
Polyester fibres	no details	100
Polyethylene foam (PE)	no details	-40 to +105
Polystyrene, expanded (EPS)	100	80–85
Polystyrene foam, extruded (XPS)	100	75
Polyurethane rigid foam (PUR)	250	-30 bis +120
Pyrogenic silicic acid	no details	950–1050
Sheep's wool	500	130–150
Cellular glass (CG)	750	-260 to +430
Exfoliated vermiculite (EV), expanded mica	no details	700–1600
3 Cellulose fibres	no details	60

Dimensional stability and temperature-induced changes in length
In order to guarantee the dimensional stability of insulating materials under defined temperature and moisture conditions, or defined compression and thermal loads, the product standards specify minimum requirements for dimensional stability. In this respect, the standards distinguish between reversible and irreversible changes.

All materials undergo material-specific dimensional changes due to temperature fluctuations caused by the changing seasons or the circumstances of their application. These dimensional changes are mostly reversible. The dimensions of plastic foam alter to a markedly greater extent than those of fibrous and other inorganic insulating materials. In the case of large-format insulating elements, possible stresses caused by thermal movements should be considered at the design stage. The behaviour of the material is expressed by its coefficient of thermal expansion measured in K^{-1}, which describes the change in length in millimetres per metre length of the material for a temperature change of 1 K (see tab. 1, p. 12). Irreversible changes in the form of shrinkage or contraction can be caused by excessive temperatures or even chemical effects. Rigid foams in particular are stored after manufacture until they reach a constant size because the gas exchange in the cells can lead to changes in length. Such processes must be complete before the boards are released onto the market.

Constant compressive loads can also lead to irreversible changes in the form of deformation or settlement. This subject is dealt with in detail in the section on compressive strength.

"Breathability"
Readers who expect an evaluation-relevant statement on the "breathability" of insulating materials at this point will be disappointed!
The breathability of building materials is not a measurable physical variable. Max von Pettenkofer's erroneous assumption has persisted since 1865. As part of his investigations into hygiene in rooms by measuring the air change rate, he

assumed that a considerable part of the air exchange necessary for hygienic conditions took place through the walls. This work later led to the term "breathing wall" being used. But building materials do not "breathe"! Indeed, considering the efforts taken these days to create sealed building envelopes in order to save energy, such a property is highly undesirable. The "breathing" idea either developed out of the unfounded fear of being "encapsulated" or the desire for hygroscopic building materials that can regulate moisture fluctuations in interiors.
Both of these ideas are unfounded because the air change rate required for hygienic conditions can only be achieved through targeted ventilation measures, and the humidity of the interior air can be regulated to a limited extent only by the interior surfaces. In this respect, loam has good properties when compared to concrete, for example, but it is still only the topmost millimetres of a layer that are involved in absorbing moisture from the air. Insulating materials do not usually participate in this process at all because they are covered by other layers. Indeed, an uncontrolled increase in moisture in an insulating material would be undesirable because of the other consequences such as an increase in the thermal conductivity and even the risk of mould growth. Advertisements for insulating products that refer to "breathing" properties are therefore not to be taken seriously!

Water vapour diffusion resistance
There is always a certain amount of water vapour in the air and also in building components. The water vapour molecules are constantly striving to distribute themselves uniformly in all directions. Building materials present a certain resistance to this distribution which depends on their microstructure.
To measure this resistance, we compare the vapour-tightness of a 1 m thick layer of air with a 1 m thick layer of material, which results in the dimensionless resistance factor μ:

$$\mu = \frac{\text{vapour-tightness of material } (d = 1\text{ m})}{\text{vapour-tightness of air } (d = 1\text{ m})}$$

The water vapour diffusion resistance index μ is used to calculate the diffusion behaviour of building components. Upper and lower values are listed for many insulating materials, which can be governed by the method of manufacture or the cell structure. The less favourable value for the application is always used in calculations.

Normally, fibrous insulating materials present very little resistance to diffusion, having an only marginally different diffusion resistance to that of air. Rigid foam products present a higher resistance to water vapour which, however, is irrelevant in customary forms of construction. Cellular glass is unique among insulating materials in that it has a μ-value of "infinite", and is therefore regarded as vapour-tight.

Water absorption
In principle, any type of water or moisture absorption is undesirable for any type of insulating material. As the thermal conductivity of water is about 20 times greater than that of stationary air, the absorption of water is always connected with an increase in the thermal conductivity. Water can infiltrate insulating materials in diverse ways. Possible causes apart from design and construction errors are construction moisture and the saturation of the insulating materials during storage, transport or installation.
Most insulating materials are not hygroscopic, i.e. they do not absorb moisture from the air, or they are given a water-repellent treatment during manufacture,

Coefficient of thermal expansion

Thermal insulating material	Coefficient of thermal expansion [K^{-1}]
Polystyrene, expanded (EPS)	5×10^{-5} to 7×10^{-5}
Polystyrene foam, extruded (XPS)	6×10^{-5} to 8×10^{-5}
Polyurethane rigid foam (PUR)	5×10^{-5} to 8×10^{-5}

1

Water vapour diffusion resistance index
(to DIN EN 12086)

Thermal insulating material	Water vapour diff. resistance index μ [–]
Cotton	1–2
Pumice	4
Foamed glass	1–5
Expanded perlite (EPB)	3–5
Expanded clay	2–8
Flax	1–2
Cereal granulate	3
Gypsum foam	4–8
Hemp	1–2
Urea-formaldehyde resin in situ foam (UF)	1–3
Wood fibres (WF)	5–10
Wood-wool boards (WW)	2–5
Calcium silicate foam	3–20
Coconut fibres	1–2
Insulation cork board (ICB)	5–10
Mineral wool (MW)	1–2
Phenolic foam (PF)	60
Polyester fibres	1–2
Polyethylene foam (PE)	7000
Polystyrene, expanded (EPS)	20–100
Polystyrene foam, extruded (XPS)	80–200
Polyurethane rigid foam (PUR)	30–200
Sheep's wool	1–5
Cellular glass (CG)	∞
Reeds	2–5
Vacuum insulation panel (VIP)	∞
Exfoliated vermiculite (EV), expanded mica	3–4
Insulating clay bricks	5–10
Cellulose fibres	1–2

2

Long-term water absorption (to DIN EN 12087)

Thermal insulating material	Long-term water absorption [% by vol.] unless stated otherwise
Cotton	12–13 kg/m²
Foamed glass	15
Hemp	4.2 kg/m²
Mineral wool (MW)	3 kg/m²
Polystyrene, expanded (EPS)	1–5
Polystyrene foam, extruded (XPS)	0.1–0.3
Polyurethane rigid foam (PUR)	1.5–3
Cellular glass (CG)	0
Exfoliated vermiculite (EV), expanded mica	≤ 5

3

Tensile strength (to DIN EN 1607)

Thermal insulating material	Tensile strength perpendicular to plane of board [kPa]
Wood fibres (WF)	2.5–50
Wood-wool boards (WW)	2.5–50
Insulation cork board (ICB)	30–50
Mineral wool (MW)	3.5–80
Phenolic foam (PF)	60
Polystyrene, expanded (EPS)	> 100
Polystyrene foam, extruded (XPS)	> 200
Polyurethane rigid foam (PUR)	40

4

so they can withstand a certain moisture load without damage. Apart from that, they generally do not support capillary action, i.e. they do not suck up or transport water. Nevertheless, it is generally advisable to avoid installing damp insulating materials because they are frequently combined with vapour check or vapour barrier layers that prevent the insulation from drying out.

Once installed, insulating materials can still be saturated by diffusion and condensation processes. If water vapour diffuses from inside to outside through the insulating material due to pressure differences, it can cool so significantly upon contact with the cold external building components that the water vapour saturation point is reached and condensation forms. Regular or frequent repetitions of this condensation process can lead to the insulating material becoming completely saturated. This also applies to insulating materials used in extremely damp environments such as upside-down roofs and in the presence of hydrostatic pressure. However, arranging the layers of the construction correctly according to building physics requirements will reliably prevent moisture absorption through diffusion and condensation.

There are defined maximum values for the majority of insulating materials which should not be exceeded in short- or long-term water absorption tests. These tests are either described in the product standards or in the national technical approvals (see also pp. 66–69).

Compressive stress, compressive strength
Generally speaking, the compressive strength of an insulating material is mainly determined by its density. In fibrous insulating materials the fineness of the fibres and their orientation is also critical. The compressive stress is defined as the stress at which an insulating material is compressed by 10% across its thickness. The compressive strength is defined as the maximum stress at which failure of the material occurs, i.e. when the sample begins to break. The lower value governs. Both values are measured in a rapid short-term test and are principally required for quality control purposes or for comparing with other products. They are in no way suitable for calculating loadbearing insulating forms of construction subjected to permanent loads.

Constant compressive stress
For those insulating materials used in applications in which they are subjected to compression, the long-term creep behaviour under permanent load is critical. Examples of such applications are industrial floors, trafficked roofs (rooftop terraces, green roofs, parking decks) and load-carrying insulation below ground floor slabs. High temperatures can reduce the load-carrying capacity of an insulating material. The insulating material standards prescribe tests for determining the behaviour under compression and thermal loads (see also pp. 66–69).

Tensile strength
For those insulating materials subjected to loads perpendicular to the plane of the board (e.g. wind suction in a thermal insulation composite system), it must be ensured that no delamination occurs within the layer of insulation. Tests are carried out according to DIN EN 1607 "Thermal insulating products for building applications – Determination of tensile strength perpendicular to faces".

Compressive stress or compressive strength, constant compressive stress
(behaviour for compressive loads to DIN EN 826,
behaviour under constant compressive stress to DIN EN 1606)

Thermal insulating material	Compressive stress at 10% deformation or compressive strength for## [kPa]	Constant compressive stress [kPa]
Foamed glass	120–140/500[1]	160[1]
Expanded perlite (EPB)	150–300	100
Wood fibres (WF)	40–200	–
Wood-wool boards (WW)	150–200	–
Insulation cork board (ICB)	100–200	–
Melamine foam (MF)	4–20	–
Mineral wool (MW)	15–80	–
Phenolic foam (PF)	120	–
Polystyrene, expanded (EPS)	60–200	20–60[2]
Polystyrene foam, extruded (XPS)	150–700	50–250
Polyurethane rigid foam (PUR)	100–500	20–30
Cellular glass (CG) (works standard)	500–1700	160–380
Vacuum insulation panel (VIP)	45–120	–
Exfoliated vermiculite (EV), expanded mica (boards)	100–450	–
Cellulose fibres (boards)	2.5	–

[1] for particle size 10/50 mm, beneath load-carrying backing boards
5 [2] special products

1 Hemp plant
2 Caulking hemp made from hemp fibres prepared exclusively by mechanical means

1

2

For example, EPS insulating materials used in a thermal insulation composite system must exhibit a tensile strength of at least 100 kPa.

Bending strength
The bending strength is an especially relevant criterion for wood-wool and wood-wool composite boards when these boards are installed without a backing material, i.e. span freely between supports, e.g. as a direct covering to timber stud construction to form a background for plaster/render, or to bridge the clear distances between the top flanges of steel beams.

The bending strength is determined according to DIN EN 12089 "Thermal insulating products for building applications – Determination of bending behaviour".

Dynamic stiffness
Airborne and structure-borne sound (in particular impact sound) place acoustic requirements on insulating materials. As with thermal insulation, the sound insulation of an insulating material depends on its cellular or fibrous microstructure. Soft, resilient materials are generally better suited to sound insulation than rigid, hard materials. There are two important parameters for evaluating the acoustic properties of insulating materials: dynamic stiffness and sound impedance per unit length.

The dynamic stiffness s´ is the most important material property for assessing impact sound insulating materials. It designates the resilience of an insulation layer. The lower the dynamic stiffness, the better is the impact sound insulation. Dynamic stiffness is determined according to DIN EN 29052 by measuring the resonant frequency of an assembly consisting of test samples of the insulating material and a known mass. Above this resonant frequency, the floor finishes attenuate the impact sound. DIN 4108-10 contains minimum dynamic stiffness values for standard insulating materials. The values are divided into stiffness steps between 5 and 90 MN/m³ for classification purposes.

In addition to insulation relevance for impact sound, the dynamic stiffness is an important parameter for wall linings plus separating and party walls where sound insulation requirements must be satisfied.

Sound impedance per unit length
Insulating materials that are used to improve the acoustics should, in principle, minimise the propagation of the sound. To evaluate insulating materials used for this purpose in acoustic ceiling systems, the sound impedance per unit length r is a critical parameter. According to DIN EN 29053, it is calculated from the sound impedance related to the material thickness and is specified in Ns/m⁴ or kPas/m². Here again, the value should be as low as possible in order that incident sound waves are essentially absorbed and no longer reflected.

Reaction to fire
With respect to fire protection, the German Building Regulations prescribe in the Model Building Code that "building constructions should be arranged and equipped such that the outbreak of a fire and the spread of flames and smoke are prevented in order to avoid risks to the lives and health of persons and animals, and that in the event of a fire, effective extinguishing operations plus the rescue of persons and animals are possible". This results in certain requirements for insulating materials concerning fire development and fire propagation plus the formation of smoke and flaming droplets/particles.

In order to classify the behaviour of insulating materials in fire, DIN 4102 "Fire behaviour of building materials and elements" contains standard provisions for determining building materials classes. Alongside this there is now DIN EN 13501 "Fire classification of construction products and building elements", which is based on the harmonised European standard. This latter standard defines seven "Euroclasses" (A1, A2, B, C, D, E, F) plus additional fire behaviour criteria regarding smoke development (s1 to s3)

Dynamic stiffness and sound impedance per unit length
(dynamic stiffness to DIN EN 29052, sound impedance per unit length to DIN EN 29053)

Thermal insulating material	Dynamic stiffness s´ [MN/m³]	Sound impedance per unit length r [kPas/m²]
Flax	no details	> 2
Hemp	no details	> 6
Wood fibres (WF)	4–8	9–100
Wood-wool boards (WW)	4–8	9–100
Melamine foam (MF)	no details	8–20
Mineral wool (MW)		
Glass wool	no details	> 5
Rock wool	7–35	6–43
Polystyrene, expanded (EPS)	10–40	k.A.
Cellulose fibres		
(boards)	3–7	43–76
(flakes)	no details	3,6–20

3

and the formation of flaming droplets/particles (d0 to d2).
As DIN EN 13501 does not yet include complete information about testing for classes A2 to D, for the time being national technical approvals that refer to DIN 4102-1 are permitted for the insulating materials of these Euroclasses.
Both classification systems may be used. To obtain a CE marking according to the harmonised European standards, however, the Euroclass must be specified, but the manufacturer can specify the DIN 4102 building materials class as well. This means that there are frequently references to existing application approvals that still contain details of the DIN 4102 classes (see also pp. 64, 70 and 102). Insulating materials requiring approvals for which there is no standard are usually labelled according to DIN 4102.

Apart from the statutory requirements, users are generally faced with the question of which hazardous substances might possibly be released from insulating materials in the event of a fire. Toxic gases such as carbon monoxide, hydrogen sulphide and PAHs (polycyclic aromatic hydrocarbons), dioxins, furans, benzpyrene or other specific substances can certainly ensue upon combustion or charring. In addition, the boron salts used as flame retardants can be washed out during extinguishing operations and contaminate the surrounding soil (see also p. 103). The quantities and concentrations of hazardous substances released during a fire depends on the particular fire situation and cannot be described in general terms.

Reaction to fire (Euroclasses to DIN EN 13501, building materials classes to DIN 4102)

Thermal insulating material	Euroclass	Bldg. materials class
Cotton	–	B1, B2
Pumice	–	A1
Foamed glass	–	A1
Expanded perlite (EPB)	C-s1, d0 to D-s1, d0	B2
Expanded clay	–	A1
Flax	B-s2, d0 to C-s2, d0	B2
Cereal granulate	–	B2
Gypsum foam	–	B2
Hemp	E	B2
Urea-formaldehyde resin in situ foam (UF)	–	B1, B2
Wood fibres (WF)	E	B1, B2
Wood-wool boards (WW)	B-s1, d0	B1
Calcium silicate foam	–	A1, A2
Coconut fibres	–	B2
Ceramic fibres, ceramic foams	–	A1
Insulation cork board (ICB)	–	B2
Melamine foam (MF)	–	B1
Mineral wool (MW)		
Glass wool	A1, A2	A2
Rock wool	A1	A1
Phenolic foam (PF)	C-s1, d0	B2
Polyester fibres	–	B1
Polystyrene, expanded (EPS)	E	B1
Polystyrene foam, extruded (XPS)	E	B1
Polyurethane rigid foam (PUR)	B-s2, d0 to C-s3, d0	B1, B2
Pyrogenic silicic acid	–	A1
Sheep's wool	E	B2
Cellular glass (CG)	A1	A1
Reeds	–	B2
Sea grass	–	B2
Exfoliated vermiculite (EV), expanded mica	–	A1, B1
Cellulose fibres	E	B1, B2

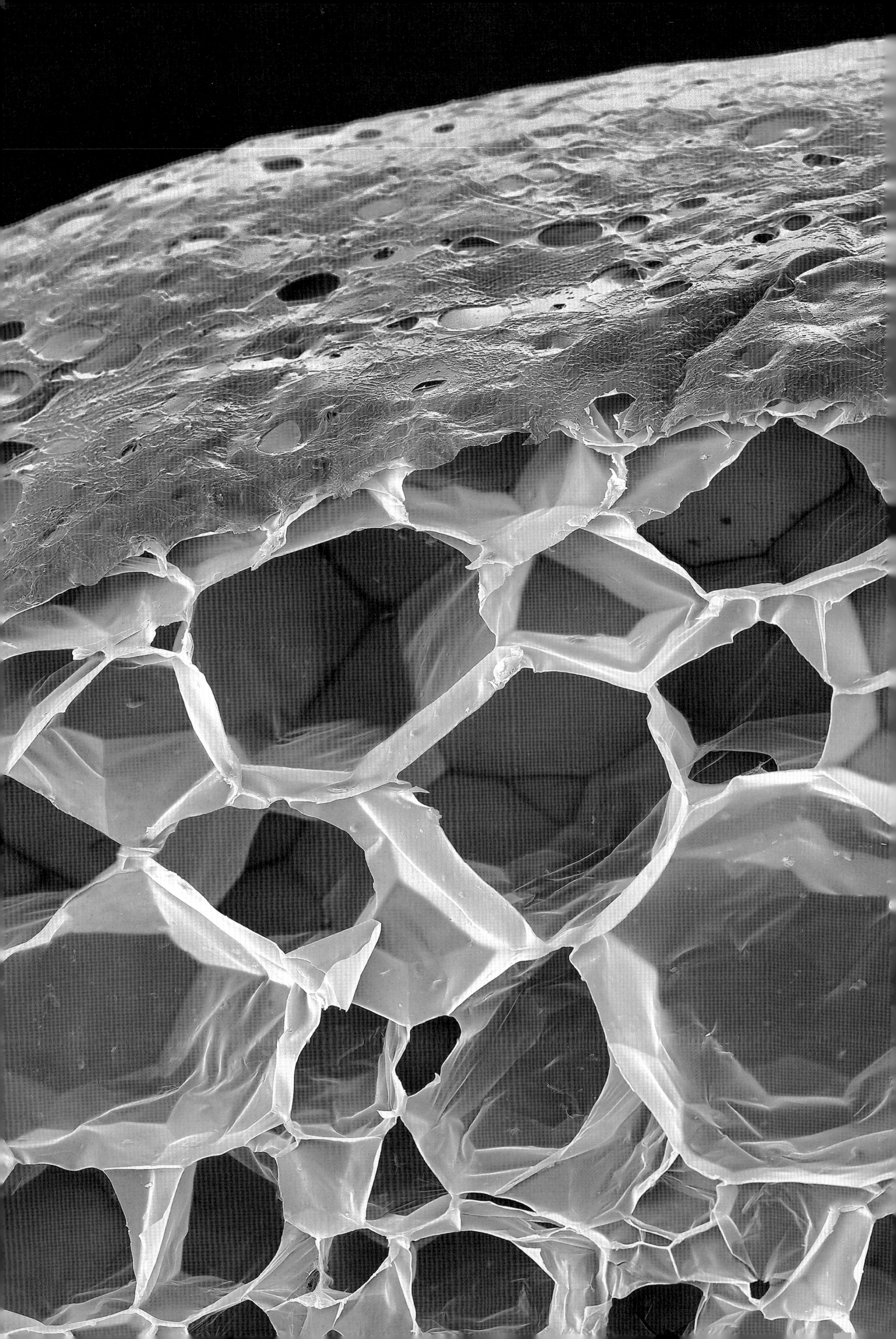

Types of insulating material

Margit Pfundstein

Classification

The classification of thermal insulating materials is carried out according to their raw materials. In doing so we distinguish between an inorganic (mineral) and organic origin for the raw material. The insulating materials within these two main groups are further subdivided into natural and synthetic materials depending on the further processing of the original raw materials. In the so-called natural products, the raw material remains essentially unchanged. However, if the mineralogical composition of the original raw material is changed due to some specific form of processing, i.e. produced commercially or assembled, we usually speak of synthetic materials.

Some of the natural insulating materials contain relatively large amounts of additives such as fire-retardant salts, impregnating substances, strengthening fibres or binders that are not natural materials. In order that such materials can still be designated "natural", the additives should not constitute more than 25% of the material (based on studies by Dr. Margit Fuehres[1]).

The overview of insulating materials on the right adheres to the above classification. The order within the groups is based on the current significance of the respective material for the market. Particularly rare insulating materials or those no longer commonly used are listed in italics. Outside this classification there are four developments that apart from nanocellular foams cannot be classified on the basis of their raw materials. These developments involve not building materials, but rather prefabricated components or systems tailored to specific functions. All the insulating materials listed here are described individually on the following pages.

Inorganic insulating materials

Synthetic	Glass wool	p. 21
	Rock wool	p. 21
	Cellular glass	p. 24
	Foamed glass	p. 26
	Calcium silicate foam	p. 27
	Ceramic fibres, ceramic foam	p. 28
	Aerogel	p. 28
	Pyrogenic silicic acid	p. 29
	Slag wool	p. 29
	Gypsum foam	p. 29
Natural	Expanded perlite	p. 30
	Exfoliated vermiculite	p. 31
	Expanded mica	p. 31
	Expanded clay	p. 32
	Pumice	p. 33
	Insulating clay bricks	p. 33

Organic insulating materials

Synthetic	Polystyrene, expanded	p. 34
	Polystyrene foam, extruded	p. 36
	Polyurethane rigid foam	p. 38
	Polyurethane in situ foam	p. 40
	Phenolic foam	p. 41
	Melamine foam	p. 42
	Polyethylene foam	p. 42
	Urea-formaldehyde resin in situ foam	p. 43
	Polyester fibres	p. 43
Natural	Wood wool	p. 44
	Wood fibres	p. 45
	Insulation cork board	p. 46
	Cellulose fibres	p. 47
	Hemp	p. 48
	Sheep's wool	p. 49
	Cotton	p. 50
	Flax	p. 50
	Cereal granulate	p. 51
	Reeds	p. 52
	Coconut fibres	p. 52
	Sea grass	p. 53
	Wood chippings	p. 53
	Giant Chinese silver grass	p. 54
	Peat	p. 54
	Straw bales	p. 54

New developments

Transparent thermal insulation	p. 55
Switchable thermal insulation	p. 56
Nanocellular foams	p. 56
Vacuum insulation panel	p. 57

[1] Source: Isoliertechnik 5/1996

Applications matrix

Application		**Inorganic**																
		Synthetic												Natural				
		Abbreviation to DIN V 4108-10	Pictogram	Glass wool (MW)	Rock wool (MW)	Cellular glass (CG)	Foamed glass	Calcium silicate foam	*Ceramic fibres, ceramic foam*	*Aerogel*	*Pyrogenic silicic acid*	*Slag wool*	*Gypsum foam*	Expanded perlite (EPB)	Exfoliated vermiculite (EV), expanded mica	Expanded clay	*Pumice*	*Insulating clay bricks*
Floor and roof	External insulation to suspended floor or roof, protected from the weather, insulation below roof covering	DAD		●	●	●		•						●	●	•		
	External insulation to suspended floor or roof, protected from the weather, insulation below waterproofing	DAA		●	●	●		•						●	●			
	External insulation to roof, exposed to the weather (upside-down roof)	DUK																
	Insulation between rafters, double-skin roof, accessible but non-trafficked topmost suspended floor	DZ		●	●		•							●	●	•		
	Internal insulation to suspended floor (underside) or roof, insulation below rafters/structure, suspended ceiling, etc.	DI		●	●	●		•			○		○	●	●			
	Internal insulation to suspended or ground floor (top side) below screed, without sound insulation requirements	DEO		●	●	●	•				○			●	●	•		
	Internal insulation to suspended or ground floor (top side) below screed, with sound insulation requirements	DES		●	●									●	●			
Wall	External insulation to wall, behind cladding	WAB		●	●	●		•		○				●	●		○	•
	External insulation to wall, behind waterproofing	WAA				●				○	○						○	•
	External insulation to wall, behind render (plinth insulation, thermal bridge insulation)	WAP		●	●	●		•			○			●	●			•
	Cavity insulation to double-leaf walls	WZ		●	●	●	•							●	●			•
	Insulation to timber-frame and timber-panel forms of construction	WH		●	●		•							●	●	•		
	Internal insulation to wall	WI		●	●	●		•			○		○	●	●	•		
	Insulation between party walls with sound insulation requirements	WTH		●	●									●	●			
	Insulation to separating walls	WTR		●	●	●									●	•		
Basement	External thermal insulation to walls in contact with the soil (on outside of waterproofing)	PW				●	•											
	External thermal insulation below ground floor slab in contact with the soil (below waterproofing)	PB				●	•											

● with defined properties to DIN V 4108-10
• with building authority approval for product or application
○ seldom used as thermal insulating material

Applications matrix

Organic																									**Application**	
Synthetic									Natural																	
Polystyrene, expanded (EPS)	Polystyrene foam, extruded (XPS)	Polyurethane rigid foam (PUR)	Polyurethane in situ foam (PUR)	Phenolic foam (PF)	Melamine foam (MF)	Polyethylene foam (PE)	*Urea-formaldehyde resin in situ foam (UF)*	*Polyester fibres*	Wood wool (WW)	Wood fibres (WF)	Insulation cork board (ICB)	Cellulose fibres	Hemp	Sheep's wool	Cotton	Flax	Cereal granulate	Reeds	Coconut fibres	*Sea grass*	*Wood chippings*	*Giant Chinese silver grass*	*Peat*	*Straw bales*		
●	●	●	◍	●						●	●	◍	◍		◍		◍	◍	◍						External insulation to suspended floor or roof, protected from the weather, insulation below roof covering	Floor and roof
●	●	●	◍	●						●	●							◍							External insulation to suspended floor or roof, protected from the weather, insulation below waterproofing	Floor and roof
	●																				○				External insulation to roof, exposed to the weather (upside-down roof)	Floor and roof
●		●		●	○		○	○	●	●	●	◍	◍	◍	◍	◍	◍	◍	◍	○					Insulation between rafters, double-skin roof, accessible but non-trafficked topmost suspended floor	Floor and roof
●	●	●		●	○		○	○	●	●	●	◍	◍	◍	◍	◍	◍	◍	◍						Internal insulation to suspended floor (underside) or roof, insulation below rafters/structure, suspended ceiling, etc.	Floor and roof
●	●	●		●					●	●	●		◍	◍					◍						Internal insulation to suspended or ground floor (top side) below screed, without sound insulation requirements	Floor and roof
●						◍				●				◍					◍						Internal insulation to suspended or ground floor (top side) below screed, with sound insulation requirements	Floor and roof
●	●	●		●					●	●	●		◍	◍	◍			◍	◍			○		○	External insulation to wall, behind cladding	Wall
●	●	●		●																		○			External insulation to wall, behind waterproofing	Wall
●	●	●		●					●	●	●							◍						○	External insulation to wall, behind render (plinth insulation, thermal bridge insulation)	Wall
●	●	●	◍	●			○			●	●								◍		○				Cavity insulation to double-leaf walls	Wall
		●						○	●	●	●	◍	◍	◍	◍	◍	◍	◍	◍	○				○	Insulation to timber-frame and timber-panel forms of construction	Wall
●		●		●	○				●	●	●	◍	◍	◍		◍		◍	◍						Internal insulation to wall	Wall
								○											◍						Insulation between party walls with sound insulation requirements	Wall
					○					●	●	◍	◍	◍	◍	◍	◍		◍						Insulation to separating walls	Wall
◍	●	◍																							External thermal insulation to walls in contact with the soil (on outside of waterproofing)	Basement
◍	●	◍																							External thermal insulation below ground floor slab in contact with the soil (below waterproofing)	Basement

● with defined properties to DIN V 4108-10
◍ with national technical approval for product or application
○ seldom used as thermal insulating material

Inorganic insulating materials – forms of supply

	Boards, batts	In situ foam	Loose fill	Blown or caulking material	Sandwich, panels, other
Synthetic					
Glass wool	•			•	
Rock wool	•			•	
Cellular glass	•				
Foamed glass	•		•		
Calcium silicate foam	•				
Ceramic fibres/foam					o
Aerogel					o
Pyrogenic silicic acid	o				o
Slag wool				o	
Gypsum foam	o				
Natural					
Expanded clay			•	•	
Expanded perlite	•		•	•	
Exfoliated vermiculite, expanded mica	•		•	•	
Pumice			o		o
Insulating clay bricks					o

• with defined properties to DIN V 4108-10
o seldom used as thermal insulating material

Organic insulating materials – forms of supply

	Boards, batts	In situ foam	Loose fill	Blown or caulking material	Sandwich, panels, other
Synthetic					
Polystyrene, expanded	•		•	•	•
Polystyrene foam, extruded	•				•
Polyurethane rigid foam	•				•
Polyurethane in situ foam		•			•
Phenolic foam	o				
Melamine foam	•				
Polyethylene foam	•				•
Urea-formaldehyde resin in situ foam		o			
Polyester fibres	o			o	
Natural					
Wood-fibre insulating materials	•			•	
Wood wool	•				•
Insulation cork board	•		•		
Cotton	•			•	
Flax	•			•	
Cereal granulate			•		
Hemp	•			•	
Coconut fibres	•			•	
Sheep's wool	•				
Reeds	•				•
Cellulose fibres	•			•	
Sea grass	o		o		
Wood chippings			o		
Giant Chinese silver grass	o				
Peat	o				
Straw bales					o

• with defined properties to DIN V 4108-10
o seldom used as thermal insulating material

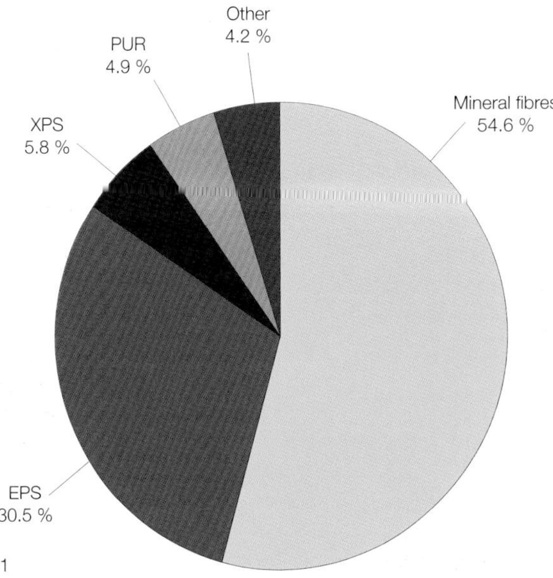

1 Market shares of insulating materials in Germany in 2005:
approx. 24.5 million cubic metres of insulating materials were used in buildings in Germany in 2005. Of this total, mineral wool, EPS, XPS and PUR rigid foam products constitute approx. 96%; a multitude of other products make up the remaining 4%. (Source: GDI – umbrella organisation for the insulating materials industry)

Mineral wool (MW)

Insulating materials made from mineral wool are covered by DIN EN 13162 a nd comply with the requirements of Construction Products List B (see p. 62).

Mineral wool is the general term for the inorganic fibrous insulating materials glass wool and rock wool, which differ merely in terms of their raw materials and some of their properties. This review therefore considers insulating materials made from mineral wool in general but adds information specific to glass wool and rock wool where necessary.

Raw materials and production
Glass wool
Glass wool consists of quartz sand, limestone and approx. 60% scrap glass (from windows and bottles) plus organic substances such as phenol-formaldehyde resin as a binder. Some products also include a hydrophobic agent and oils to minimise the dust.

Rock wool
Rock wool is produced from various rock types such as diabase, dolomite and limestone. The binders plus dust-reducing and hydrophobic agents added are the same as for glass wool.

The raw materials are melted in tanks at approx. 1400–1500°C and subsequently fed into a pulverising machine, the operation of which depends on the particular manufacturer. For example, in the centrifugal method the molten material is spread over rotating discs or drums where it is thrown off the perimeter as fibres by the centrifugal force, whereas in the blowing method a thin jet of steam is blown through the molten material and this breaks it down into fibres. The binder, dissolved in water, is added during these processes. In doing so, the water vaporises and the fibres cool so rapidly that they vitrify. The fibres are then spread over a conveyor belt and pass through a tunnel furnace at 200–250°C to enable the binder to cure, which gives the products their stability. After that, they are cut to size and coated or laminated if required.
The degree of compaction, the amount of binder and the orientation of the fibres in the wool are critical for the respective properties of each type of product.

Development and market significance
Glass wool
The manufacture of glass wool can be traced back to the glass-blowers of the Thuringia Forest who in the 18th century were already making so-called fairy's or angel's hair for decorative purposes. The potential of the material for further large-scale technical applications was discovered around 1900. The 1930s saw the development of the stem drum drawing method which enabled the manufacture of spinnable glass threads with a precisely defined diameter. These could be sold in reels and that marked the start of the industrial production of insulating materials made from glass wool.

Rock wool
The possibility of producing rock wool was discovered in 1935 in New Jersey, USA. A Swedish manufacturer purchased the rights to use the technology and started producing rock wool batts. Owing to the high proportion of granulate in the wool, these batts were initially very heavy. It was in the 1970s that new methods started to appear which enabled the production of lighter wools with lower densities. Glass wool and rock wool production methods have continued to develop since then and today a large range of products is available, optimised for the most diverse applications.

In Europe, mineral wool is by far the most popular type of insulating material. Its market share in Germany, for instance, is about 55%.

Properties and applications
With a thermal conductivity of 0.035–0.045 W/mK, mineral wool insulating materials exhibit a good insulating capacity and are very open to diffusion (see "Physical properties", p. 23). They are resistant to mould, rot and vermin, also weak alkalis, acids, organic solvents and ultraviolet radiation. Such properties make mineral wool a suitable thermal insulating material for many applications (see "Applications for mineral wool", p. 23).

Mineral wool products also exhibit good sound insulation properties – depending on their density and fibre structure – which can be exploited in steep pitched roofs, thermal insulation composite systems and lightweight party and separating walls. Typical sound insulation applications include impact sound insulation and insulation in acoustic ceilings. Mineral wool's favourable reaction to fire also means it is preferred where higher fire protection requirements apply (Euroclasses and DIN 4102 classes A1 and A2). Besides such applications, mineral wool to worksheet Q 132 of the Industrial Buildings Study Group (AGI) is also suitable as an insulating material for industrial installations (insulating material code 10.01.02.62.10).

However, besides the aforementioned common features, glass wool and rock wool also differ in some respects, which makes one or the other ideal for specific applications:

1 Glass wool
2 Rock wool

Glass wool

The colour of glass wool varies from light to dark yellow depending on the mixing proportions and the quantity of binder.
Glass wool is not suitable for applications where the insulating material is subjected to compression loads. However, for the imposed loads normal in housing, it is sufficiently firm and stable to be used as impact sound insulation.
Another advantage of many glass wool products is their flexibility. They are suitable as an infill material where, cut slightly oversize, they can be forced into place and remain clamped in place without the need for any further fixings.
The flammability is influenced by the proportion of binder. For example, special grades without binders have been developed for industrial applications which can withstand long-term thermal loads up to 500°C.

Rock wool

Rock wool is usually a grey-olive green colour and is used in many different applications where insulation against heat and cold, fire protection and sound insulation is required.
Compared to glass wool, rock wool products are less flexible owing to their (usually) higher density. However, handled appropriately, they are also suitable as an infill material. For example, in conjunction with wedges of insulating material they can be fitted exactly, without waste and without the need for any further fixings.
Their temperature stability is very high. Without binders, rock wool products can withstand constant temperatures up to 750°C. Their melting point is usually in excess of 1000°C.
Certain rock wool products with an especially high density and compressive strength are used in roadbuilding, as sound insulation in noise barriers and for damping vibrations under railway tracks.

Forms of supply

Mineral wool insulating materials can be supplied in many forms, also with water-repellent properties if required:

- Loose in sacks as a caulking material
- Rolls, laminated/unlaminated
- Batts, laminated/unlaminated
- Boards, laminated/unlaminated
- Quilted mineral wool batts on a wire mesh
- Lamella products
- Preformed insulation for pipes and vessels
- Rock wool: triangular wedges

The following dimensions are customarily available:

- Rolls:

thickness	70–240 mm
width	600–200 mm
length	to 9000 mm

- Boards:

thickness	12–200 mm
width	400–625 mm
length	800–2000 mm

- Batts (rolled):

thickness	15–70 mm
width	400–625 mm
length	to 10000 mm

Installation advice

Insulating materials made from mineral wool are usually easy to transport and install. Rolled products in particular can be compressed during packaging to save space. The material is easy to cut exactly to size with the help of a sharp knife and a straightedge – and the materials are frequently printed with markings to make cutting to size even easier. No additional protective measures are required during the work.

The handling of mineral wool insulating materials on the building site is described in detail in part 1 of TRGS 521, the technical rules for hazardous materials.

The general principles of industrial hygiene that apply to all materials containing fibres should be observed when working with products complying with modern standards, e.g.:

- careful handling of products, offcuts and waste to minimise contamination of the workplace
- wearing of loose-fitting, full-protection overalls and suitable gloves
- wearing of a suitable dust mask, and suitable protective goggles when working overhead
- washing off dust after completing the work

Health and ecological aspects

Since May 1994, a regulation has been in force in Germany that demands a certain composition for glass wool in order that it can be regarded as a non-hazardous substance. At the same time, definitions for rock wool were introduced regarding the biosolubility in the body.

In order to comply with European legislation as well, the revised Chemicals Prohibition Act and the Hazardous Substances Act, in which biopersistence criteria for fibres are described, have been in force since May 2000. According to these laws, synthetic mineral fibres may only be used for thermal and sound insulation in buildings, also for lagging to pipes and vessels, when at least one of the following three criteria is satisfied:

- A suitable intraperitoneal test (fibres injected below the abdominal wall in tests on animals) do not show any excessive cancerogenic indications.
- The half-life after intratracheal instillation (fibres introduced into the respiratory tract in tests on animals) is max. 65 days for a defined fibre size.
- The carcinogenity index (KI-40 KMF standard) determined is at least 40.

Products installed prior to 1996 should be classified as carcinogenic. Since 1998 only mineral wool insulating materials not classed as possibly carcinogenic may be used in Germany, and these are marked with the RAL quality symbol 388 "mineral wool product". Caution should be exercised with products obtained from outside Europe.

From the ecological viewpoint, the good availability of the raw materials and the short transport distances are among the advantages of mineral wool. This applies to the raw materials for glass wool products and to a large extent also the raw materials of rock wool products which are obtained in Europe from open-cast mining operations. Just 1 m³ of raw materials can be used to produce, for example, approx. 100 m³ of rock wool.

Recycling
Mineral wool is partially recyclable or may be simply reused. For example, production waste can be fed back into the production process or used as an aggregate in the production of clay bricks or tiles.

Mineral wool can be disposed of in landfill and disposed of like mineral building debris. Products made from mineral wool with the RAL quality symbol are allocated to waste code No. 17 06 04. Older mineral wool products whose origins cannot be identified are generally allocated to waste code No. 17 60 03 and may no longer be used as an insulating material.

Physical properties – glass wool

Property	Unit	Values
Density	kg/m³	15–150
Thermal conductivity	W/(mK)	0.035–0.045
Specific heat capacity	J/(kgK)	840–1000
Reaction to fire		
Euroclass	A1, A2	
Bldg. materials class	A2 (incombustible)	
Water vapour diffusion resistance index	–	1–2
Long-term water absorption	kg/m²	≤ 3
Maximum service, temperature, long-term		
with binder	°C	100–200
without binder	°C	up to 500
Compressive strength for imposed load (impact sound insulating materials)	kPa	3.5
Sound impedance	kPas/m²	≥ 5

Physical properties – rock wool

Property	Unit	Values
Density	kg/m³	20–200
Thermal conductivity	W/(mK)	0.035–0.045
Specific heat capacity	J/(kgK)	600–840
Reaction to fire		
Euroclass	A1	
Bldg. materials class	A1 (incombustible)	
Water vapour diffusion resistance index	–	1–2
Long-term water absorption	kg/m²	≤ 3
Maximum service, temperature, long-term		
with binder	°C	100–200
without binder	°C	600–750
Compressive stress at 10% deformation or compressive strength	kPa	15–80
Compressive strength for imposed load (impact sound insulating materials)	kPa	5–20
Sound impedance	kPas/m²	6–43

Applications for mineral wool

Roof and suspended floor:

DAD	• External insulation, protected from the weather, below roof covering (zero or high compressive strength)
DAA	• External insulation, protected from the weather, below waterproofing
DZ	• Insulation between rafters, double-skin roof, topmost suspended floor
DI	• Internal insulation below suspended floor, below rafters or loadbearing structure
DEO	• Below screed, without sound insulation requirements
DES	• Below screed, with sound insulation requirements (higher or low compressibility)

Wall:

WAB	• External insulation behind cladding
WAP	• External insulation behind render (with low to high tensile strength)
WZ	• Cavity insulation to double-leaf walls
WH	• Timber-frame and timber-panel forms of construction
WI	• Internal insulation to wall (zero, low or high tensile strength)
WTR	• Insulation to separating walls
WTH	• Between party walls with sound insulation requirements (higher or low compressibility)

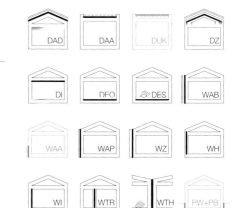

DAD DAA DUK DZ
DI DEO DES WAB
WAA WAP WZ WH
WI WTR WTH PW+PB

Cellular glass (CG)

DIN EN 13167 applies to factory-made solid insulating materials made from closed-cell glass. Cellular glass conforms to the requirements of Construction Products List B (see p. 62).

Raw materials and production
Cellular glass consists of quartz sand and dolomite plus calcium and sodium carbonate. In some cases recycled glass is also used. Carbon is used as a blowing agent.

The raw materials are melted at a temperature of 1400°C to form glass, then cooled, crushed and milled to a glass powder. The powder is reheated to over 1000°C in special moulds while introducing carbon; the carbon oxidises and forms gas bubbles which foam up the mixture. The resulting blocks are cooled in stages before being cut to the final board dimensions. This insulating material contains no blowing agents, flame retardants or binders.

Development and market significance
Cellular glass was developed in the 1930s by the French Saint-Gobain Group. The production of insulating materials made from cellular glass began in the early 1940s.

Owing to the relatively high cost of production and installation, the market share of cellular glass is max. 1%. Although there are only a few manufacturers, the products are, however, generally well known and readily available.

Properties and applications
Besides good thermal insulation properties and closed cells, a high compressive strength and imperviousness to water vapour are the typical properties of cellular glass.
It is dimensionally stable, water-repellent, frost-resistant to DIN 52104, ageing-resistant and incombustible.
Cellular glass exhibits a generally good resistance to chemicals. This also applies to all organic solvents, acids (except hydrofluoric acid) and weak alkalis. It is 100% resistant to insects and rodents and does not rot.
As cellular glass is very brittle and can fracture easily under concentrated loads, it is necessary to coat the material completely in bitumen. In doing so, care should be taken to ensure that the bitumen does not have a detrimental effect on the behaviour of the components in fire, depending on the particular application, or prevent the deconstruction, recycling or disposal of the components. As an alternative, synthetic resin can be used instead of bitumen for lagging to pipes and vessels.

Cellular glass boards can be used in many different ways as an insulating material in floors, walls and roofs. However, cellular glass is not suitable for sound insulation or for impact sound insulation.
Typical applications are those where high compressive and moisture loads are expected, e.g. trafficable flat roofs, industrial floors and external basement insulation.
External basement insulation applications are covered in DIN 4108-2. National technical approvals are available for external basement insulation applications in groundwater and when cellular glass is used as a loadbearing thermal insulating material beneath ground floor slabs.
Besides the traditional applications in buildings, cellular glass can also be used to lag pipes and vessels. According to the technical rules for insulation work in industrial installations, see worksheet Q 131-4 of the Industrial Buildings Study

Group (AGI), cellular glass has insulating material code 10.01.02.62.10.

Forms of supply
Cellular glass insulating materials are available in the following sizes as standard:

- Boards: length 300, 600 mm
  width 450, 600 mm
  thickness 40–180 mm
- Moulded parts for industrial applications:
  pipe diameters
  DN 8 – DN 300
  thickness 40–100 mm

Installation advice
The boards or moulded parts are supplied in convenient formats. Any cutting to size required is usually best carried out with a handsaw.
As cellular glass is very brittle, it cannot accommodate any concentrated loads. The boards must therefore lie flat, be supported across their full area and also be covered with a flat material. Cellular glass boards are therefore bonded to the substrate across their full area with hot bitumen, and all joints should be filled with hot bitumen. This bonding can also be carried out in several layers.
The installation work is often carried out by two persons, one pouring the bitumen and the other laying the boards in it.
Unlaminated insulating boards are usually finished with a coat of hot bitumen that fills the cells, on which the actual waterproofing – bitumen sheeting or similar to suit the application – is laid. The bitumen consumption varies between 2 and 5 kg/m^2, depending on the application.

Although the boards are not vulnerable to moisture, the cut cells on the surface should not be allowed to come into contact with water because if this water freezes, it can lead to local destruction of the board structure.

Health and ecological aspects
Small amounts of sulphur hydroxide can be released from the cells during installation. This leads to an unpleasant, putrid smell, but the ensuing concentrations are not critical.

Physical properties – cellular glass

Property	Unit	Values
Density	kg/m^3	115–220
Thermal conductivity	W/(m•K)	0.040–0.060
Specific heat capacity	J/(kg•K)	800–1100
Coefficient of thermal expansion	K^{-1}	8×10^{-6} to 10×10^{-6}
Reaction to fire		
Euroclass	A1	
Bldg. materials class	A1 (incombustible)	
Water vapour diffusion resistance index	–	∞ (infinite)
Long-term water absorption	kg/m^2	–
Maximum service temperature, long-term	°C	-260 to +430
Compressive strength (works standard)	kPa	700–1700
Constant compressive stress	kPa	160–480

Applications for cellular glass

Roof and suspended floor:
- DAD • External insulation, protected from the weather, below roof covering
- DAA • External insulation, protected from the weather, below waterproofing (high, very high and extremely high compressive strength)
- DI • Internal insulation below suspended floor, below rafters or loadbearing structure
- DEO • Below screed, without sound insulation requirements

Wand:
- WAB • External insulation behind cladding
- WAA • External insulation behind waterproofing
- WAP • External insulation behind render
- WZ • Cavity insulation to double-leaf walls
- WI • Internal insulation to wall
- WTR • Insulation to separating walls

External basement insulation:
- PW • Walls in contact with the soil (high and very high compressive strength)
- PB • Ground floor slabs in contact with the soil (high and very high compressive strength)

Health problems can be caused by glass dust during cutting or from the use of synthetic resin adhesives when installing lagging to pipes and vessels. It is therefore advisable to wear a dust mask and protective goggles when cutting cellular glass.

Recycling
Provided there is no bitumen adhering to it, cellular glass can be reused, e.g. as frost protection under roads. In most applications, however, the cellular glass boards are combined with bitumen and the two materials cannot be properly separated upon deconstruction. Such waste must be disposed of as building debris in landfill sites, but can be compressed to approx. 5% of its original volume. However, the bitumen residue adhering to the boards does lead to an environmental problem that has not yet been resolved. Incineration for energy generation is not possible.

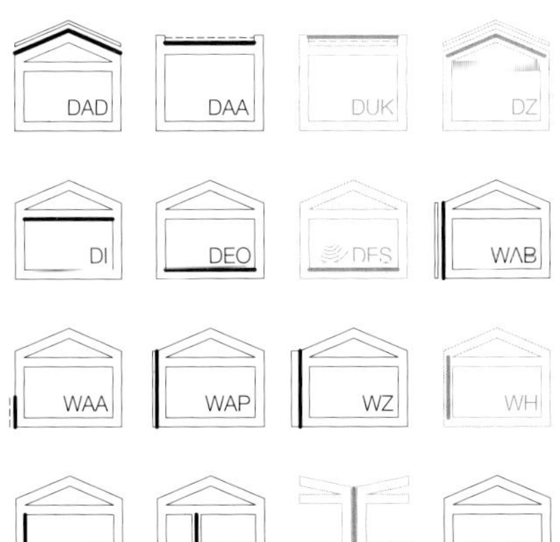

Physical properties – foamed glass

Property		Unit	Values
Density		kg/m³	150–230
Thermal conductivity	loose fill granulate (design value)	W/(mK) W/(mK)	0.070–0.093 0.14
Specific heat capacity		J/(kgK)	800–1000
Reaction to fire	building materials class	A1 (incombustible)	
Water vapour diffusion resistance index		–	1–5
Long-term water absorption after 28 days storage underwater		Vol.-%	15
Maximum service temperature, long-term		°C	600–700
Compressive strength or compressive stress after 10% deformation		kPa kPa	120–140 500[1]
Constant compressive stress			kPa 160[1]

[1] for grain size 10/50 mm, with approval also below loadbearing ground floor slabs

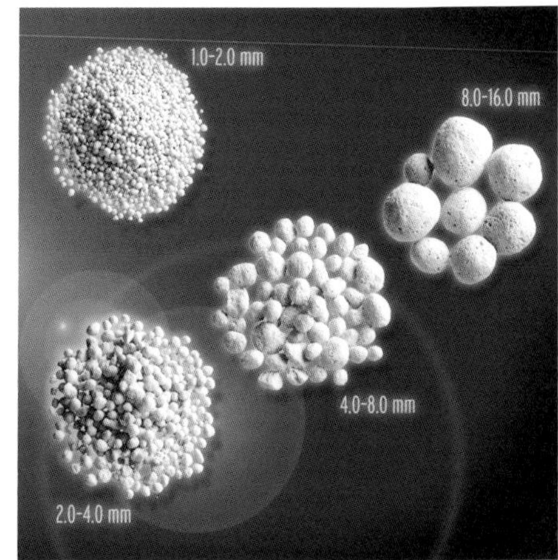

Foamed glass

Insulating products made from foamed glass require a national technical approval. This also applies to cellular glass frost protection under roads, which is here classed as foamed glass.

Raw materials and production
The raw materials are scrap glass and a blowing agent. The broken glass is milled to form a fine glass powder and then mixed with water, binder and a blowing agent, the so-called activator. Following the foaming process at approx. 900°C, the material is either spread over a conveyor belt and broken down into various particle sizes during cooling (coarse ballast for roads) or processed with the help of a dish granulator to form rounded foamed glass granulate.

Development and market significance
Foamed glass is a relatively new product and is employed primarily as an aggregate. Its use as a loose fill insulating material is still relatively unknown. It is impossible to put a figure to the market share, but is certainly very small.

Properties and applications
Foamed glass exhibits only moderate thermal insulation properties and a considerable thickness must be employed to achieve a certain insulating effect. Further typical properties are its low density, high strength and good sound-attenuating capacity. Foamed glass is incombustible and meets the requirements of DIN 4102 building materials class A1. Owing to their closed-cell form, cellular glass grains and beads are themselves watertight and do not promote capillary action. However, the constant presence of moisture can lead to water being absorbed into the interstitial spaces, which results in a higher thermal conductivity for the overall insulation.

Foamed glass does not swell or shrink. It has a high chemical resistance to acids, alkalis and organic solvents, and its alkali resistance means it is suitable for use with lime and cement. Foamed glass does not provide any nutrients for pests or fungi.

Typical applications for foamed glass are as loose fill – without binders, but also with cement and resin binders – with grain sizes of 2/4 mm or 4/8 mm for voids in roof, floor and wall structures. In small grain sizes from 0.1 to 8 mm, foamed glass can be used as a thermal insulating aggregate in plaster, render, mortar, filling compounds, prefabricated components and acoustic boards.
Ballast made from cellular glass with a grain size of 10/50 mm is suitable as external basement insulation and as loadbearing insulation below ground floor slabs. National technical approvals are required for such applications. Ballast is used, however, mainly as a blinding layer or frost-resistant layer beneath buildings and roads.

Forms of supply

• Loose fill:	grains	2/4 or 4/8 mm
	sacks	55 l and 100 l
	big bags	1.5–2.5 m³
	silos	
• Ballast:	grains	10/50 mm

Applications for foamed glass

Roof and suspended floor:	
DZ	• Insulation between rafters, double-skin roof, topmost suspended floor
DEO	• Below screed, without sound insulation requirements
Wall:	
WZ	• Cavity insulation to double-leaf walls
WH	• Timber-frame and timber-panel forms of construction
External basement insulation (with approval only):	
PW	• Walls in contact with the soil
PB	• Ground floor slabs in contact with the soil

Installation advice
The installation of foamed glass does not call for particular protective measures. According to a report by the stone quarry employers' insurance liability association, there is no risk of silicosis.

Health and ecological aspects
Health risks during installation and use are not known. Foamed glass is a recycled product that can be easily used again. The relatively high energy requirements during production are offset by the good availability and comparatively short transport distances.

Recycling
The material can be disposed of in landfill as building debris or domestic waste with waste code No. 20 01 02. Owing to the activator content as a blowing agent, waste from calcium-sodium foamed glass granulate is water risk class 1.

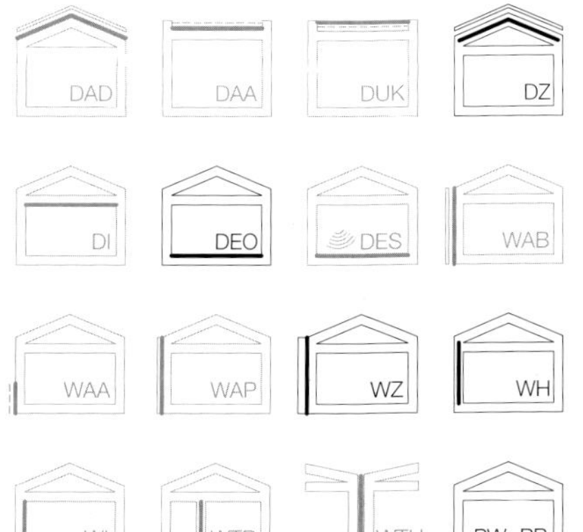

Calcium silicate foam

Calcium silicate foam boards with slightly different aggregates are also known as mineral foam or mineral insulating boards. The products have been awarded national technical approvals (see p. 60). A European standard is in preparation (prEN 14306).

Raw materials and production
The raw materials are calcium and silicon oxide plus an aggregate of 3 – 6% cellulose. These are mixed with water to form a slurry and this produces calcium silicate hydrate (CSH). The cellulose content improves flexibility and edge stability. The mixture is poured into moulds and then autoclaved (high pressure + steam). The result is a fine-pore, open-cell, rigid foam which is subsequently cut into boards and treated with metallic soaps or siliconates to give it hydrophobic properties.

Development and market significance
Insulating materials made from calcium silicate foam have not been available for very long and are therefore not yet widely used.

Properties and applications
The boards exhibit moderate insulating properties, are good in compression and highly dimensionally stable. Their high capillary action enables them to absorb moisture, store this and release it quickly again. Calcium silicate foam is therefore preferred for internal insulation, especially in timber-frame houses and buildings protected by preservation orders (see p. 83). Calcium silicate foam is incombustible and can be allocated to DIN 4102 building materials classes A1 and A2. It shows an alkali reaction and should not be allowed to come into contact with acids. The boards inhibit the growth of mould, do not rot and have a very high temperature stability.

Forms of supply
Boards with the following dimensions are generally available:
- Length: 250, 2500 mm
- Width: 50, 100 mm
- Thickness: 25–100 mm

Installation advice
The material, like autoclaved aerated concrete, can be cut, sawn and drilled. Owing to the dust generated during such work, the wearing of a dust mask and protective goggles is recommended. When used as internal insulation, the boards should be bonded to walls and soffits with a suitable adhesive spread over the entire area in order to rule out any hidden air cavities which can have an unfavourable building physics effect. In addition, the joints between boards should be bonded or filled. Silicate paints (open to diffusion) or lightweight wallpapers are the recommended finishes. In contrast to other common internal insulating materials, a vapour barrier or vapour check should not be installed. Despite their good moisture control properties, the boards should be stored and installed in dry conditions. Water that subsequently freezes can very easily damage the boards.

Applications for calcium silicate foam

Roof and suspended floor:

DAD	• External insulation, protected from the weather, below roof covering
DAA	• External insulation, protected from the weather, below waterproofing
DI	• Internal insulation below suspended floor, below rafters or loadbearing structure.

Wall:

WAB	• External insulation behind cladding
WAP	• External insulation behind render
WI	• Internal insulation to wall
	• Dämmung von Raumtrennwänden

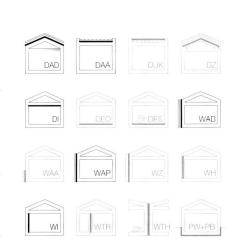

Health and ecological aspects
Apart from the dust during cutting and drilling, no health risks are known for this material. The raw materials are available in sufficient quantities and the transport distances are short. The production process, however, does require a relatively high amount of energy.

Recycling
It is easy to reuse this material provided is not contaminated by other waste. It can also be disposed of in landfill as building debris according to the local regulations.

Physical properties – calcium silicate foam

Property	Unit	Values
Density	kg/m³	115–300
Thermal conductivity	W/(mK)	0.045–0.065
Specific heat capacity	J/(kgK)	1000
Maximum service temperature, long-term	°C	300
Reaction to fire Building materials class		A1 and A2, (incombustible)
Water vapour diffusion resistance index	–	3–20
Compressive stress at 10% deformation or compressive strength	kPa	500–1500
Bending strength	kPa	800–1000

DAD DAA DUK DZ
DI DEO DES WAD
WAA WAP WZ WH
WI WTR WTH PW+PB

Ceramic fibres, ceramic foams

Ceramic fibres and foams are polycrystalline structures based on aluminium and silicon oxide.

The fibres are processed in different ways, e.g. to form fire-resistant textiles, to form reinforcement for ceramic products, and as a substitute for asbestos for insulating purposes in industrial plants and apparatus.
Ceramic foams are used as insulating materials in filter, burner and catalysis technologies and are undergoing further research.
Ceramic fibres and foams are not used for conventional thermal insulation tasks in buildings.

Ceramic fibre insulating materials are tear-resistant, resilient, chemical-resistant and in some cases can resist temperatures up to 1000°C.

The characteristic physical properties of ceramic fibres are given in the table below.

Corresponding figures for ceramic foams are not yet available.

Physical properties – ceramic fibres

Property	Unit	Values
Density	kg/m³	120–560
Thermal conductivity	W/(mK)	0.030–0.070
Specific heat capacity	J/(kgK)	1040
Reaction to fire Building materials class	A1 (incombustible)	

Aerogel

Aerogel is an extremely lightweight, highly porous, solid material. Metal oxides or polymers are among the various raw materials possible. However, aerogel is primarily manufactured from silicates (SiO_2) which liquefy to a gel upon addition of a catalyst. This gel is subsequently dried under extreme conditions to a non-brittle consistency. This sol-gel process was developed as long ago as 1930 and over the course of time the mix of raw materials has been varied and improved. In the meantime, pore sizes in the nanometre range down to five-millionths of a millimetre have become possible. With a thermal conductivity of just 0.017–0.021 W/mK, aerogel exhibits excellent thermal insulation properties; it is also good as sound insulation and remains stable in temperatures up to approx. 1200°C. Aerogels have a density of 60 – 80 kg/m³. They are resistant to moisture and mould growth and do not discolour even after long exposure to ultraviolet radiation. Experience has shown that the properties of aerogels remain stable in the long-term.

The main applications result from the good insulating properties in conjunction with the high optical transparency of the silicate aerogels. These enable particular architectural applications, e.g. as transparent thermal insulation behind panes of glass. The appearance of aerogels is matt to transparent, and against a dark background they appear milky blue. Specially developed products using carbon aerogels can even absorb electromagnetic radiation.
Despite their excellent insulating properties, aerogels are not widely used – partly due to their high price.

Pyrogenic silicic acid

Pyrogenic silicic acid is produced by burning silicon tetrachloride in a hydrogen flame. In conjunction with a stabiliser, this produces a microporous insulating material. In order to minimise the release of radiant heat, opacifiers such as titanium oxide (TiO_2) or, for high-temperature applications, zirconium oxide (ZrO_2), are added.

This mixture, together with reinforcing fibres, is compressed under high pressure to form boards with densities of up to 300 kg/m^3. Depending on the density, this results in rigid or flexible boards with a microporous structure that significantly impedes the migration of gas molecules and hence reduces the thermal conductivity down to 0.021 W/mK.

Insulating boards made from pyrogenic silicic acid are used mainly in the construction of industrial plant and apparatus, and in buildings in the form of the recently introduced vacuum insulation panels (VIP). With a maximum service temperature of 950–1050°C, they exhibit a high thermal stability, are incombustible (DIN 4102 building materials class A1) and are resistant to chemicals. Dimensional stability and easy working are further advantages.

No organic binders are required for the production of pyrogenic silicic acid boards, and so they can be classed as physiologically harmless.
Pyrogenic silicic acid is currently an insignificant player on the insulating materials market, but in future could play a role as the core in vacuum insulation panels (see also p. 57).

Slag wool

Slag wool belongs to the group of mineral-fibre insulating materials and is produced from slag which occurs as a waste product of combustion processes. Blastfurnace slag is modified to suit the particular intended purpose, spun into fibres and bonded.

Slag wool has similar physical properties to the traditional mineral-fibre products (see table below). It is sound-attenuating, insoluble in water and elastic. As slag wool is manufactured from waste products, it can contain heavy metals, potentially carcinogenic fibres and other undesirable substances.

Slag wool is therefore no longer used on a large scale. In recent years it has been used occasionally as a caulking material in the construction of industrial plants and vessels.

No information is available for the handling of slag wool and legacy materials. The general principles of industrial hygiene that apply to the use of mineral wool insulating materials must be observed as a minimum (see p. 22).
Owing to its possible contamination, disposal of this material is correspondingly problematic.

Physical properties – slag wool

Property	Unit	Values
Density	kg/m^3	27
Thermal conductivity	W/(mK)	0.035–0.040
Specific heat capacity	J/(kgK)	840–1000
Reaction to fire Building materials class	A1 (incombustible)	

Gypsum foam

The addition of a polymer to a mixture of water and gypsum causes a foaming action that produces a porous mass which can be cured in various moulds for the production of a whole range of products with different shapes and sizes.
The gypsum used for this is frequently obtained from flue-gas desulphurisation plants. However, the final products cannot be recycled.

The relevant physical properties of gypsum foam are shown in the table below.

The gypsum foam boards available on the market are used primarily for sound absorption and then principally in open-plan offices.
It plays no role as a thermal insulation material.

Physical properties – gypsum foam

Property	Unit	Values
Thermal conductivity	W/(mK)	0.045
Specific heat capacity	J/(kgK)	1000
Reaction to fire Building materials class	B2 (flammable)	
Water vapour diffusion-resistance index	–	4–8

Physical properties – expanded perlite

Property		Unit	Values
Density	loose fill boards	kg/m³ kg/m³	90–490 150–210
Thermal conductivity		W/(mK)	0.045–0.070
Specific heat capacity		J/(kgK)	1000
Reaction to fire, loose fill	Euroclass Building materials class	A1 A1 (incombustible)	
Reaction to fire, boards	Euroclass Building materials class	C-s1, d0 to D-s1, d0 B2 (flammable)	
Water vapour diffusion resistance index		–	3–5
Maximum service temperature, long-term		°C	110–800
Compr. stress at 10% deformation or compr. strength (boards)		kPa	200–300
Constant compressive stress (boards)		kPa	100

Expanded perlite, expanded perlite boards (EPB)

Boards and composite boards made from expanded perlite are covered by DIN EN 13169 and comply with the requirements of Construction Products List B. A national technical approval is required for the use of expanded perlite as a loose fill insulating material (see p. 60).

Raw materials and production
Expanded perlite is produced from perlite, a vitreous rock from the lava of underwater volcanoes. The finely ground grains of perlite are abruptly heated to approx. 1000°C, whereupon they expand to 15 to 20 times their original volume.
To produce perlite boards, ground expanded perlite is mixed with cellulose fibres, bonded with starch and pressed in moulds. Synthetic resin or bitumen emulsions can be added to give the material hydrophobic properties.
Expanded perlite boards can be combined with a layer of mineral wool for impact sound insulation applications. Such composite boards can be assembled from different layers in various thicknesses.

Development and market significance
Expanded perlite has been used for insulation purposes since about 1955, is a well-known product and is readily available. The market share is about 1.1%.

Properties and applications
These insulating materials are characterised by moderate to good thermal insulation properties. They exhibit an excellent temperature stability and in the form of boards can also be used for applications where high compressive loads are involved. Untreated expanded perlite is classed as incombustible complying with DIN 4102 building materials class A1, but boards only as class B2 (flammable) owing to their additives. The behaviour with regard to moisture depends heavily on the hydrophobic treatment. Unprotected grains are vulnerable to moisture and must be suitably protected. Generally, however, expanded perlite does not rot and does not promote mould growth.
It is resistant to chemicals and traditional building materials. Rodents and insects do not attack perlite.

Forms of supply
The customary forms of supply are:

• Loose fill:	sacks	100 l
	grains	2–8 mm
• Boards:	length	1200 mm
	width	600 mm
	thickness	20–80 mm

Installation advice
Cutting and working the boards is easy and does not call for any special safety measures. Owing to the dust, the wearing of a dust mask is recommended when installing loose fill. Blown insulation should only be installed by specialist contractors who are aware of and can allow for the settlement behaviour of the material.

Health and ecological aspects
Neither the processing nor the use of this insulating material results in any health risks.
The majority of perlite is obtained from southern Europe and South America. This is a finite resource and its use is coupled with long transport distances.

Recycling
Loose fill can be reused as insulating material or as an aggregate for mortar and concrete. Only rarely can bonded boards be reused and so they must be disposed of as building debris according to local regulations; composite boards should be treated depending on their make-up.

Applications for expanded perlite

Roof and suspended floor:	
DAD	• External insulation, protected from the weather, below roof covering
DAA	• External insulation, protected from the weather, below waterproofing (with very high compressive strength)
DZ	• Insulation between rafters, double-skin roof, topmost suspended floor
DI	• Internal insulation below suspended floor, below rafters or loadbearing structure
DEO	• Below screed, without sound insulation requirements
DES	• Below screed, with sound insulation requirements
Wand:	
WAB	• External insulation behind cladding
WAP	• External insulation behind render
WZ	• Cavity insulation to double-leaf walls
WH	• Timber-frame and timber-panel forms of construction
WI	• Internal insulation to wall
WTR	• Insulation to separating walls
WTH	• Between party walls with sound insulation requirements

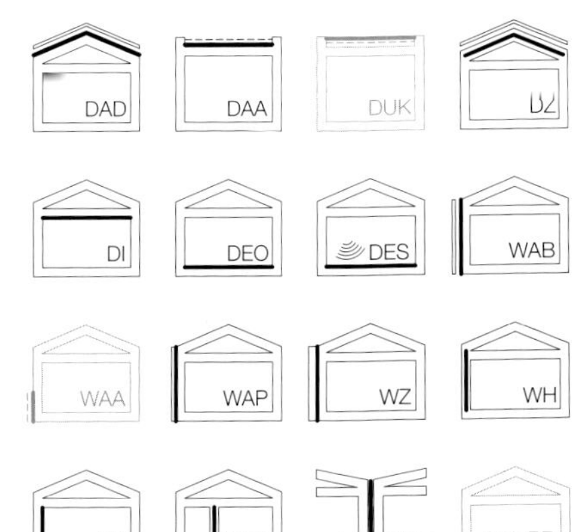

Physical properties – vermiculite, mica

Property	Unit	Values
Density	kg/m³	70–160
Thermal conductivity	W/(mK)	0.046–0.070
Specific heat capacity	J/(kgK)	800–1000
Reaction to fire untreated granulate boards		 A1 (incombustible) B1 (not readily flammable)
Water vapour diffusion resistance index	–	3–4
Long-term water absorption	% by vol.	≤ 5
Maximum service temperature, long-term	°C	700–1600
Compressive stress at 10% deformation or compressive strength (boards only)	kPa	100–450

Exfoliated vermiculite (EV), expanded mica

Exfoliated vermiculite and expanded mica are dealt with together here because they are very similar. An approval is required for applications in building (see p. 60). Standardising regulations are available for exfoliated vermiculite aggregate (EVA), coated (EVC), bitumen-coated (EVB), hydrophobic (EVH) and pre-mixed vermiculite (EVM). These products are also listed in Construction Products List B.

Raw materials and production
Vermiculite is an aluminium-iron-magnesium silicate. In terms of both its appearance and its microstructure, it resembles the expanded mica minerals – sheet silicates in which the bonding forces are weak and therefore easy to split. Both vermiculite and mica are granulated and abruptly heated to more 1000°C. The water inclusions between the layers of rock vaporise due to the abrupt rise in temperature and in doing so expand the granulate to 15 to 20 times its original size (exfoliation). Boards and moulded parts are mostly produced from vermiculite granulate which is pressed in moulds with the addition of bitumen, silicates or synthetic resin.

Development and market significance
In recent years, expanded mica has been used as an inexpensive substitute for window panes. The production methods and the use as an insulating material first appeared in the 21st century. With a market share of much less than 1%, vermiculite and mica insulating materials play only a minor role in the market.

Properties and applications
The thermal and impact sound insulation properties are moderate to good. Their reaction to fire varies from incombustible to not readily flammable depending on the additives used. They do not rot, are resistant to acids and alkalis and are uninteresting for insects and rodents. In building work, vermiculite and mica are preferred for applications in the voids of roofs and suspended floors. The granulate can also be used to level uneven floors or flat roofs. Boards are suitable for all floating screeds plus applications with hot bitumen.
Further applications include lagging to industrial plant and back-panel insulation in household appliances.

Forms of supply
The insulating materials can be supplied as

- Boards: length 1000, 2500 mm; width 610, 1250 mm; thickness 15–80 mm
- Moulded parts: for pipe diameters DN 15–273 mm; length 667 mm; thickness 30–50 mm
- Loose fill: grains 0–15 mm; sacks, big bags, silos

Applications for exfoliated vermiculite

Roof and suspended floor:	
DAD	• External insulation, protected from the weather, below roof covering
DAA	• External insulation, protected from the weather, below waterproofing (with very high compressive strength)
DZ	• Insulation between rafters, double-skin roof, topmost suspended floor
DI	• Internal insulation below suspended floor, below rafters or loadbearing structure.
DEO	• Below screed, without sound insulation requirements
DES	• Below screed, with sound insulation requirements
Wall:	
WAB	• External insulation behind cladding
WAP	• External insulation behind render
WZ	• Cavity insulation to double-leaf walls
WH	• Timber-frame and timber-panel forms of construction
WI	• Internal insulation to wall
WTR	• Insulation to separating walls
WTH	• Between party walls with sound insulation requirements

Installation advice
Blown insulation should only be installed by specialist contractors. Loose fill insulation can be readily compacted and if necessary cemented in place with binders such as lime, clay, gypsum, loam, cement or resin.
Boards are easy to install. The wearing of a dust mask is recommended when cutting larger quantities.
Material without a hydrophobic treatment is hygroscopic and should be protected against moisture.

Health and ecological aspects
Various ecology institutes have confirmed that vermiculite and mica do not involve any health risks.
The main deposits are found in South Africa, the USA and the Russian Kola peninsular. The raw material obtained from open-cast mines is used in large quantities outside the building sector, e.g. for cat litter.

Recycling
Untreated granulate and boards can be reused directly or for loosening soils, or disposed of in landfill as mineral building debris. Bonded boards and bitumenised granulate must be disposed of by special means.

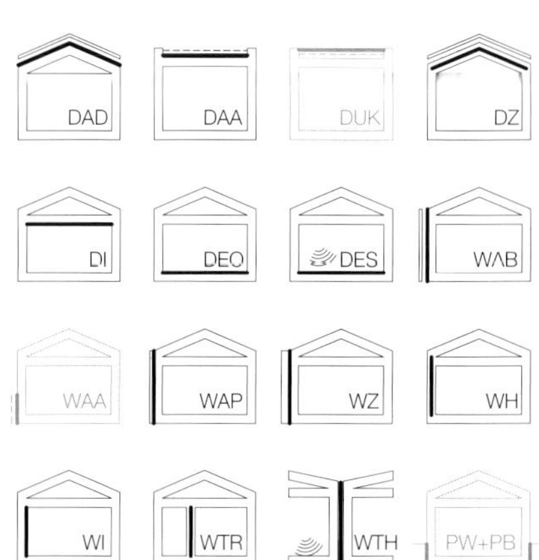

Expanded clay

When used as a thermal insulating material, expanded clay does not have to comply with any standard and therefore does not require a national technical approval (see p. 60).

Raw materials and production
The raw material is low-lime clay. It is ground, granulated and expanded at a temperature of 1000–1200°C in rotary kilns. During this process, the outer skin of the clay beads is sintered. At the same time, an expansion effect takes place inside due to the splitting of oxygen molecules and the decomposition of carbon compounds. Heavy oils are sometimes used as blowing agents. The resulting beads exhibit a stable outer skin and a fine-pore core.

Development and market significance
Expanded clay was first developed around 1917 in the USA, and since 1955 has also been produced in Germany. Its position in the insulating materials market is insignificant; its more usual use is as an aggregate in other materials.

Properties and applications
Expanded clay has only moderate thermal insulation properties. It is very open to diffusion and can absorb a considerable amount of moisture. It is an incombustible material to DIN 4102 building materials class A1 and is also highly resistant to chemicals. Rodents and insects find no nutrients in expanded clay; however, fungi can grow on it if moisture is constantly present.

When used as a thermal insulation material, expanded clay is mainly used to fill voids and, for example, contributes to improving the sound insulation of suspended floor constructions. It cannot be used in applications where compression is expected.
Expanded clay is also used as an aggregate in the manufacture of masonry units and precast concrete elements, and in a small grain size for improving the insulation properties of mortar, render and plaster.

Forms of supply
Dry loose fill is supplied as follows:
- Sacks: 50 l
- Big bags: 1000 or 2500 l
- Silos: for blown insulation application

Installation advice
This loose fill material is easy to use without any special measures, in DIY or projects. There is no significant dust build-up or static discharge. The loose fill is merely levelled with a straightedge. As expanded clay absorbs moisture quickly, it must be stored in dry conditions and protected against moisture during installation.

Health and ecological aspects
Processing and use do not involve any health risks.

Applications for expanded clay

Roof and suspended floor:	
DAD	• External insulation, protected from the weather, below roof covering
DZ	• Insulation between rafters, double-skin-roof, topmost suspended floor
DEO	• Below screed, without sound insulation-requirements
Wall:	
WH	• Timber-frame and timber-panel forms of construction
WI	• Internal insulation to wall
WTR	• Insulation to separating walls

The raw materials are readily available locally and the transport distances are short. However, the extraction of clay in open-cast mining operations is associated with a major intervention in the natural environment, which is why attention should be given to restoration measures.

Recycling
Loose fill can very easily be reused for insulating purposes, in the construction of green roofs, in hydroponics and for ground improvement measures.
Disposal in landfill as building debris does not involve any problems.

Physical properties – expanded clay

Property	Unit	Values
Density	kg/m³	260–500
Bulk density	kg/m³	275–420
Thermal conductivity	W/(mK)	0.085–0.100
Specific heat capacity	J/(kgK)	1100
Reaction to fire Building materials class	A1 (incombustible)	
Water vapour diffusion resistance index	–	2–8

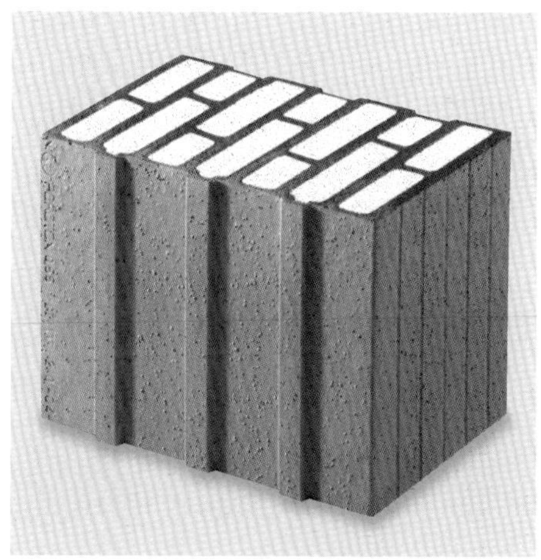

Pumice

Pumice is a vesicular volcanic rock. The pores that ensue during eruptions ensure a light weight and moderate thermal insulation properties.

Natural, angular pumice with an aggregate of expanded perlite can be used as loose fill for insulating purposes. Furthermore, the use of pumice as an aggregate in the manufacture of concrete bricks, so-called pumice-concrete bricks, or in lightweight mortars, is well known.

The characteristic physical properties of pumice are given in the table below.

Natural pumice does not rot. Untreated material can be reused or disposed of in landfill without any problems.

Pumice plays no significant role as a thermal insulation material. There are therefore no suppliers who market pumice for insulation purposes.

Physical properties – pumice

Property	Unit	Values
Density	kg/m^3	175–285
Thermal conductivity	W/(mK)	0.060–0.080
Specific heat capacity	J/(kgK)	1000
Water vapour diffusion resistance index	–	4
Reaction to fire Building materials class	A1 (incombustible)	

Insulating clay bricks

Since the late 1990s, the brickmaking industry has been offering special masonry units with a thermal conductivity < 0.1 W/mK. Their insulating effect is therefore comparable with that of thermal insulating materials.

The clay content of the bricks was reduced by optimising the arrangement of the internal webs to such an extent that the loadbearing capacity for normal structural requirements is still sufficient but at the same time the thermal insulating properties are considerably better than in the past.
The arrangement of the webs results in a highly porous internal structure but the sizes of the voids vary among the different products and are either left hollow or filled with an insulating material. Expanded perlite or a special mineral granulate (similar to rock wool) is used as a filling material.

Insulating clay bricks meet the requirements of DIN 4102 building materials class A1. Walls plastered on both sides can fulfil the requirements of fire resistance class F 90-A, depending on overall thickness. Such bricks may not, however, be used for fire compartment walls.

In order to reduce the mortar's influence on the thermal conductivity of the wall, these products are constructed exclusively as precision bricks laid in thin-bed mortar. In the majority of cases these clay bricks cannot be chased horizontally for pipes and cables, or at best only to a very limited extent, because this has a serious effect on the structural properties. Cutting to size, chases and drilled holes can lead to the insulating material being lost from large voids and hence to a reduction in the insulating effect. Such matters must be taken into account when installing services.

Requirements and the detailed regulations covering usage are described in the respective national technical approval documents for each product.

Physical properties – insulating clay bricks

Property	Unit	Values
Density	kg/m^3	500–750
Thermal conductivity	W/(mK)	0.080–0.140
Water vapour diffusion resistance index	–	5–10
Reaction to fire Building materials class	A1 (incombustible)	

1 

2 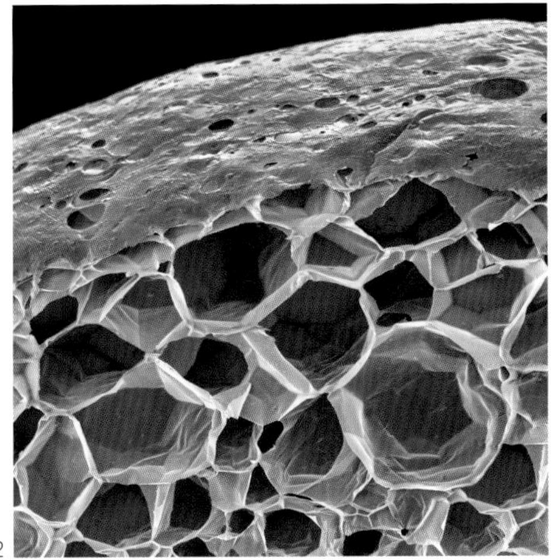

1 Insulating boards made from expanded polystyrene
2 Cell structure of IR-modified EPS

Expanded polystyrene (EPS)

DIN EN 13163 is valid for factory-made expanded polystyrene products. They meet the requirements of Construction Products List B (see p. 62).

Raw materials and production
EPS is produced from polystyrene, a blowing agent (pentane), a flame retardant (HBCD) and stabilisers.
The production of EPS insulating materials takes place in several stages. Firstly, the polystyrene granulate is obtained through the polymerisation of styrene and the addition of a blowing agent. In the next stage, this granulate of glass-like beads with a diameter of up to 3 mm is expanded by 20 to 50 times its original volume through steam treatment. During this process, the blowing agent vaporises. Following a cooling phase, the beads are expanded for a second time with steam and this causes them to join together – plastic and slightly sticky – to form a homogeneous material. This results in large-format blocks which, following a period of storage, are cut to form boards and sections. Individual boards with finished surfaces and edges can be produced in special automatic foaming plants, which with appropriate densities and owing to their closed-pore surface can also be used for external basement insulation.

Development and market significance
Expanded polystyrene was first developed in 1951 and the name Styropor is a registered trademark of BASF. In the German-speaking countries, Styropor is frequently used as a synonym for EPS.
The well-known white EPS foam underwent further development in the mid-1990s: the inclusion of graphite particles in the cell structure enabled the thermal conductivity to be reduced even further. The graphite particles are the reason for the silver-grey colour of the foam material and they act as an infrared absorber which reflects much of the heat radiation and prevents it passing through the material. Such "IR absorber-modified EPS" has lowered the thermal conductivity even at low densities, and values as low as 0.032 W/mK have been measured. To achieve such figures, conventional EPS would need to be twice as dense.

EPS insulating materials are inexpensive and readily available; their market share in Germany is about 30%. EPS boards are particularly popular for thermal insulation composite systems.

Properties and applications
EPS insulating materials have good to very good insulating properties, are not hygroscopic and do not rot; their compressive strength depends on the particular type of board.
Special "elasticised" boards are also suitable as impact sound insulation and can achieve improvements of up to 30 dB on hard substrates.

The production parameters enable a wide range of products with various qualities which depend heavily on the density and the degree of adhesion between the individual beads. The spectrum ranges from large beads joined at only a few points, e.g. for bitumenised drainage boards, to degrees of adhesion in which there are almost no interstitial spaces between the beads and which, for example, are used for thermal insulation composite systems or, in higher densities, for applications subjected to compression loads. EPS with hydrophobic treatment can be used for external basement insulation.
The new IR absorber-modified qualities can be used for the well-known standard applications apart from external basement insulation.

Many board types carry national technical approvals for use as external basement insulation or as part of a thermal insulation composite system. Some manufacturers can supply approved special products for use on upside-down roofs and as load-bearing thermal insulation below ground floor slabs with a moderate loading.
EPS boards are also used as the frost protection layer below roads and in landscaping projects. In addition, EPS can be processed to form a multitude of custom and shaped parts, e.g. for roller shutter housings and as decorative elements on plastered surfaces.

Some suppliers can also provide EPS as a loose fill material for insulating voids. A national technical approval is, however, required in such instances.

When exposed to ultraviolet radiation for some time (several weeks or months), the surface of EPS will discolour and become brittle. Covering materials and finishes should therefore be applied without delay. Polystyrene is very vulnerable to solvents, also fuels and mineral oils. However, EPS is not affected significantly by the majority of acids and alkalis. EPS is not suitable for use in conjunction with hot bitumen or mastic asphalt.

Forms of supply
Typical dimensions of EPS boards:
- Length: 1000 mm
- Width: 500 mm
- Thickness: 10–300 mm

The edges are usually finished plain, but for special applications edges with straight or lipped rebates can be supplied.

Other board forms can also be supplied depending on the application:

- Customised insulating boards incorporating falls
- Large-format boards for prefabricated roof elements
- Combined EPS/waterproofing segmented rolls for flat roofs
- Insulating boards profiled on one side for the corrugated and trapezoidal profile sheeting of industrial sheds
- Boards with profiled surfaces for external basement insulation
- Boards with slits on alternate sides for clamping between rafters

Installation advice

EPS is easy to install. Thinner boards can be cut with a knife, thicker ones with a circular-saw or bandsaw. Individual beads can be lost when cutting boards with a loose structure; a hot-wire cutter or hot knife is therefore recommended for accurate cutting. Cutting, sawing and drilling on site do not result in any dust or other unpleasant effects. However, individual particles can pick up a static charge or be blown around in draughts.

Health and ecological aspects

Polystyrene is classed as biologically neutral and is also approved as a material for the packaging of foodstuffs.
The processing and use of EPS insulating materials does not involve any health risks. As has been confirmed by measurements, the emission of residual styrene monomers lies below the recommended maximum workplace concentration and the amounts are so low that they cannot be verified in the interior air. However, during a fire, styrene and polycyclic aromatic hydrocarbons (PAH) are released.
The pentane used as a blowing agent has, in principle, a low environmental impact, and some manufacturers even recover the pentane within the production process.

Recycling

In Germany, clean offcuts and waste from building sites are collected at approx. 1500 depots, where it is crushed and recycled to form, for example, packaging materials or a lightweight aggregate for concrete, masonry units, mortar, render and plaster.
If recycling is not possible, EPS waste can be disposed of in special landfill sites according to valid regional regulations under waste code No. 17 06 04 for insulating material or No. 17 09 04 for mixed building and demolition debris. Many waste incineration plants use plastic foam waste to assist the firing. If the ensuing energy is used for generating heat, the energy content of the plastic foam can be recovered.

Applications for EPS

Roof and suspended floor:	
DAD	• External insulation, protected from the weather, below roof covering
DAA	• External insulation, protected from the weather, below waterproofing (moderate to high compressive strength)
DZ	• Insulation between rafters, double-skin roof, topmost suspended floor
DI	• Internal insulation below suspended floor, below rafters or loadbearing structure
DEO	• Below screed, without sound insulation requirements
DES	• Below screed, with sound insulation requirements (low to higher compressibility)
Wall:	
WAB	• External insulation behind cladding
WAA	• External insulation behind waterproofing (moderate to high compressive strength)
WAP	• External insulation behind render
WZ	• Cavity insulation to double-leaf walls
WI	• Internal insulation to wall
External basement insulation (with approval only):	
PW	• Walls in contact with the soil
PB	• Ground floor slabs in contact with the soil

Physical properties – EPS

Property	Unit	Values
Density	kg/m³	15–30
Thermal conductivity	W/mK	0.032–0.040
Specific heat capacity	J/kgK	1500
Coefficient of thermal expansion	K^{-1}	$5 \times 10^{-5} - 7 \times 10^{-5}$
Reaction to fire		
Euroclass	E	
Bldg. materials class	B1 (not readily flammable)	
Water vapour diffusion resistance index	–	20–100
Long-term water absorption	% by vol.	1–5
Maximum service temperature, long-term	°C	80–85
Compressive stress at 10% deformation or compressive strength	kPa	60–200
Constant compr. stress	kPa	20–60
Tensile strength perpendicular to plane of board	kPa	> 100
Bending strength	kPa	≥ 50
Dynamic stiffness	MN/m³	10–40

Extruded polystyrene foam (XPS)

DIN EN 13164 is valid for factory-made insulating materials made from extruded polystyrene foam. They meet the requirements of Construction Products List B (see p. 62).

Raw materials and production
XPS is manufactured from polystyrene and blowing agents (usually CO_2 or HFC), dyes and fire retardants (HBCD – hexabrom cyclododecane).
This process involves melting a milky-opaque polystyrene granulate at approx. 200°C in an extruder, mixing it with additives and extruding it continuously through a slot die onto a conveyor belt. In doing so, the molten material under pressure expands considerably and takes on a homogeneous structure with 98% closed cells and the characteristic smooth foam skin on both sides. After cooling, the foam material can be cut to size and the edges profiled.

Development and market significance
In 1941 the American Ministry of Defence financed the development of a lightweight foam material whose specification called for it to be waterproof and have a high compressive strength. The intention was to use the material as a floating and buoyancy aid for crossing rivers. It soon became clear that the new foam material also possessed good thermal insulation properties. Up until the end of the 1980s, the blowing agents used for extruded foam were fully halogenated chlorofluorocarbons (CFC 12). As a result of new legislation, more environmentally-friendly, partly halogenated chlorofluorocarbons (CFC 142b) were employed thereafter. Today, manufacturers use zero-chlorine blowing agents (CO_2, HFC 134a or HFC 152a) exclusively.
With a market share of about 6%, XPS is used primarily for those applications in which high demands are placed on moisture resistance and good compressive strength.

Properties and applications
Extruded polystyrene foam combines three essential properties: low thermal conductivity, high compressive strength and moisture resistance. XPS does not provide a home for insects or pests and does not rot.

It was not until the advent of these properties that applications such as external basement insulation and upside-down roofs could even be considered.
As XPS laid underwater absorbs virtually no water, it is the only insulating material that can be installed in hydrostatic pressure conditions without an additional protective layer.
XPS is not suitable for use as impact sound insulation.

Besides the traditional applications in ground floors, walls and roofs, extruded polystyrene foam is also used for thermally insulated, unclad soffits in warehouses and agricultural buildings plus the ground floors of cold stores and ice rinks.

XPS insulating materials comply with requirements of Construction Products List B, but currently must be regulated via national technical approvals because products with the blowing agents used these days have been in use for only a relatively short period of time. According to DIN 4108-2, XPS may also be used as standard as external basement insulation plus for gravel-surfaced upside-down roofs. However, use as external basement insulation in groundwater, loadbearing external basement insulation beneath ground floor slabs (see p. 84) and insulation in parking decks according to the upside-down principle (see pp. 80–81) all require national technical approvals.

For sanitary applications, XPS is available as a so-called tiling element which is covered with a fabric on both sides ready to receive ceramic tiles – for separating walls and showers.
In addition, the material is used as the sandwich filling to door and facade elements, in vehicles and as the frost protection layer below roads and railways.

Forms of supply
The extrusion method means that only boards can be produced. The following dimensions are available as standard:

- Length: 1250, 2500 mm
- Width: 600 mm
- Thickness 20–180 mm
- Edges: plain, rebate, tongue and groove

Besides the production-related smooth surface finish, surfaces with embossed patterns or with the smooth skin "planed" off can also be supplied (both intended to provide a key for following work), also fluted surfaces laminated with fleece for drainage purposes.
XPS can also be supplied as a formwork element for thermal bridge insulation.

Installation advice
The processing of the material on the building site does not call for any special safety measures. The stable boards can be easily cut, sawn and chased with conventional tools. Special cutting is carried out with a hot-wire cutter, hot knife or CNC cutting equipment.
Several layers of XPS can be laid in ground floor, wall and internal applications, also warm deck roof constructions. However, this is not possible in an upside-down roof for building physics reasons because

diffusion and condensation can lead to an increase in the moisture absorption in the lower layer of boards over time; the upper layer of boards prevents the lower layer drying out (see p. 81).

Only boards with a rough or profiled surface are suitable as a backing for concrete, adhesives, render and plaster because boards with a smooth foam skin do not provide an adequate key.

Extruded polystyrene foam is not resistant to ultraviolet radiation. In the case of long-term exposure (several months), the surface initially becomes discoloured (yellow to brown) and after further exposure becomes "dusty". However, the internal cell structure of the material remains unchanged. If a damaged surface is to be used as a substrate for render or plaster, it must be thoroughly brushed down and its soundness checked.

When installing XPS, it must be remembered that solvents, adhesives and mineral oils can dissolve the surface and at higher concentrations even destroy the material completely.

Health and ecological aspects
The processing and use of XPS boards does not involve any health risks. Contact with precipitation, moisture in the soil and groundwater does not cause any substances to be released.

From the ecological viewpoint, XPS products produced exclusively with CO_2 as a blowing agent are to be preferred because the quantity of CO_2 required for the production is often matched by the CO_2 equivalent saving in the heating energy over six months. Compared with this, an HFC blowing agent has a much higher GWP (Global Warming Potential, see p. 98).

Physical properties – XPS

Property	Unit	Values
Density	kg/m³	25–45
Thermal conductivity	W/mK	0.030–0.040
Specific heat capacity	J/kgK	1300–1700
Coefficient of thermal expansion	K^{-1}	6×10^{-5} to 8×10^{-5}
Reaction to fire Euroclass Bldg. materials class	 E B1 (not readily flammable)	
Water vapour diffusion resistance index μ	–	80–200[1]
Long-term water absorption	% by vol.	0.1–0.3
Maximum service temperature, long-term	°C	75
Compressive stress at 10% deformation or compressive strength	kPa	150–700
Constant compr. stress	kPa	50–250

[1] depends on board thickness: thin boards have a high μ-value

Applications for XPS

Roof and suspended floor:

DAD	• External insulation, protected from the weather, below roof covering
DAA	• External insulation, protected from the weather, below waterproofing (medium, high and very high compressive strength)
DUK	• External insulation exposed to the weather (upside-down roof), (high, very high and extremely high compressive strength)
DI	• Internal insulation below suspended floor, below rafters or loadbearing structure, topmost suspended floor
DEO	• Below screed, without sound insulation requirements (high and very high compressive strength)

Wall:

WAB	• External insulation behind cladding
WAP	• External insulation behind render
WZ	• Cavity insulation to double-leaf walls
WI	• Internal insulation to wall

External basement insulation:

PW	• Walls in contact with the soil (medium, high and very high compressive strength)
PB	• Ground floor slabs in contact with the soil (medium, high and very high compressive strength)

Recycling
Used, clean XPS insulating materials can be disposed of in landfill according to regional regulations as an insulating material (waste code No. 17 06 04) or as mixed building and demolition debris (No. 17 09 04).
In the ideal case, undamaged insulating material obtained from deconstruction measures can be reused directly.
Energy generation through combustion in waste incineration plants is also possible.

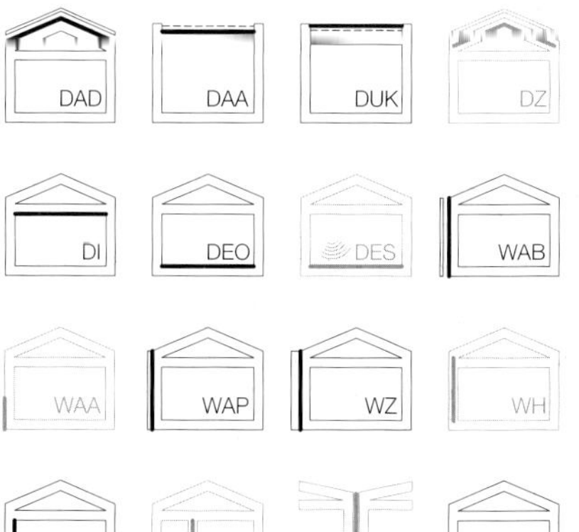

Polyurethane rigid foam (PUR)

DIN EN 13165 covers factory-made products of polyurethane rigid foam. PUR rigid foam complies with the requirements of Construction Products List B (see p. 62).

Raw materials and production
Polyurethane is produced from two main components: polyalcohol and polyisocyanate (P-MDI). Polyalcohols can be obtained from crude oil or, alternatively, from sugar beet, maize or potatoes. The blowing agents used are mainly pentane and CO_2/ pentane mixtures, the flame retardant usually TCPP (tri-(dichlorisopropyl)-phosphate). The group of PUR foams includes PIR-modified polyurethanes. PIR (polyisocyanurate) is based primarily on isocyanurate rings, which bring about a stronger cross-linking of the foam material. Their temperature stability and reaction to fire is therefore better. For technical reasons, these foams are produced from a PUR/PIR mixture which with just a small amount of flame retardant achieves DIN 4102 building materials class B2.

The manufacture of PUR rigid foam boards is carried out according to the lamination method. Here, the two-part mixture is spread via nozzles onto a conveyor belt where it foams up and adheres to upper and lower facings of fleece, bitumen flexible sheeting, metal foils or composite sheeting, depending on the intended application.
Blocks are produced in the so-called slabstock method in which the reaction mixture is fed from a mixing head into a block mould. Following the foaming-up process and storage, the blocks (up to 5 m long) are cut into boards or shaped parts.

Development and market significance
The industrial manufacture of polyurethane began as long ago as 1937. As this material can be processed in many ways and is suitable for diverse applications, it also plays a major role outside the construction industry, e.g. for shoe soles, as synthetic leather or as foam for upholstered furniture.
It was during the 1960s and 1970s that polyurethane started to gain importance as a thermal insulation material. The CFC (chlorofluorocarbon) blowing agents common at that time were replaced from the late 1980s onwards by more environmentally friendly partly halogenated CFCs and later by zero-chlorine HFCs. Today, pentane (hydrocarbon) is the most widespread blowing agent.
Polyurethane rigid foams enjoy a market share of 5% in Germany.

Properties and applications
PUR rigid foams have more than 90% closed cells and are characterised by very low thermal conductivities and high compressive strengths. Without facings they are open to diffusion and exhibit a favourable reaction to fire.
Combined with vapour-tight facings, PUR boards can achieve particularly low thermal conductivities, and these values may be assumed over the long-term because ageing processes such as the slow release of the cell gas through diffusion are already allowed for in the design values.

PUR exhibits good resistance to the solvents in adhesives, bituminous materials or sealing compounds, and also to the plasticisers contained, for example, in PVC sheeting. Fuels, mineral oils and diluted acids and alkalis attack PUR to only a limited degree. It does not rot and is resistant to mould, but suffers when constantly exposed to ultraviolet light.
The main applications for insulating boards are flat roofs, pitched roofs and floors. Another major application is as the insulating core in metal sandwich elements for roof and facade constructions and industrial structures. Furthermore, PUR makes a good insulating infill in door and facade elements, overhead doors, roller shutters and in the sections for post-and-rail constructions and window frames.

PUR rigid foam boards are frequently used in floors not required to meet impact sound insulation requirements because they combine high compressive strength and good insulating properties, which leads to a thinner overall floor construction.
Boards with very high compressive strengths up to 500 kPa can also be used in heavily loaded industrial floors and parking decks. Special boards made from recycled material with compressive strengths up to 900 kPa and a thermal conductivity around 0.070 W/mK are also possible.
PUR rigid foam has good temperature stability and can briefly withstand temperatures up to 250°C, which means it can be used in conjunction with hot bitumen without any problems. Special PUR products are available for special applications such as the insulation of tanks for liquid gas subjected to constant temperatures of -196°C, or for the insulation of steam lines at temperatures of up to +200°C.

Some products have been granted national technical approvals that permit their use in special applications such as thermal insulation composite systems and external basement insulation.

Forms of supply
The method of manufacture means that PUR insulating materials can be supplied as boards and moulded parts. Many products are provided with facings of glass-fibre fleece, lightweight bitumen flexible sheeting or aluminium foil. Sandwich elements are frequently combined with sheet metal, aluminium foil or plastic sheeting, even wood-based products.

Typical dimensions for boards in building work are:

- Length: 600, 1000, 1200, 2400 mm
- Width: 500, 600, 800, 1020 mm
- Thickness: 20–300 mm
- Edges: plain, rebate, tongue and groove

Custom products can be supplied – also in very large dimensions, e.g. sandwich elements in lengths up to 24 m.
Moulded parts made from PUR are available for insulating pipes of various diameters.

Installation advice
No special safety measures are necessary when working the material on the building site. The stable boards are easy to cut, saw and chase with conventional tools. They can be laid in one or more layers and also in conjunction with hot bitumen as an adhesive.
The surface of PUR foam can be damaged by ultraviolet radiation where it is left exposed. Any such damage must be vigorously brushed away before using the material.

Health and ecological aspects, recycling
Neither the processing nor use of PUR rigid foams are linked with any physiological problems.

Besides the reuse of undamaged boards, a number of other recycling options are available:

- Compression moulding (materials recovery), in which the ground foam material is mixed with PUR binders and pressed to form moisture-resistant boards.
- Glycolysis (raw materials recovery), in which PUR with a known composition is liquidised by glycol and can then be reused to produce new PUR foam materials.
- Incineration (thermal reuse) in modern waste incineration plants with energy recovery.
- Disposal in landfill according to the local regulations is also possible.

Applications for PUR rigid foam

Roof and suspended floor:

DAD	• External insulation, protected from the weather, below roof covering
DAA	• External insulation, protected from the weather, below waterproofing (high and very high compressive strength)
DZ	• Insulation between rafters, double-skin roof, topmost suspended floor
DI	• Internal insulation below suspended floor, below rafters or loadbearing structure
DEO	• Below screed, without sound insulation requirements (high and very high compressive strength)

Wall:

WAB	• External insulation behind cladding
WAA	• External insulation behind waterproofing
WAP	• External insulation behind render
WZ	• Cavity insulation to double-leaf walls
WH	• Timber-frame and timber-panel forms of construction
WI	• Internal insulation to wall

External basement insulation (with approval only):

PW	• Walls in contact with the soil
PB	• Ground floor slabs in contact with the soil

Physical properties – PUR rigid foam

Property	Unit	Values
Density	kg/m³	30–100
Thermal conductivity	W/mK	0.024–0.030
Specific heat capacity	J/kgK	1400–1500
Coefficient of thermal expansion	K^{-1}	5×10^{-5}–8×10^{-5}
Reaction to fire		
Euroclass		C-s3, d0 B-s2, d0 (sandwich panel)
Bldg. materials class		B1 (not readily flammable) B2 (flammable)
Water vapour diffusion resistance index		
without coating	–	30–200
with dense facings	–	∞ (vapour-tight)
Long-term water absorption	% by vol.	1.3–3
Water absorption in diffusion test	% by vol.	6
Maximum service temperature, long-term	°C	-30 to +120
Compressive stress at 10% deformation or compressive strength	kPa	100–500
Constant compressive stress (2% deformation after 50 years)	kPa	20–30
Tensile strength perpendicular to plane of board	kPa	40

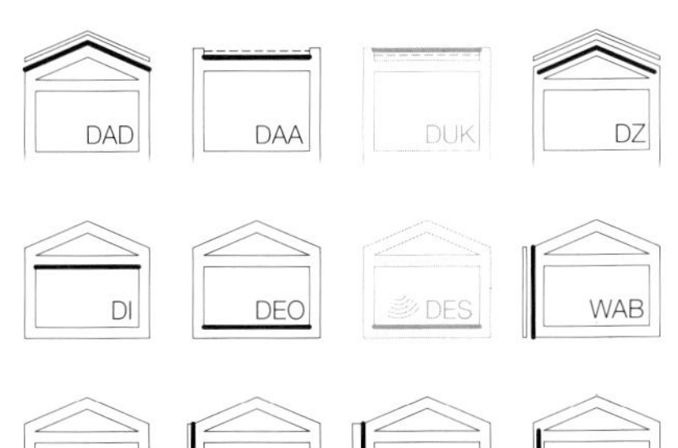

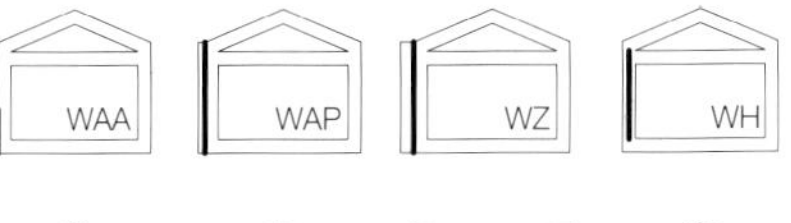

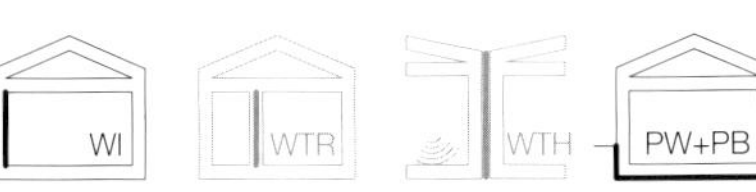

Physical properties – PUR in situ foam

Property	Unit	Values
Density	kg/m³	35–65
Thermal conductivity (characteristic value)	W/mK	0.030
Specific heat capacity	J/kgK	1400–1500
Coefficient of thermal expansion	K^{-1}	5×10^{-5} to 8×10^{-5}
Reaction to fire	B2 (flammable)	
Water vapour diffusion resistance index	–	60–110
Water absorption after 7 days storage in water	% by vol.	1.4–2.1
Maximum service temperature, long-term	°C	-30 to +120
Compressive strength at 7% deformation	kPa	210–420

Polyurethane in situ foam (PUR)

PUR in situ foams carry national technical approvals. A European standard, prEN 14315 "Thermal insulation products for buildings – In-situ formed sprayed rigid polyurethane foam (PUR) products", is in preparation.

Raw materials and production
The raw materials for PUR in situ foam are, like for PUR rigid foam, isocyanates (MDI) and polyalcohols, with the addition of HFC and CO_2 as blowing agents and TCPP as a flame retardant.
PUR spray foams are employed when applying insulation to large areas.
In the spray method, the two liquid components are mixed in situ with mobile high-pressure apparatus, pumped via heated hoses to a spray gun where they are thoroughly mixed as they are ejected. Trained operatives spray the reactive mixture onto the prepared substrate, where it foams up and cures immediately without the need for any seams or joints.

Development and market significance
Sprayed PUR foam for large areas is not common as thermal insulation in northern and central Europe. In southern Europe, however, it is a popular thermal insulation system for industrial, residential and agricultural buildings. This material is much better known in the form of PUR foam in spray cans, which is used during the installation of doors and windows or for filling smaller voids. As this material is not classified as in situ foam, nor as an insulating material, it is not included in this review.

Properties and applications
PUR in situ foam is characterised by excellent thermal insulation properties and a high compressive strength. It can withstand weak acids and bases, industrial fumes, fuels and mineral oils, but suffers when exposed to ultraviolet radiation.

Sprayed PUR foam offers advantages primarily in the case of complicated surfaces with many penetrations such as rooflights, pipes and floor- or roof-mounted structures. It adheres to almost all sound substrates and can be sprayed seamlessly onto floors, walls and soffits, even around complicated shapes. This prevents air leaks and thermal bridges.
When used in conjunction with suitable coatings, sprayed PUR foam acting as the thermal insulation and, at the same time, the waterproofing to industrial roofs, is resistant to flying sparks and radiant heat. However, an additional UV-resistant coating with a national technical approval must be used in such instances.
Owing to the variable application options, PUR in situ foam can also be used for filling voids, for covering the surfaces of profiled components, for insulating pipes and vessels, and in shipbuilding.

Installation advice
The application of sprayed PUR foam may only be carried out by approved, specialist contractors. The foam may only be applied to clean, dry and dust-free substrates, and the weather conditions (temperature, humidity, wind) must be taken into account during the work. As a rule, at least three layers of sprayed foam each with a thickness of 10–30 mm will usually be required, depending on the particular application. The sprayed foam hardens relatively rapidly and cures within a few minutes.

Forms of supply
The components are supplied in transportable drums or containers depending on the amount required.

Health and ecological aspects, recycling
Like PUR rigid foam, PUR in situ foam involves no physiological problems, and the same recycling options are available. However, the removal of the foam material from composite products is laborious and expensive. In such cases incineration or disposal in landfill according to local regulations is probably the better option.

Applications for PUR in situ foam

Roof and suspended floor:	
DAA	• External insulation, protected from the weather, below waterproofing
DZ	• Insulation between rafters, double-skin roof, topmost suspended floor
DI	• Internal insulation below suspended floor, below rafters or loadbearing structure
DEO	• Below screed, without sound insulation requirements (high and very high compressive strength)
Wall:	
WZ	• Cavity insulation to double-leaf walls
WI	• Internal insulation to wall

Phenolic foam (PF)

Factory-made thermal insulating materials of phenolic resin are covered by DIN EN 13166. They comply with the requirements of Construction Products List B (see p. 62).

Raw materials and production

The raw materials for producing the foam are phenolic resin and pentane as the blowing agent.

The phenolic resin is mixed with the blowing agent and a hardener and foamed in a continuous process on a conveyor belt. While on the belt, the initially viscous foam is laminated on both sides with glass fleece, which fixes the product. After curing and drying, the edges can be profiled.

Development and market significance

Phenolic resins were used around 1909 to produce the first plastic materials, e.g. Bakelite. Insulating boards made from phenolic resin, also known as resol rigid foam boards, first appeared on the market in the 1970s. Phenolic foam is used as an insulating material in building applications to a limited extent only and is available from only a few manufacturers.

Properties and applications

Phenolic foam (also known as phenolic resin foam) is a brittle foam material with excellent thermal insulation properties because the high proportion of closed cells in the material prevents the loss of the highly insulating blowing agent almost completely.

The material's reaction to fire enables it to be classified in Euroclass C-s1, d0 because it is almost impossible to ignite. In the event of a fire, formaldehyde is released and a charcoal-like residue remains which continues to glow for a long time.

Phenolic foam exhibits good resistance to chemicals, insects and rodents. The insulating boards are ideal for applications in pitched roofs, e.g. as insulation above the rafters, on flat roofs and beneath steel trapezoidal profile sheeting.

Provided there are no impact sound insulation requirements to be satisfied, the boards can also be used under all types of subfloors and screeds, especially mastic asphalt, and under floors subjected to heavy loads.

Furthermore, phenolic foam can be used as the core insulation in sandwich elements.

Forms of supply

Phenolic foam is available in board form:

- Length: 1200 mm
- Width: 600, 1000 mm
- Thickness: 20–120 mm
- Edges: rebate
- Surface finish: laminated with glass fleece

Installation advice

Owing to its relatively high density, it is easy to cut with a saw, but owing to its brittleness, cutting the material to fit exactly between rafters, for example, is time-consuming. If the boards are laid below hot bitumen, an intermediate layer of expanded perlite boards is recommended. Direct contact between phenolic foam and metal should be avoided. When in contact with moisture, sulphonic acid can dissolve out of the phenol, which leads to corrosion damage (white rust).

Health and ecological aspects, recycling

Sound advice and information on the ecology of phenolic foam and possible recycling options for the products are unavailable. Incineration would seem to be the only option.

Applications for phenolic foam

Roof and suspended floor:	
DAD	• External insulation, protected from the weather, below roof covering
DAA	• External insulation, protected from the weather, below waterproofing
DZ	• Insulation between rafters, double-skin roof, topmost suspended floor
DI	• Internal insulation below suspended floor, below rafters or loadbearing structure
DEO	• Below screed, without sound insulation requirements (high and very high compressive strength)
Wall:	
WAB	• External insulation behind cladding
WAA	• External insulation behind waterproofing
WAP	• External insulation behind render
WZ	• Cavity insulation to double-leaf walls
WI	• Internal insulation to wall

Physical properties – phenolic foam

Property	Unit	Values
Density	kg/m³	40
Thermal conductivity	W/mK	0.022–0.040
Specific heat capacity	J/kgK	1500
Reaction to fire Euroclass Bldg. materials class	C-s1, d0 B2 (flammable)	
Water vapour diffusion resistance index	–	60
Maximum service temperature, long-term	°C	150
Compressive stress at 10% deformation or compressive strength	kPa	120

Melamine foam (MF)

Insulating materials made from melamine foam (also known as melamine resin foam) are not covered by any standards. An approval or a national test certificate is required for applications in buildings (see p. 60).

Melamine resin is the raw material used to which a blowing agent is added in a special method. This mixture foams up into blocks which are subsequently cut into boards and shaped parts.
The typical characteristic of melamine foam is its delicate three-dimensional network structure formed by slender and hence easily deformable webs.
This foam material has open cells, is very light and elastic, and exhibits good thermal insulation properties, a high sound-attenuation capacity and a high temperature stability. Even without the addition of flame retardants, it meets the requirements of DIN 4102 building materials class B1. For acoustic applications, an additional coating enables it to comply with DIN 4102 building materials class A2.
Melamine foam absorbs moisture readily and can tear under point loads, but new developments have resulted in very flexible product variants. This insulating material is, however, not permanently resistant to acids, bases and water, but is suitable for use in conjunction with solvent-based adhesives and reaction resins.

Melamine has been available since the 1980s. It is insignificant as a thermal insulating material but is frequently used for acoustics applications, as lagging to pipes and vessels, and in vehicles. Very different board formats are available, depending on application and manufacturer, but all are easy to work. Dust masks or dust extraction should be used when working with this material to ensure that the dust does not enter the respiratory tract.
The raw materials used mean that small amounts of formaldehyde are emitted, but these remain below the limits prescribed by legislation.
Melamine foam waste can be incinerated or disposed of in landfill according to local regulations.

Physical properties – melamine foam

Property	Unit	Values
Density	kg/m³	8–11
Thermal conductivity	W/mK	0.035
Reaction to fire Building materials class	B1 (not readily flammable)	
Water vapour diffusion resistance index	–	1–2
Maximum service-temperature, long-term	°C	220
Compressive stress at 10% deformation or compressive strength	kPa	4–20
Degree of sound absorption d = 50, f = 2000 Hz	%	> 90
Sound impedance	kPas/m²	8–20

Polyethylene foam (PE)

Insulating materials made from polyethylene foam carry national technical approvals. The ethylene ($CH_2{=}CH_2$) obtained from crude oil polymerises through cross-linking to form polyethylene. Isobutane is used as a blowing agent in the production of polyethylene foam.
The first soft foams made from polyethylene appeared as early as 1954. They play no role as thermal insulation materials in the building industry, but are very widespread as sound insulation batts and perimeter strips for floating screeds. However, the most frequent application for polyethylene foam is as lagging to hot and cold pipes in plumbing, heating, ventilation and air-conditioning systems, also in industrial plants and installations. PE foam's widespread use as pipe lagging is due to its high flexibility, high water vapour diffusion resistance and its usefulness over a wide range of temperatures. It is usually supplied as batts or on rolls or as strips for impact sound insulation. Polyethylene tubes for lagging pipes are mostly supplied with self-adhesive tabs, are easy to work and are quickly fitted around pipes. Furthermore, a multitude of products for the sport and leisure industries is available.

Physical properties – polyethylene foam

Property	Unit	Values
Density	kg/m³	50–110
Thermal conductivity at 10°C mean temperature	W/mK	0.033
Reaction to fire Bldg. materials class	B1 (not readily flammable)	
Water vapour diffusion resistance index	–	7000
Maximum service temperature, long-term	°C	-40 to +105

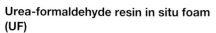

Urea-formaldehyde resin in situ foam (UF)

The use of urea-formaldehyde resin in situ foam for lagging hot and cold pipes is covered by DIN 18159 part 2. UF in situ foam complies with the requirements of Construction Products List A (see p. 62).

For the production of UF in situ foam, an aqueous formaldehyde resin solution is mixed with an aqueous urea surfactant solution foamed up by compressed air and hardened with a catalyst. The individual components are first foamed up in situ and sprayed directly onto the components to be insulated.
Owing to its formaldehyde content, the use of UF foam is subject to building authority requirements with respect to its emissions behaviour and the diffusion-tightness of the construction.
UF in situ foam is used to a considerable extent in mining for sealing against methane and occasionally in industrial installations.

Urea-formaldehyde resin in situ foam is a very light, primarily open-cell foam with good insulating properties. It is waterproof, open to diffusion, very elastic and exhibits excellent resilience. The foaming-up in situ makes it ideal for insulating voids, for filling the cavity in double-leaf masonry and chases around pipes.
The directive for UF in situ foam published by the Committee for Standard Technical Building Provisions (ETB) should be adhered to when working with this material; the wearing of protective goggles and gloves is mandatory.

Polyester fibres

An approval is required for using this material as an insulating material in buildings (see p. 60).

Polyesters (PES) are synthetic hydrocarbon compounds based on ethene which are polymers esterified together. The production of insulating fleeces involves arranging spun polyester fibres in a loose structure and cross-linking them by applying heat. This insulating material contains no binder, flame retardant or other additives.
Polyester batts are soft and elastic and have a coarse, fibrous surface. They retain their contours and form, are very open to diffusion and can withstand temperatures of up to 100°C.
In principle, polyester fibres can be used just like any other fibrous insulating material, but not where compressive loads are expected. One special area of use is in membrane roofs. Polyester fibres are, however, rarely used as a thermal insulating material and play no role in the market.
Thin batts can be easily cut with scissors or knives, thicker batts with a hot-wire cutter or hot knife. As the fibres are very elastic and do not break during cutting, no dust ensues that could irritate the skin or respiratory tract. Polyester fibres are non-toxic and do not cause allergies, and exhibit good resistance to chemicals, insects and rodents.
Uncontaminated insulating materials can be almost fully recycled to form new fibres. They are also suitable for incineration because they have a high calorific value comparable to that of coal.

Physical properties – urea-formaldehyde resin in situ foam

Property	Unit	Values
Density	kg/m^3	10
Thermal conductivity	W/mK	0.035–0.040
Specific heat capacity	J/kgK	1500
Reaction to fire Building materials class	B1 (not readily flammable) B2 (flammable)	
Water vapour diffusion resistance index	–	1–3
Maximum service temperature, long-term	°C	110

Physical properties – polyester fibres

Property	Unit	Values
Density	kg/m^3	15–20
Thermal conductivity	W/(m•K)	0.035–0.045
Reaction to fire Building materials class	B1 (not readily flammable)	
Water vapour diffusion resistance index	–	1–2
Maximum service temperature, long-term	°C	100

1 Wood-wool composite board with mineral wool core

Wood-wool boards (WW), wood-wool composite boards (WW-C)

The materials and qualities of these lightweight building boards are specified in DIN EN 13168. DIN 1102 covers the use and working of wood-wool boards and wood-wool composite boards.

Raw materials and production
Wood-wool building boards consist of long-fibre wood wool from softwoods that are bonded together with Portland cement or calcined magnesite.
Properly stored waste from the woodworking industry is broken down mechanically into wood wool, moistened and mixed with a magnesite or cement suspension. This mass is pressed into moulds and cut to size after drying.

Development and market significance
A patent for the invention of magnesite-bonded wood-wool boards was granted as early as 1908. Production reached its climax in the mid-1960s. Since then, wood-wool boards have proved their worth in many applications. Even though their share of the insulating materials market is only around 1%, they have secured a place for themselves in certain applications.

Properties and applications
Wood-wool boards exhibit low thermal insulation properties. Composite boards therefore combine the good insulating properties of polystyrene or mineral wool with the advantages of wood wool, mostly in the form of a three-ply board with EPS or MW core and two wood-wool boards for the outer plies, which are open to diffusion and dimensionally stable and present a surface that is ideal for plaster or render.
Although wood-wool boards are dimensionally stable and not particularly sensitive to moisture, they do swell and shrink. They should therefore be protected against saturation, especially when used externally.
In the form of acoustic panels, wood-wool boards offer excellent sound absorption, and are frequently used in basement car parks owing to their good fire protection characteristics.

Physical properties – wood-wool boards (WW), wood-wool composite boards (WW-C)

Property	Unit	Values
Density		
wood-wool boards (WW)	kg/m³	350–600
composite boards with EPS	kg/m³	60–300[1]
composite boards with MW	kg/m³	180–300[1]
Thermal conductivity (WW)	W/mK	0.090
Specific heat capacity (WW)	J/kgK	1600–2100
Reaction to fire		
Euroclass	B-s1, d0	
Bldg. materials class	B1 (not readily flammable) B2 (flammable)	
Water vapour diffusion resistance index	–	2–5
Maximum service temperature, long-term	°C	110
Compressive stress at 10% deformation or compressive strength		
wood-wool boards (WW)	kPa	150–200
composite boards with EPS	kPa	> 50
composite boards with MW	kPa	> 30
Bending strength		
wood-wool boards (WW)	kPa	400–1000
composite boards with EPS	kPa	400–1000
composite boards with MW	kPa	300–900
Sound impedance (WW)	kPas/m²	9–100

[1] depends on thickness

Forms of supply, installation advice
Standard boards are 500 mm wide, 1000 or 2000 mm long and between 15 and 150 mm thick. Custom dimensions are also possible.
The boards are easy to cut with a circular-saw, but the wearing of a dust mask is recommended while doing so. Depending on the particular application, they can be attached with cement, adhesive or mechanical fasteners.

Health and ecological aspects, recycling
The use of wood-wool boards does not involve any health risks. As the renewable raw material originates from indigenous stocks, the energy requirement for production and transport is comparatively low. However, the boards cannot be recycled. As they are often used in conjunction with cement, plaster or render, separation during deconstruction and hence reuse is hardly possible. Waste can be disposed of in landfill as building debris.

Applications for wood-wool boards and wood wool multi-ply boards

Roof and suspended floor:	
DZ	• Insulation between rafters, double-skin roof, topmost suspended floor
DI	• Internal insulation below suspended floor, below rafters or loadbearing structure
DEO	• Below screed, without sound insulation requirements
Wall:	
WAB	• External insulation behind cladding
WAP	• External insulation behind render
WH	• Timber-frame and timber-panel forms of construction
WI	• Internal insulation to wall

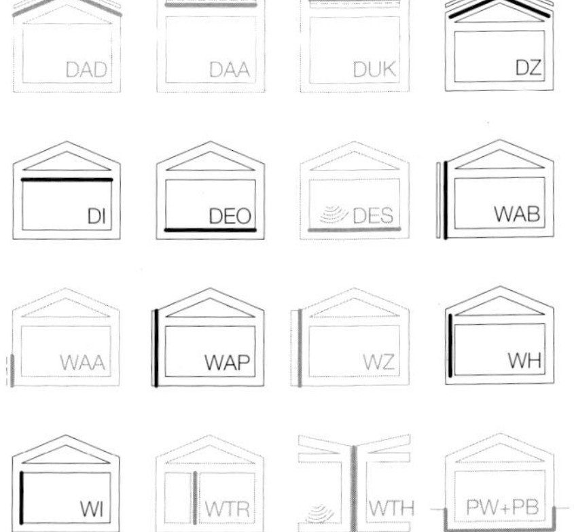

Physical properties – wood fibres

Property	Unit	Values
Density		
blown insulation	kg/m³	30–60
wood-fibre boards	kg/m³	40–270
Thermal conductivity	W/mK	0.040–0.090
Specific heat capacity	J/kgK	1600–2100
Reaction to fire		
Euroclass	E	
Building materials class	B1 (not readily flammable) B2 (flammable)	
Water vapour diffusion resistance index	–	5–10
Maximum service temperature, long-term	°C	110
Compr. stress at 10% deform. or compressive strength	kPa	40–200

Wood fibres (WF)

Boards made from wood fibres are covered by DIN EN 13171 and comply with the requirements of Construction Products List B. Loose wood fibres require an approval (see p. 60).

Raw materials and production
Long-fibre softwood and sometimes also hardwood – waste products from the woodworking industry – constitutes the raw material for wood-fibre insulating materials. Depending on the method of production, latex or a wax emulsion with aluminium sulphate is used as the binder. Boric acid is added to provide protection against pests and fire. Some types of board are given an additional hydrophobic treatment in the form of a bitumen or natural resin emulsion.
There are two production methods: wet or dry. Both methods involve breaking down the wood first in a chipping machine, then turning it into a pulp in autoclaves before pulverising it between grinding wheels. The fibres are then either mixed dry with latex adhesive and pressed to form boards, or mixed with water and the other additives to form a pulp, pressed and then dried. In the wet method, the resins present in the wood itself bond the fibres together.

Market significance, properties and applications
Wood fibres account for less than 1% of the insulating materials market.
Wood-fibre boards exhibit good thermal and sound insulation properties. They are very open to diffusion, have a good specific heat capacity and help to regulate the humidity. Boards with higher densities can accommodate considerable compression loads, but their insulation properties are poorer. Lighter wood-fibre products in particular can absorb moisture and release it again relatively quickly. Due to this characteristic, the products tend to swell easily. However, this means they can also readily accommodate the swelling and shrinkage effects of adjoining structural timber members.
Wood-fibre boards exhibit good resistance to mould and vermin.

Forms of supply
Various formats in board and wedge form are available:

- Boards: length 1000–2500 mm
  width 560–780 mm
  20–200 mm
  (tongue and groove possible with higher densities)
- Wedges: length 1000 mm
  width 600 mm
  (boards split diagonally)
  thickness 60–120 mm

In addition, loose wood fibres can be supplied in various containers for blown insulation.

Applications for wood fibres

Roof and suspended floor:

DAD	• External insulation, protected from the weather, below roof covering (with low, medium and high compressive strength)
DAA	• External insulation, protected from the weather, below waterproofing
DZ	• Insulation between rafters, double-skin roof, topmost suspended floor
DI	• Internal insulation below suspended floor, below rafters or loadbearing structure (zero or medium compressive strength)
DEO	• Below screed, without sound insulation requirements (low, medium and very high compressive strength)
DES	• Below screed, with sound insulation requirements (higher and low compressibility)

Wall:

WAB	• External insulation behind cladding (low, medium and very high compressive load)
WAP	• External insulation behind render
WZ	• Cavity insulation to double-leaf walls
WH	• Timber-frame and timber-panel forms of construction
WI	• Internal insulation to wall (zero or medium compressive strength)
WTR	• Insulation to separating walls

Installation advice
Conventional woodworking tools can be used for cutting the boards to size. Harder boards with higher densities can be drilled and chased and also fixed securely with nails and screws. Owing to the considerable amounts of dust, the wearing of a dust mask and protective goggles is recommended. Wood fibres for blown insulation should be installed by specialist contractors only.

Health and ecological aspects
Wood-fibre insulating materials do not involve any health risks. A positive aspect from the ecological viewpoint is that wood is a renewable raw material, although these days more wood is being consumed than can be regrown. The majority of raw materials are found in central Europe, but are also imported from northern and eastern Europe.

Recycling
Undamaged wood-fibre insulating materials can be reused. Non-bitumenised wood-fibres can be composted, pulverised insulating materials for loosening soils. Wood-fibre insulating materials can also be disposed of in landfill under waste code Nos. 17 06 04, 03 01 05 and 70 201, or incinerated in waste incineration plants.

Physical properties – insulation cork board

Property	Unit	Values
Density	kg/m³	100–220
Thermal conductivity	W/mK	0.045–0.060
Specific heat capacity	J/kgK	1700–2100
Reaction to fire Building materials class		B2 (flammable)
Water vapour diffusion resistance index granulated cork pressed cork board	 – –	 2–8 5–10
Maximum service temperature, long-term	°C	110–120
Compressive stress at 10% deformation or compressive strength	kPa	100–200
Bending strength	kPa	140–200

Insulation cork board (ICB)

Factory-made products are covered by standard DIN EN 13170 and comply with the requirements of Construction Products List B. Granulated cork requires a national technical approval.

Raw materials and production
The raw material is exclusively cork from the cork oak, sometimes also recycled cork. The cork is first ground to form a granulate with a grain size of 2–5 mm and then expanded in autoclaves at approx. 350°C to form granulated cork (3–12 mm). In the case of pressed cork board, the granulate is pressed to form blocks as it expands. The suberin released from the cork's own resin acts as the binder. The products can be impregnated by adding bitumen, occasionally also formaldehyde resin.

Development and market significance
There is evidence that cork has been used since the 2nd century. Industrial production, however, first began in the 19th century. Besides its principal use for sealing bottles, cork is also used as a floor finish, in the manufacture of linoleum and as an insulating material. The market share for cork insulating materials in Germany is about 0.1%.

Properties and applications
Cork exhibits good sound and thermal insulation properties, is very light and elastic, and has a high resilience. Despite its imperviousness with respect to air and liquids, it permits diffusion. Cork can accommodate heavy loads, does not age or rot, and provides no nutrients for rodents or insects. Cork insulating materials are resistant to acid and alkalis, but are flammable without a flame retardant (DIN 4102 building materials class B2). When used as an insulating material, not only boards should be considered, but also granulated cork as a loose fill for voids and as a lightweight aggregate for loam products.

Forms of supply
The standard board formats for pressed cork boards and impregnated cork are:
- Length: 1000, 1200 mm
- Width: 500, 600 mm
- Thickness: 10–320 mm

Granulated cork with a grain size of 3–12 mm is available in sacks.

Installation advice
Insulating materials made from cork can be cut and sawn without the need for special safety measures. Cutting exactly to size is, however, difficult owing to the elasticity of the material.
If granulated cork is to be installed in voids, subsequent settlement is unavoidable and it will be necessary to "top up" the filling.
The good temperature stability of the products means they can be used together with hot bitumen without any problems. The cork cells can, however, expand subsequently if the temperature remains above 120°C for a long time.

Applications for insulation cork board

Roof and suspended floor:	
DAD	• External insulation, protected from the weather, below roof covering
DAA	• External insulation, protected from the weather, below waterproofing
DZ	• Insulation between rafters, double-skin roof, topmost suspended floor
DI	• Internal insulation below suspended floor, below rafters or loadbearing structure (zero or high compressive strength)
DEO	• Below screed, without sound insulation requirements
Wall:	
WAB	• External insulation behind cladding (zero or high compressive strength)
WAP	• External insulation behind render
WZ	• Cavity insulation to double-leaf walls
WH	• Timber-frame and timber-panel forms of construction
WI	• Internal insulation to wall (zero or high compressive strength)
WTR	• Insulation to separating walls

Health and ecological aspects
Cork does not bring any health risks with it. When used extensively indoors, a persistent but harmless odour may be noticeable.
Critical from the ecological viewpoint is the overharvesting of the relatively limited stocks of the cork oak tree and the long transport distances, mostly from Portugal. Cork grows slowly and the bark can be removed only every nine years or so. Phenols and PAH (polycyclic aromatic hydrocarbons) can be released at very high temperatures, in the event of fire also alcohols, aldehydes and acetic acid.

Recycling
Untreated cork can be processed to form granulated cork or new boards, and can also be used for loosening soils. As there are no additives, composting is another option. Owing to its bitumen content, impregnated cork cannot be composted, but it can be reprocessed to form new impregnated cork products, or can be incinerated for energy purposes.

Physical properties – cellulose fibres

Property		Unit	Values
Density		kg/m³	30–80
Thermal conductivity		W/mK	0.040–0.045
Specific heat capacity		J/kgK	1700–2150
Reaction to fire	Euroclass Building materials class	E boards: B1 (not readily flammable) flakes: B2 (flammable)	
Water vapour diffusion resistance index		–	1–2
Maximum service temperature, long-term		°C	60
Spontaneous ignition temperature			°C 280
Compressive stress at 10% deformation or compressive strength		kPa	2.5 (boards)
Dynamic stiffness		MN/m³	3–7
Sound impedance		kPas/m² kPas/m²	43–76 (boards) 3.6–20 (flakes)

Cellulose fibres

A European standard, prEN 15101, is in preparation for cellulose insulating materials. Conventional products carry national technical approvals, in some cases European technical approvals (ETA), and they comply with Construction Products List B (see p. 62).

Raw materials and production
Cellulose insulating materials are produced from scrap paper. Other constituents are 8–20% by wt. powdered boric salts, which improves the reaction to fire, and in the manufacture of boards also tall resin and aluminium sulphate or lignin sulphonate as a binder plus polyolefin fibres or jute twine as stabilisers.
The loose insulating material – wool-type flakes – is obtained directly from the milling of scrap paper. To produce the boards, the flakes are mixed with fibres and binders, pressed together in steam and cut to size after drying.

Development and market significance
In the USA and Sweden, cellulose insulating materials have been used since 1920. In Germany they first appeared on the market in the mid-1980s. They account for about 1% of the market.

Properties and applications
Cellulose insulating materials achieve good thermal insulation, are open to diffusion and can compensate for minor humidity fluctuations. However, as they are highly hydrophilic and swell up, they must be protected against moisture. They are dimensionally stable and elastic, but cannot accommodate any compression. Acids and alkalis attack cellulose fibres. Typical applications for cellulose flakes are filling the voids in timber joist floors/roofs and timber-stud walls.
Cellulose boards are relatively flexible and are suitable for fitting between rafters and timber studs, and with appropriate spacer screws can also be laid on top of the rafters.

Forms of supply
Cellulose insulation is available in the form of flakes and boards:

- Flakes: in sacks or silos
- Boards: length 1000, 1200, 1250 mm
  width 570, 600, 625 mm
  thickness 25–180 mm

Installation advice
Cellulose flakes are usually blown into prepared voids and compacted to form a seamless layer of insulation. Correctly installed by approved contractors, the flakes do not settle and leave uninsulated voids, but if simply tipped into place, there is a risk of settlement over time. Another installation method is to blow the cellulose flakes in a light water spray onto a surface. Using this method, thicknesses of up to 200 mm can be sprayed on and trowelled smooth if required. A dust mask must be worn during such work. Boards are easy to work, but the fibrous nature of the material means that cut edges tend to fray.
Cellulose insulating materials must be stored in the dry with good air circulation and may not be stacked. According to the approval, the installation moisture of the structural timber should not exceed 20%, or 35% in the case of roofs.

Health and ecological aspects, recycling
Cellulose insulating materials do not involve any health risks. The recycled raw materials are available in large quantities without long transport distances.
Composting is not allowed owing to the possible danger of the boric salts contaminating the groundwater. In the event of a fire there is also the risk of boric salts being leached out by extinguishing water. Uncontaminated materials can either be reused or returned to the manufacturer. Incineration in waste incineration plants with energy recovery is a good option because of the high calorific value.

Applications for cellulose fibres

Roof and suspended floor:

DAD	• External insulation, protected from the weather, below roof covering (zero compressive strength)
DZ	• Insulation between rafters, double-skin roof, topmost suspended floor
DI	• Internal insulation below suspended floor, below rafters or loadbearing structure

Wall:

WH	• Timber-frame and timber-panel forms of construction
WI	• Internal insulation to wall (low tensile strength)
WTR	• Insulation to separating walls

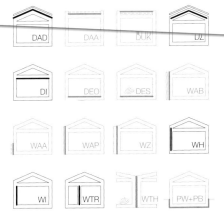

DAD DAA DUK DZ
DI DEO DES WAB
WAA WAP WZ WH
WI WTR WTH PW+PB

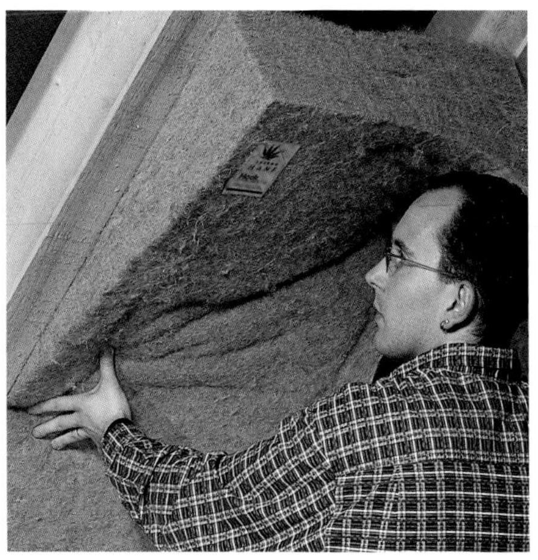

Hemp

The standard products carry national technical approvals and in some cases a European technical approval (ETA) (see p. 60).

Raw materials and production
Hemp insulating materials are made from the shives (chaff, splinters) and fibres of the hemp plant (*Canabis sativa*). Depending on the particular product, various additives are introduced such as bicomponent fibres (heat-treated, usually polyester), potato starch, water glass, sodium carbonate or boric salt as a flame retardant and bitumen as a waterproofing agent.

The shives can be used directly for loose insulation and levelling purposes, whereas hemp fibres are used to produce insulating fleece. The fibres, sometimes mixed with flax fibres, are bundled, roasted and subsequently worked into a felt. The addition of polyester fibres (approx. 10%) improves the dimensional stability but at the same time the flexibility and resilience of the felt. Straps and cords made from spun hemp twine are used to seal joints.

Development and market significance
Hemp has been cultivated for thousands of years and has a long tradition. In Europe, cord made from hemp, so-called caulking cord, has long been used for sealing joints. The logs of old log houses, too, were caulked with hemp fibres. Cultivation was prohibited for many years, but low-narcotics grades have now been approved for cultivation and have been grown in Germany since 1996. Up until now, hemp has played only a minor role in the insulating materials market.

Properties and applications
Hemp insulating materials exhibit good sound and thermal insulating properties and allow diffusion. The products, however, are unsuitable for use where compression and moisture loads are anticipated.
As hemp does not contain any proteins valuable to insects, attack by pests is unlikely. The resistance against mould has been proved in tests, but hemp has only a limited resistance to acids and alkalis.

Forms of supply
Hemp insulating materials are mainly supplied in rolls or as batts, but also as unbonded fibres for use as a blown insulation or for sealing purposes. Hemp twine for caulking is also available.

- Batts: various formats up to 1000 × 2000 mm, thickness 30–200 mm
- Rolls: length 6–10 m, width 580, 625 mm, thickness 30–80 mm
- Shives: in sacks

Installation advice
The materials can be cut to size with hand or power saws; no special protective measures are necessary. However, hazardous substances can be caused by organic fibres and dust. Blown insulation should always be carried out by an authorised contractor.

Health and ecological aspects, recycling
The hemp used for insulating materials comes mainly from southern Germany and is readily available to meet current demands. Untreated hemp is easy to recycle, but flame retardants and polyester fibres complicate the composting and recycling options.

Applications for hemp

Roof and suspended floor:	
DAD	· External insulation, protected from the weather, below roof covering (low compressive load)
DZ	· Insulation between rafters, double-skin roof, topmost suspended floor
DI	· Internal insulation below suspended floor, below rafters or loadbearing structure
DEO	· Below screed, without sound insulation requirements (low compressive load)
Wall:	
WAB	· External insulation behind cladding (low compressive load)
WH	· Timber-frame and timber-panel forms of construction
WI	· Internal insulation to wall (no compressive load)
WTR	· Insulation to separating walls

Physical properties – hemp

Property	Unit	Values
Density	kg/m³	20–68
Thermal conductivity	W/(mK)	0.040–0.050
Specific heat capacity	J/(kgK)	1500–2200
Reaction to fire Euroclass Bldg. materials class	 E B2 (flammable)	
Water vapour diffusion resistance index	–	1–2
Water absorption	kg/m²	≤ 4.2
Maximum service temperature, long-term	°C	100
Sound impedance	kPas/m²	> 6

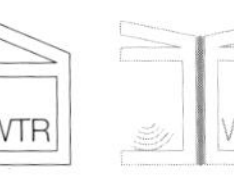

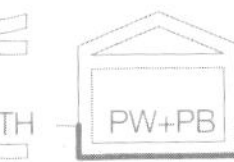

Sheep's wool

Insulating materials made from sheep's wool require a national technical approval (see p. 60).

Raw materials and production
The insulating material consists of pure sheep's wool which in some cases is obtained from recycled sheep's wool. Additives such as sodium salt (borax) or urea derivatives, also boric salts in some cases, protect the wool against moths and improve the fire resistance. Batts < 100 mm thick also contain polyester fibres, frequently in combination with natural latex milk.
The first step in the production involves cleaning the raw wool with the help of soap and soda, followed by spraying with the additives. The thin (15–50 µm) fibres up to 300 mm long are then separated from the wool by machine and carded to form so-called carded fleece.
These fleeces are laid over each other diagonally, compacted in a needle-punch machine and needled to form batts, sometimes on a backing fleece made from compacted sheep's wool.

Development and market significance
In the form of warm clothing, sheep's wool is certainly one of the oldest "insulating materials". Sheep's wool has been available on the German building market since about 1992 and currently accounts for a market share of < 1%.

Properties and applications
Sheep's wool has good insulating properties, does not aggravate the skin and is essentially rot-resistant. Sheep's wool can absorb up to 33% of its weight in moisture and also release this again relatively quickly. Sheep's wool insulating batts are mainly used as an infill between structural members and as impact sound insulation in housing. Furthermore, sheep's wool can also be used for sealing joints around doors and windows.

Forms of supply
Sheep's wool is available as a caulking material or in the form of rolled batts and fleeces:

- Batts: 6000 mm × 500–800 mm, thickness 40–180 mm
- Fleeces: 2000 mm × 10–30 mm, thickness 4–14 mm

The products can also be laminated with aluminium foil.

Installation advice
Sheep's wool is very easy to work and owing to its flexibility is ideal for installing between the members of timber frames, for example. Thin fleeces should be stapled in place in pitched roofs and glued to plasterboard or wood-based board products in partitions. When working overhead, the wearing of a dust mask and protective goggles is recommended.

Health and ecological aspects
From the ecological viewpoint, the use of sheep's wool, a natural product, is offset by the comparatively high consumption of cleaning agents during production and the large quantity of flame retardant and moth protection. Furthermore, in the event of a fire, the keratin in the wool gives rise to toxic substances.
As a sheep can supply 2–4 kg of wool per year, the high demand for insulating materials cannot be met by such a limited supply. The transport distances are usually very long because the raw wool comes mainly from New Zealand, although some is obtained from Austria and the UK.

Recycling
Undamaged, clean insulating materials can be reused. Wool without boric salt additives can also be composted. If the wool has been impregnated with boric salts for fire resistance purposes, it must be disposed of in landfill or incinerated in a waste incineration plant.

Applications for sheep's wool

Roof and suspended floor:	
DZ	• Insulation between rafters, double-skin roof, topmost suspended floor
DI	• Internal insulation below suspended floor, below rafters or loadbearing structure
DEO	• Below screed, without sound insulation requirements
DES	• Below screed, with sound insulation requirements
Wall:	
WAB	• External insulation behind cladding
WH	• Timber-frame and timber-panel forms of construction
WI	• Internal insulation to wall
WTR	• Insulation to separating walls

Physical properties – sheep's wool

Property	Unit	Values
Density	kg/m³	25–30
Thermal conductivity	W/(mK)	0.040–0.045
Specific heat capacity	J/(kgK)	960–1300
Reaction to fire		
Euroclass	E	
Bldg. materials class	B2 (flammable)	
Water vapour diffusion resistance index	–	1–5
Maximum service temperature, long-term	°C	130–150

Physical properties – cotton

Property	Unit	Values
Density	kg/m^3	20–60
Thermal conductivity	W/(mK)	0.040
Specific heat capacity	J/(kgK)	840–1300
Reaction to fire Bldg. materials class		B1 (not readily flammable) B2 (flammable)
Water vapour diffusion resistance index	–	1–2
Water absorption	kg/m^2	12–13
Maximum service temperature, long-term	°C	100

Cotton

There is no standard covering insulating materials made from cotton. Such products require a national technical approval.

Raw materials and production
Cotton insulating materials are produced from the fibres in the seed pods (bolls) of the cotton plant.
The wool-type flakes with a boric salt flame retardant impregnation can be used directly as an insulating material. In order to produce batts, the cotton is carded, which strengthens it mechanically, and subsequently impregnated.

Development and market significance
Cotton has only been available as a thermal insulation material in the German-speaking countries for about 10 years. Its share of the insulating materials market is very small.

Properties and applications
Cotton exhibits good thermal and sound insulation properties. It is very elastic and is very pleasant to the touch.
Owing to its high absorbency, it can absorb up to 80% of its weight in water and requires a relatively long time to dry out again. As an insulating material it should not be exposed to longer periods of saturation because it is not resistant to mould. Problems with moths are unlikely because the larvae eat only animal fibres. Loose flakes are mainly used as blown insulation for voids or for caulking, batts are primarily fitted between timber members.

Forms of supply
Rolls and batts up to 200 mm thick, flakes for blowing in and caulking, also caulking cord.
Installation advice
Special protective measures are unnecessary. However, a dust mask is recommended for blown insulation measures because the concentrations of fibres in the interior air can reach high levels.

Health and ecological aspects, recycling
Cotton for insulating materials is mostly transported over long distances from Asian countries. This renewable raw material is frequently cultivated in large monocultures where the use of pesticides is normal.
Composting is not possible owing to the flame retardant, which is a danger to groundwater. Residue and waste should be disposed of in landfill sites or in waste incineration plants.

Applications for cotton

Roof and suspended floor:

DAD	• External insulation, protected from the weather, below roof covering
DZ	• Insulation between rafters, double-skin roof, topmost suspended floor
DI	• Internal insulation below suspended floor, below rafters or loadbearing structure.

Wall:

WAB	• External insulation behind cladding (low compressibility)
WH	• Timber-frame and timber-panel forms of construction
WTR	• Insulation to separating walls

DAD DAA DUK DZ
DI DEO DES WAB
WAA WAP WZ WH
WI WTR WTH PW+PB

Flax

An approval is required (see p. 60) for insulating materials made from flax (linen).

To produce an insulating material, the short fibres of the flax plant are processed to form a fibrous fleece after removing the bast layer. During the processing, potato starch (approx 10%) is added as a binder and boric salt (approx. 10%) as a flame retardant, also polyester fibres to strengthen thicker boards.

Flax has been used for more than 4,000 years for the production of linen cloth and linseed oil, but the large-scale use of its fibres for creating an insulating material is a new development. Flax exhibits good insulating properties, helps to regulate the humidity, resists alkalis and is very resistant against moisture and mould, but not if it is permanently wet.

Flax insulating materials can be supplied as:
- Caulking material
- Batts: 625 mm × 1000 mm, thickness 40–200 mm
- Rolls: for impact sound insulation 1000 mm × 25 lfm, thickness 2, 5, 8 mm

Applications for flax

Roof and suspended floor:

DAD	• External insulation, protected from the weather, below roof covering
DZ	• Insulation between rafters, double-skin roof, topmost suspended floor
DI	• Internal insulation below suspended floor, below rafters or loadbearing structure
DEO	• Below screed, without sound insulation requirements
DES	• Below screed, with sound insulation requirements

Wall:

WAB	• External insulation behind cladding
WH	• Timber-frame and timber-panel forms of construction
WI	• Internal insulation to wall
WTR	• Insulation to separating walls

Cutting to size can be carried out easily and cleanly with a panel saw or circular-saw, but owing to possible high fibre concentrations, the wearing of a dust mask is recommended during installation. Flax insulation contains no hazardous substances.
This renewable raw material stems mainly from organic farms in Germany and Austria. The insulating materials can only be composted in specially equipped composting plants owing to the boric salt content, which is a danger for groundwater, and the non-decomposable polyester fibres. Direct reuse and incineration are other options.

Physical properties – flax

Property	Unit	Values
Density	kg/m³	20–80
Thermal conductivity	W/(mK)	0.03–0.045
Specific heat capacity	J/(kgK)	1300–1640
Reaction to fire Euroclass Bldg. materials class	 B-s2, d0 to C-s2, d0 B2 (flammable)	
Water vapour diffusion resistance inde	–	1–2
Sound impedance	kPas/m²	> 2

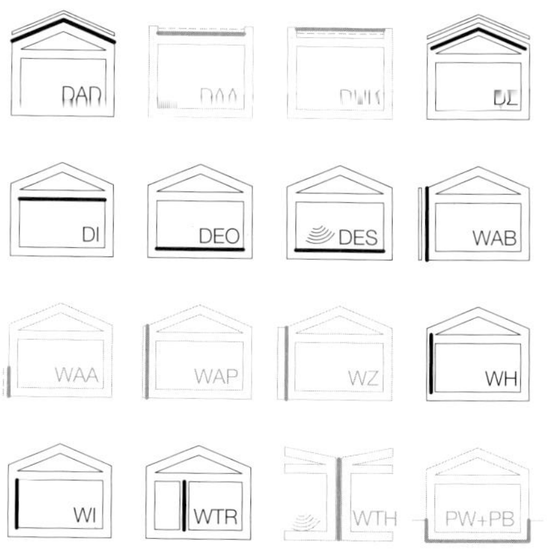

Cereal granulate

An approval is required when using cereal granulate as a thermal insulation material.

The granulate is obtained by extrusion from fine rye grains, rye pulp, whey, water glass and slaked lime. Its use as an insulating material first developed during the 1990s and so far has not become widespread.
Cereal granulate has good insulating properties, a relatively high density and is open to diffusion. It is, however, sensitive to moisture and cannot accommodate compression loads. Additives introduced during manufacture makes the granulate resistant to mould, insects and rodents. In contact with water, cereal granulate exhibits a marginally alkaline behaviour.
It is used for insulating voids in walls and suspended floors. In the case of the latter, a check should be carried out to ensure that the relatively high weight of this loose fill material does not cause structural problems. When installing the insulation, the relative humidity of the air should not be higher than 80%. The inclusion of a vapour barrier is highly advisable in rooms where the activities cause a high vapour pressure.

Applications for cereal granulate

Roof and suspended floor:	
DAD	• External insulation, protected from the weather, below roof covering
DZ	• Insulation between rafters, double-skin roof, topmost suspended floor
DI	• Internal insulation below suspended floor, below rafters or loadbearing structure
Wall:	
WH	• Timber-frame and timber-panel forms of construction
WTR	• Insulation to separating walls

The granulate is supplied as a loose material in sacks, or in silos for blown insulation. Settlement amounting to approx. 5% during installation of the loose fill should be allowed for by suitable compaction. Apart from the dust during installation, no health risks are known.
The use of a renewable raw material from indigenous sources is positive from the ecological viewpoint, also the possibility of reusing the material directly for insulation. Cereal granulate can also be composted or incinerated without causing any problems.

Physical properties – cereal granulate

Property	Unit	Values
Density	kg/m³	105–115
Thermal conductivity	W/(mK)	0.050
Specific heat capacity	J/(kgK)	1950
Reaction to fire Bldg. materials class	 B2 (flammable)	
Water vapour diffusion resistance index	–	3

Reeds

When used as an insulating material, reeds require a national technical approval.

The stalks of reed plants are pressed mechanically and bound together with galvanised iron wire or nylon cords to form firm but flexible batts. In the form of a thermally insulating roof covering (thatch) or as a plaster background beneath timber joist floors, reeds can look back on a long tradition in many regions. However, the market share as a pure insulating material is currently very small.

Reeds exhibit only moderate thermal insulation properties. The plant is naturally water-resistant, dimensionally stable and essentially resistant to ageing and rotting, but should still be protected against the effects of permanent wetting. Owing to the high silicic acid content, reeds are fire-retardant. The use of reeds does not involve any health risks.
The following formats are available:

- Reed batts: 200, 100 cm long; 100, 125 cm wide; 20–100 mm thick
- Bound stalks for thatched roofs
- Lightweight loam building boards with reeds

Reed products can be cut with a circular-saw. When laying, it should be noted that the batts are very resistant to breakage in the direction of the stalks, but buckle or deflect easily in the direction of the wires. The manufacturers obtain their raw materials primarily from Poland, Austria, Hungary and the Danube Delta, which means that the transport distances are not short. On the other hand, the energy required for production is very low. Uncontaminated reeds can either be reused or composted. Treated insulating materials can sometimes be composted, but certainly can be disposed of in landfill as building debris, or incinerated for energy purposes.

Physical properties – reeds

Property	Unit	Values
Density	kg/m³	120–225
Thermal conductivity	W/(mK)	0.055–0.090
Specific heat capacity	J/(kgK)	1200
Reaction to fire Bldg. materials class	B2 (flammable)	
Water vapour diffusion resistance index	–	2–5

Applications for reeds

Roof and suspended floor:

DAD	• External insulation, protected from the weather, below roof covering
DZ	• Insulation between rafters, double-skin roof, topmost suspended floor
DI	• Internal insulation below suspended floor, below rafters or loadbearing structure

Wall:

WAB	• External insulation behind cladding
WAP	• External insulation behind render
WH	• Timber-frame and timber-panel forms of construction
WI	• Internal insulation to wall

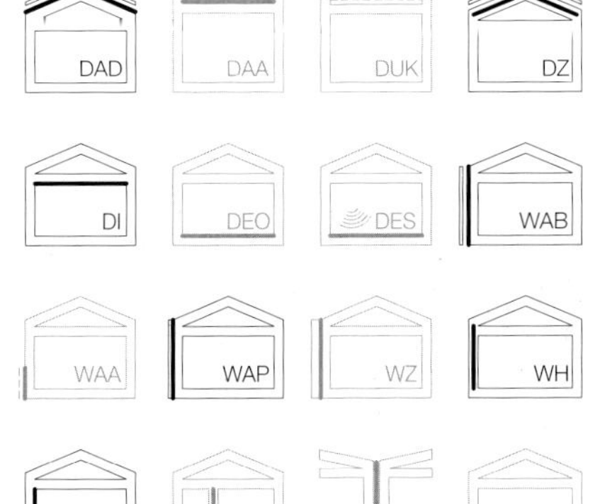

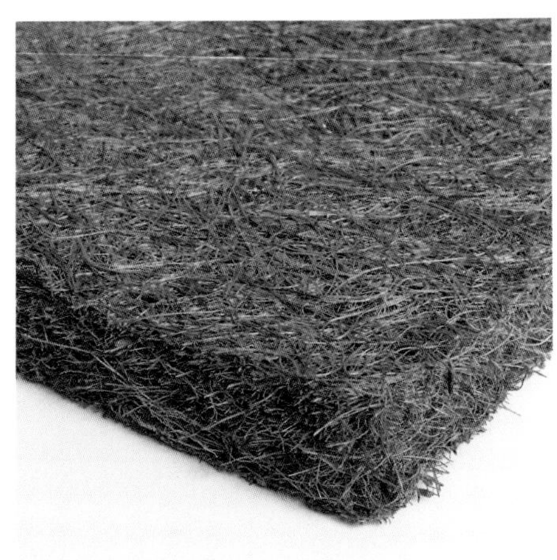

Coconut fibres

Insulating materials made from coconut fibres require an approval (see p. 60).

The raw materials are the fibres of the coconut shell plus ammonium sulphate or borax as a fire retardant. After preparation, the fibres are carded and needled to form fleeces or batts. Bitumen, latex or synthetic dispersions then being added as a water-repellent if required.
Coconut fibres have been used for about 100 years, mainly for textile floor coverings.
In the form of an insulating material they are only available from a few manufacturers at the present time, mostly in the form of batts or rolls up to 120 mm thick. They exhibit good sound and thermal insulation properties, are open to diffusion and help to adjust the humidity. The elastic batts are dimensionally stable and the plant's own tanning agents make this material resistant to rotting and vermin.
The batts can be worked with conventional tools, but in doing so high concentrations of fibres and dust can be expected, and so an appropriate mask should be

Applications for coconut fibres

Roof and suspended floor:

DAD	• External insulation, protected from the weather, below roof covering
DZ	• Insulation between rafters, double-skin roof, topmost suspended floor
DI	• Internal insulation below suspended floor, below rafters or loadbearing structure
DEO	• Below screed, without sound insulation requirements
DES	• Below screed, with sound insulation requirements

Wall:

WAB	• External insulation behind cladding
WZ	• Cavity insulation to double-leaf walls
WH	• Timber-frame and timber-panel forms of construction
WI	• Internal insulation to wall
WTR	• Insulation to separating walls
WTH	• Between party walls with sound insulation requirements

worn. Apart from that, coconut fibres are totally harmless. Occasionally they can give off a mild but harmless odour.
The ecological benefits of this renewable raw material are offset by the long transport distances from South-East Asia.
Recycling is not a problem, provided the fibres have not been treated. They can be composted or used for loosening soils. Bitumenised products, however, can only be disposed of in landfill or incinerated.

Physical properties – coconut fibres

Property	Unit	Values
Density (felt, boards)	kg/m³	70–120
Thermal conductivity	W/(mK)	0.040–0.050
Specific heat capacity	J/(kgK)	1300–1600
Reaction to fire Bldg. materials class	B2 (flammable)	
Water vapour diffusion resistance index	–	1–2
Compressive stress at 10% deformation or compressive strength	kPa	10

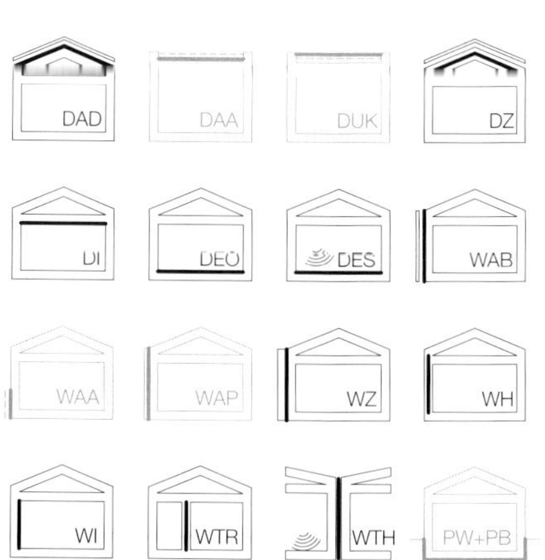

Sea grass

If used as a thermal insulation material, sea grass requires a national technical approval.

Sea grass (*Zostera marina*, *Zostera noltii*) grows in almost all the seas of the world and was used as an insulating material in buildings along the coast of the Baltic Sea hundreds of years ago. The long, narrow leaves of the plant grow at depths of 3 to 10 m. Uprooted plants are washed up onto the beaches, especially in summer and autumn, and can be "harvested" there.
The leaves are dried and either processed to form batts or, in several steps, pellets. The salt from the sea contained in the sea grass makes it fire-retardant without any further additives and it achieves DIN 4102 building materials class B2 (flammable). With a thermal conductivity of 0.043 to 0.050 W/mK, sea grass exhibits its good insulating properties. It helps to adjust the humidity, does not rot and is resistant to mould growth.

Sea grass insulation is supplied loose in big bags and also in the form of batts in various sizes made from pure sea grass or a combination of sea grass and flax. Sea grass installed loose in voids can be installed by DIY enthusiasts or by specialist contractors with blowing apparatus. The bulk density is 75 kg/m³.
In order to keep beaches attractive for tourists, sea grass is collected continuously, and the lack of demand means it is frequently disposed of on meadows and fields, where it rots very slowly and contaminates the soil as the salt leaches out. Its use as an insulating material must therefore be actively encouraged.

Wood chippings

There are no standards covering wood chippings. A national technical approval is required when wood chippings are used as an insulating material.

The raw material for this insulating product consists of waste chippings of spruce, pine or fir that occur in great quantities in the woodworking industry. To improve the fire resistance and reduce the risk of fungal attack, the wood chippings are impregnated with whey, soda lye or cement. This loose fill insulating material is installed with the help of special equipment and compacted by vibration.
Wood chippings as an independent product are hardly available on the market, rather found mainly as part of a building system, e.g. prefabricated timber houses.

Physical properties – wood chippings

Property	Unit	Values
Density	kg/m³	90–140
Thermal conductivity	W/(mK)	0.055
Specific heat capacity	J/(kgK)	2100
Reaction to fire Building materials class	B 2 (flammable)	
Water vapour diffusion resistance index	–	2

Giant Chinese silver grass

This insulating material is not covered by any material standard and therefore requires an approval (see p. 60).

Giant Chinese silver grass (*Miscanthus giganteus*) – sometimes erroneously called elephant grass – is a species of grass from Asia which is very similar to the reeds of Europe. This modest plant has been grown on a small-scale in Europe since the 1930s.
As a result of dwindling fossil fuel resources, the initial idea was to cultivate and use giant Chinese silver grass as a renewable raw material on a large scale. However, cultivation is in the early years coupled with high costs and low harvests, and hitherto giant Chinese silver grass has not been able to achieve a major breakthrough.
Nevertheless, giant Chinese silver grass is an ideal plant for producing a reed-type insulating material because it grows fast and offers greater harvests than indigenous reed species. Ground to powder, it can be used as an aggregate for plasters, renders and screeds. Chopped coarsely and mixed with cement as a binder, it is possible to produce blocks with a low thermal conductivity for infilling between timber members. But even for this application, the production of insulating materials from giant Chinese silver grass has not been able to establish itself in the market. Up until now, its use has been confined to a few isolated projects.

Peat

Peat is an organic sediment of the moors. It consists to a large extent of dead moss (*Sphagnum fallax*) and is frequently used in gardens to improve the soil.
In contrast to humus (topsoil), more than 30% of peat is vegetable constituents. This is also the reason for its high calorific value and the reason why it has been used as a fuel for many centuries. However, peat mosses were also widely used as an insulating material in log buildings. Damp peat moss was used in sufficiently thick layers as an insulating material between the individual logs and maintained the form it had been given even after drying out. Due to its antibiotic and humidity-regulating characteristics, peat has a positive effect on the durability of the timber construction.
During the 20th century, compressed and impregnated peat boards were sold under the name of "Torfoleum" for use as an insulating material in buildings and railway rolling stock. This product is no longer available.
On the whole, peat no longer plays a role in the insulating materials market, which from the ecological viewpoint is highly desirable because the excavation of peat destroys rare, non-renewable habitats and CO_2 sinks.

Straw bales

Insulation made from bales of straw requires an approval – and in 2006 a German manufacturer obtained just such a national technical approval.

Straw can be used for insulating purposes either in the form of whole bales or as an additive for loam. Lightweight straw loam, which has only a low insulating effect, is not reviewed here.
The building of houses made from load-bearing straw-bale walls covered with a loam render/plaster began in the late 19th century in North America parallel with the development of the mechanical bale press. Nowadays, manufacturers from the Netherlands and Austria offer straw bales for insulation purposes.
The bales are preferably fitted between timber studs, but can also be installed between or above the rafters and either rendered or clad with suitable materials.
Straw bales exhibit very diverse qualities. The degree of pressing and the surface quality depends on the type of bale press. They also differ in terms of length and in the orientation of the stalks in the bales.
The insulating capacity of straw bales also varies depending on the type of straw, its density and the moisture content after drying (5–15% by wt.). The thermal conductivity can fluctuate between 0.038 and 0.072 W/mK. The approved products achieve a value of 0.045 W/mK, after allowing for a 20% safety factor.
Studies of the airtightness, the resistance to mould and pests, and the fire behaviour confirm that straw bales are suitable for the aforementioned applications provided they are produced and installed correctly.

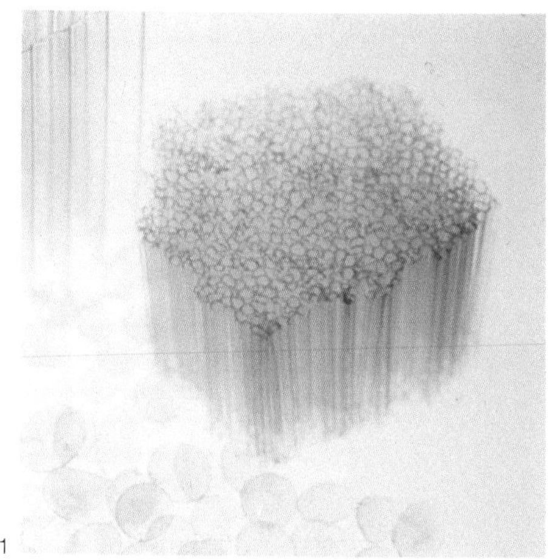

1

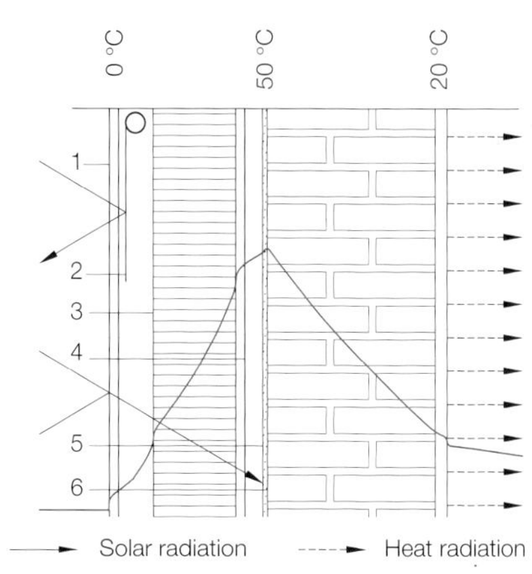

2

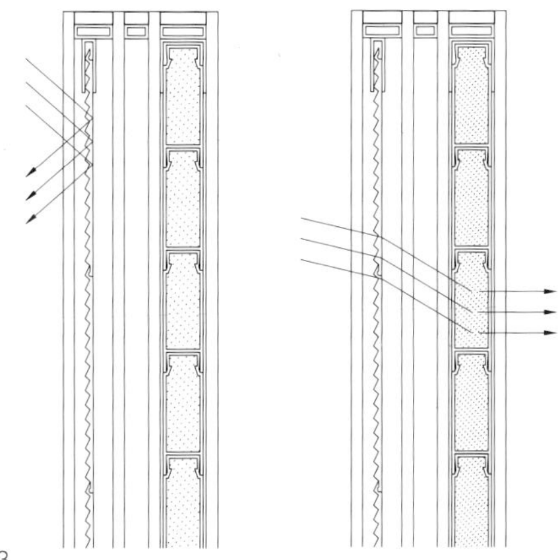

3

Transparent thermal insulation (TWD)

TWD is part of an insulating system consisting of light-permeable materials with a thermal insulating effect which enables solar energy to be used for heating purposes in conjunction with an opaque external wall. We distinguish between three methods of function:

Solid wall system
The TWD layer with its honeycomb, capillary-like hollow chamber structures of glass or plastic (PC, PMMA) is fitted behind a pane of glass or a coat of transparent glass render on the outside. The solar radiation can penetrate these structures easily in the case of a low angle of incidence in the winter and heat up the wall behind (absorber), which is usually painted a dark colour. The heat gain either radiates into the interior after a delay (see also p. 90) or can be used to heat hot water via a system of pipes incorporated in the wall.

Direct gain system
TWD in glass facades has a light-scattering effect and can exploit the solar radiation for the direct heating of the interior after a delay if a phase change material (PCM), e.g. salt hydrate, is used as the translucent material. As a latent heat store, salt hydrate can first store solar energy by melting (change of state) and then release it again by solidifying as the ambient temperature drops (see also p. 91). The sequence of layers in the glazing unit ensures the directed release of heat into the interior. Shading elements, e.g. prisms, incorporated in the glazing ensure that the bright sunshine is cut out in the summer and the heat store is therefore "charged up" only during the cooler seasons.

Thermally decoupled systems
Convective and hybrid systems still undergoing development make use of controllable layers of air or water decoupled from the storage wall. For example, according to the principle of a curtain wall of opaque glass, the temperature rise of the intermediate layer of air achieves a good insulating effect.

All TWD systems require effective sunshading to protect against overheating during the summer, which increases the costs considerably.

1 Various transparent thermal insulating materials
2 TWD element with shading and temperature gradient (solid wall system)
 1 Glass
 2 Shading element
 3 TWD
 4 Glass
 5 Absorber
 6 Masonry
3 Sketch of principle of TWD glass facade shown in Fig. 4:
Multi-pane insulating glass unit with integral shading prisms and polycarbonate double-wall sheets with salt hydrate filling as latent heat store which releases the heat into the interior after a delay (direct gain system).
4 Glass facade with TWD in the form of a phase change material (direct gain system); sheltered housing in Domat/Ems, Switzerland
Architect: Dietrich Schwarz

4

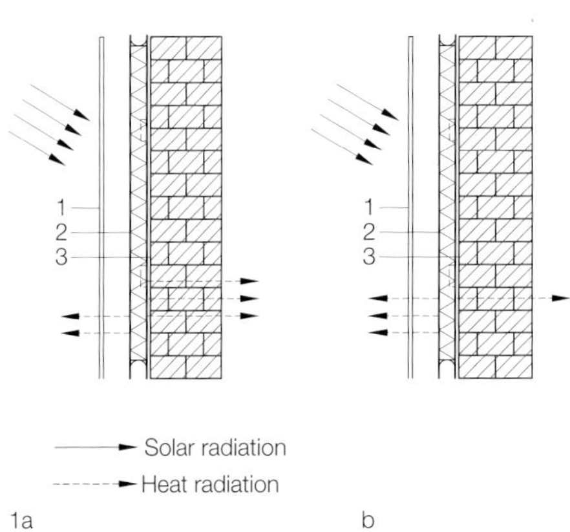

Switchable thermal insulation (SWD)

Switchable thermal insulation is essentially a vacuum system consisting of an approx. 20 mm thick panel with a stainless steel enclosure and a core of glass fibre from which the air has been evacuated and whose thermal conductivity can be changed by means of an electric current.

Inside the panel there is an electrically heated capsule with metal hydrite. Heating this up to approx. 300°C releases a small amount of bound hydrogen in the insulating element which raises the pressure in the glass-fibre core from < 0.01 mbar to approx. 50 mbar. By cooling the capsule, the hydrogen is re-absorbed and the pressure drops again, thus decreasing the thermal conductivity considerably.
Using this system, SWD panels can be switched between a highly insulating and a highly thermally conductive state.
The switching is controlled by a sensor that reacts to the external temperature. However, electrical power of about 5 W/m^2 panel area is required for the thermally conductive state.

Theoretically, an SWD system could transport about 150 kWh/m^2 p.a. of the incident solar energy via a storage wall into the interior as usable heat. By switching the SWD panels into the highly insulating state, the heat is retained at night or during cloudy periods without changing the appearance of the facade.
Depending on the wall construction behind the SWD panels, U-values of approx. 0.2 W/m^{2}K in the insulating state and approx. 10.0 W/m^{2}K in the thermally conductive state are obtained.
This new technology requires further development and has yet to be tried in practice.

Nanocellular foams

It is known that the cell size of foam materials has a considerable influence on their insulating properties. The smaller and finer the cell structure, the lower is the heat transfer by way of convection within the cells.

The aim of the development of nanocellular foams is therefore the production of cells not in the micrometre range common these days, but rather in the nanometre range.
In these foam materials, the size of the cells is to be reduced to such an extent that they match the mean free path length of a gas molecule. The "mean free path length" is the average distance travelled by a particle without interaction with other particles. An exchange of heat is practically impossible without this interaction. The insulating effect of a foam material could therefore be improved by more than 50% or, looked at another way, the thickness of material required for a certain level of insulation could be cut by more than half.
Various organic materials can be used as the raw materials, and polyurethane foams would seem to be ideal for a realistic implementation.
These materials are currently undergoing development and it is not yet possible to predict when they may become available.

1 Switchable thermal insulation (SWD)
   a in heat transfer mode (heating period and sunshine)
      1 Glass
      2 Panel in heat transfer mode
      3 Masonry
   b in insulating mode (all other times)
      1 Glass
      2 Panel in insulating mode
      3 Masonry
2 Insulating a rooftop terrace using vacuum insulation panels
3 Insulation to thermal bridge: vacuum insulation panels for insulating a concrete column in a double-leaf external wall

2

3

Vacuum insulation panel (VIP)

The use of vacuum insulation panels generally requires individual approval for each project (see p. 60).

Raw materials and production
Vacuum insulation panels consist of a gas-tight enclosure and a rigid core from which the air has been evacuated. Complex multi-ply laminates with metallised polyethylene or polypropylene are used for the high-barrier foils of the enclosure. Pyrogenic silicic acid is preferred for the core along with mineral wool, polystyrene and polyurethane. A VIP is therefore not an insulating material in the conventional sense, but rather a prefabricated highly efficient insulating element.

Development and market significance
The principle of the vacuum insulation panel has been used successfully in refrigerators and freezers since the 1970s. In the building industry there have been a number of studies and practical trials.
However, the high price in comparison to conventional insulating materials and the vulnerability of these panels in practical situations has prevented their widespread use up to now.

Properties and applications
Extremely low thermal conductivities of 0.002–0.008 W/mK can be achieved with VIPs. These values are about 5 to 10 times better than conventional good insulating materials, which means that excellent insulating effects can be achieved with VIPs.
The very nature of these panels means that they are absolutely vapour-tight and also exhibit a high compressive strength. However, up until now they have not been used in applications where this high compressive strength is really of benefit.

The prerequisite for the permanent functioning of the panels is the imperviousness of the enclosure. The initial gas pressure is approx. 1–5 mbar, but it is supposed that the gas pressure will increase by 2 mbar annually because the vacuum cannot be fully maintained permanently, which means that, theoretically, the thermal conductivity could reach approx. 0.008 – 0.014 W/mK after 25 years. For comparison, the value for nanocellular silicic acid is only about 0.005 W/mK. But even damaged panels still exhibit excellent values of, for example, 0.020 W/mK, depending on the filling material used.

Vacuum insulation panels are suitable for many different applications, e.g.:

- rooftop terraces and balconies, in order to avoid steps
- insulation of thermal bridges
- door cores
- spandrel panel elements for post-and-rail facades
- underneath underfloor heating pipes
- internal insulation with inner lining
- thermal insulation composite systems combined with other materials as a protective layer or substrate for render
- around dormer windows

VIPs are used, in particular, where their specific advantages, i.e. high insulation performance in conjunction with a thin material, outweigh the high cost.
Vacuum insulation systems are especially interesting in the case of refurbishment work where there is insufficient space for thick layers of insulation and the original appearance has to remain intact.

Forms of supply
VIPs are available in thicknesses of 10–50 mm (in 5 mm steps).
The usual formats are:

- 600 × 500 mm
- 1200 × 500 mm
- 1000 × 600 mm.

Custom panels are also possible, but the cost of such panels can be twice that of standard panels. Panels with rounded geometry cannot be produced at present.

Installation advice
As the vacuum enclosure may not be damaged, requirements must be measured exactly – cutting is impossible because the insulating effect is then lost. Remaining areas that cannot be filled with standard panels require accurately made custom panels.
Care must be taken to ensure that all panels are installed free of all restraint. The panels must be protected against damage during installation and also during use, which means that appropriate constructional measures must be planned (cladding, covering, building into prefabricated elements, etc.).
Joints between the panels, likewise junctions with adjoining components, should be minimised as far as possible in order to avoid weak spots.

Health and ecological aspects, recycling
A consideration of the health risks and ecological aspects depends on the core and enclosing materials used.
No information on the recycling of vacuum insulation panels is yet available.
If the elements cannot be reused, costly disposal must be reckoned with because the enclosing foils must be separated.

Statutory instruments and insulating material standards

Roland Gellert

Binding legislation on the one hand and standards and approvals on the other have created an extensive set of rules and regulations covering the manufacture of insulating materials and their use in construction. The standards and approvals are by definition not mandatory, but do become so when statutory instruments make reference to them.

In order to bring transparency into the European market for manufacturers and designers, and to guarantee legal security for all those involved, national regulations have been subjected to a process of harmonisation at European level. The current transitional phase is characterised by the coexistence of European and national regulations, the validity of which must be carefully considered.

This chapter takes this aspect into account for the standards and approvals applicable to insulating materials and also the relevant statutory instruments (European Construction Products Directive and German Construction Products Act) together with the building legislation instruments for their implementation (Model Building Code and Construction Products List). The final part of this chapter explains the various quality control measures for construction products (attestation of conformity, CE marking, voluntary product certification).

Construction Products Directive (CPD) and Construction Products Act (BauPG)

It was in 1989 that the "Council Directive 89/106/EEC of 21 December 1988 on the approximation of laws, regulations and administrative provisions of the Member States relating to construction products (89/106/EEC)" was published in the Official Journal of the European Communities (OJ).

This so-called Construction Products Directive (CPD) states that construction products – and the technical specifications that describe them – must be of such a form that their use does not have a detrimental effect on the levels of safety and protection that apply to the construction works. Such levels can vary, depending on the location of the works, their use or other circumstances.

The levels of safety and protection are divided into six primary requirements listed in Annex I of the CPD:

1. Mechanical resistance and stability
2. Safety in case of fire
3. Hygiene, health and the environment
4. Safety in use
5. Protection against noise
6. Energy economy and heat retention.

For the implementation of the CPD, the European Commission has provided detailed explanations and commentaries of individual parts in the form of interpretive documents and Guidance Papers; the Member States and the CEN (Comité Européen de Normalisation – European Committee for Standardisation) have to take into account these non-binding documents in their national legislation. The Federal Republic of Germany has incorporated this directive into its national legislation in the form of the 1998 Construction Products Act [1] (BauPG).

According to article 1 "Purpose", the provisions of the BauPG regulate the placing on the market of construction products and the free movement of goods with respect to construction products to and from the Member States of the European Union or other contracting states to the agreement on the European Economic Area (EEA).

It is important that in doing so the national public-law provisions concerning the requirements and the use of construction products, e.g. insulating materials, remain unaffected.

The definitions specified in BauPG article 2, which will be referred to later, are given below:

- Construction products
  are any products "produced for incorporation in a permanent manner in construction works, including both buildings and civil engineering works" (CPD).
- Harmonised standards
  are technical rules (EN) drawn up on the basis of mandates of the Commission of the European Communities by the European standardisation organisations with respect to the essential requirements; they are implemented in corresponding national standards (e.g. DIN EN). Normally, national and state governments contribute to the drafting of harmonised standards within the scope of the participation of interested parties in order to incorporate into European standardisation the latest technical requirements achieved in the Federal Republic of Germany as a result of public-law instruments and public-sector procurement.
- Acknowledged standards
  are technical rules valid for construction products in the Member States of the European Union or other contracting states to the agreement on the European Economic Area (EEA), where owing to one of the methods carried out according to the Construction Products Directive it is presumed that they conform to the essential requirements.

[1] Law covering the placing on the market and free movement of goods with respect to construction products for the implementation of directive 89/106/EEC of the European Council dated 21 December 1988 for harmonising the legislative and administrative instruments of the Member States with regard to construction products and other acts of law of the European Communities (Construction Products Act – BauPG) in the version of the notification of 28 April 1998 (German Federal Law Gazette I, p. 812)

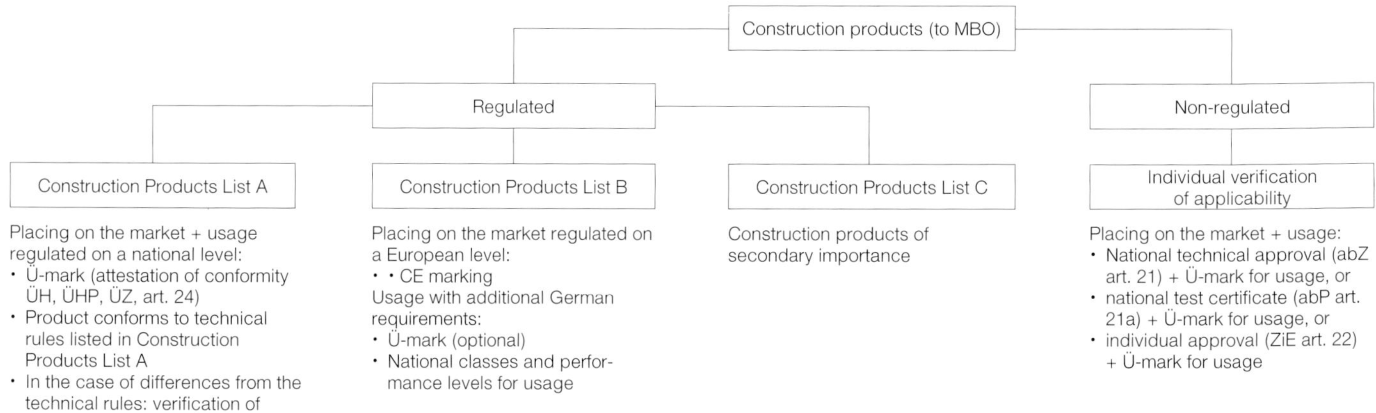
Construction products (to MBO)
Regulated
Non-regulated
Construction Products List A
Construction Products List B
Construction Products List C
Individual verification of applicability
Placing on the market + usage regulated on a national level:
• Ü-mark (attestation of conformity ÜH, ÜHP, ÜZ, art. 24)
• Product conforms to technical rules listed in Construction Products List A
• In the case of differences from the technical rules: verification of applicability abZ or abP (art. 21)
Placing on the market regulated on a European level:
• • CE marking
Usage with additional German requirements:
• Ü-mark (optional)
• National classes and performance levels for usage
Construction products of secondary importance
Placing on the market + usage:
• National technical approval (abZ art. 21) + Ü-mark for usage, or
• national test certificate (abP art. 21a) + Ü-mark for usage, or
• individual approval (ZiE art. 22) + Ü-mark for usage
1

- European Technical Approval Guidelines (ETAG) are principles "drafted by and for the EOTA Approval Bodies as a result of a mandate from the European Commission and EFTA. [The] basic aim is to establish how Approval Bodies should evaluate the specific characteristics/requirements of a product or family of products." (EOTA website)
- European Technical Approvals (ETA) are favourable technical assessments of fitness for an intended use issued to a manufacturer for his construction products by certain Approval Bodies according to this law or the legislation adopted by other Member States of the European Union or other contracting states to the agreement on the European Economic Area (EEA).

The provisions of this act (BauPG article 3) apply to construction products for which either
- the European Commission has published the references of harmonised or acknowledged standards in the Official Journal of the European Communities (OJ), or
- European Technical Approval Guidelines (ETAGs) have been drawn up, or
- European Technical Approvals (ETAs) have been issued without Guidelines having been drawn up.

Examples from the area of insulating materials are given here (see table 2, p. 62).

Construction legislation instruments

The Model Building Code and the Construction Products List are the two construction legislation instruments available in Germany for regulating the technical characteristics and applications of insulating materials.

Model Building Code (MBO)
The conference of ministers and senators responsible for urban planning, building and housing (ARGEBAU) coordinates the building regulations of the 16 German federal states. The federal minister responsible for building also regularly takes part in this conference. The experts of the ARGEBAU have drawn up a model for the building regulations of the federal states. The building regulations of all the federal states are based on this "Model Building Code" and therefore contain almost identical provisions. They differ only in terms of a few minor details, e.g. the designation of the paragraphs, which are called "articles" in Bavaria, for instance. The current edition of the Model Building Code dates from 2002. Important for the topic of insulating materials is the third section "Construction products and construction forms", especially the following articles:

Article 20 Construction products
They "may be used for the erection, modification and maintenance of buildings and structures only if they, for the intended purpose,
1. do not or not significantly differ from the technical rules publicised according to paragraph 2 (regulated construction products) or are permissible according to paragraph 3 and if they are marked with the conformity symbol (Ü-mark) on the basis of the attestation of conformity according to article 24, or
2. according to the provisions
   a) of the Construction Products Act (BauPG),
   b) for implementing directive 89/106/EEC of the European Council for harmonising the legislative and administrative instruments of the Member States with regard to construction products (Construction Products Directive) dated 21 December 1988 (OJ L 40, 11 Feb 1989, p. 12) by other Member States of the European communities and other contracting states to the agreement on the European Economic Area (EEA), or
   c) for the implementation of other directives of the European Communities insofar as these take into account the essential requirements,

   may be placed on the market and traded, are marked with the symbol of the European Communities (CE marking) in particular and this marking identifies the classes and performance levels specified according to paragraph 7 No. 1.
3. Construction products for which technical rules have been published in Construction Products List A according to paragraph 2 and which differ significantly from these or for which there are no technical building regulations or generally acknowledged technical rules (non-regulated construction products) must have
   1. a national technical approval (article 21), or
   2. a national test certificate (article 21a), or
   3. an individual approval (article 22)."

Article 21 National technical approval (abZ)
"The German Institute for Building Technology (DIBt) issues national technical approvals for non-regulated construction products if their usability in the meaning of article 3 para. 2[1] has been verified. The documents necessary to substantiate the application must be appended.
If necessary, test samples must be made available by the applicant or obtained by experts, who can be appointed by the

[1] MBO article 3, para. 2: Construction products may be used only if their use means that the properly maintained buildings and structures fulfil the requirements of this Act for a period of time appropriate to the purpose and are fit for the intended purpose.

1 Conditions for the use of construction products
Products with CE marking may be placed on the European market. They are listed in Construction Products List B. When using such products, the respective national requirements for construction works and the national codes of practice must be taken into account.
Products without CE marking are limited to national markets and must comply with the rules applicable in those markets regarding their placing on the market and usage.

DIBt, or tests on samples carried out under the supervision of the experts.
The DIBt can stipulate the expert institute for performing the test and the time and location of the tests on samples. The national technical approval is issued for a certain length of time, generally five years, and is revocable.
The DIBt publishes the objects and essential contents of the national technical approvals it issues."

Article 21a National test certificate (abP)
"Construction products
1. whose use does not serve the fulfilment of substantial requirements for the safety of buildings and structures, or
2. those assessed according to generally acknowledged test procedures,

require a national test certificate instead of a national technical approval. The DIBt announces this in Construction Products List A by specifying the relevant technical rules and, insofar as there are no generally acknowledged technical rules, by designating the construction products in agreement with the highest building authority.
A national test certificate is issued for non-regulated construction products by a testing laboratory if their usability is verified in the meaning of article 3, para. 2."

Article 22 Individual approval (ZiE)
"Provided the highest building authority agrees,
1. construction products that may be placed on the market and traded exclusively according to the Construction Products Act or according to other regulations for implementing the directives of the European Communities, but do not fulfil their requirements, and
2. non-regulated construction products-may be used if their usability is verified in the meaning of article 3, para. 2.

The lower building authority shall issue the approval for building products according to para. 1 that are to be used in, for example, buildings covered by preservation orders."

Article 24 Attestation of conformity (Ü-mark)
"Construction products require attestation of their conformity with the technical rules according to article 20, para. 2, the national technical approvals, the national test certificates or the individual approvals; conformity also applies to a difference that is not significant.
The attestation of conformity is achieved through
1. the manufacturer's declaration of conformity (article 24a), or
2. a certificate of conformity (article 24b).

Attestation by way of a certificate of conformity can be prescribed in the national technical approval, in the individual approval or in Construction Products List A, if this is necessary for verifying the proper manufacture.
The declaration of conformity and the declaration that a certificate of conformity has been issued must be specified by a manufacturer by labelling his construction products with the conformity symbol (Ü-mark) which includes an indication of the use.
The Ü-mark is to be provided on the construction product or its packaging or, if this is not possible, on the accompanying commercial documents."

Article 24a Manufacturer's declaration of conformity
"The manufacturer may only submit a declaration of conformity if he guarantees through factory production control measures that the construction product manufactured by him complies with the relevant technical rules, the national technical approval, the national test certificate or the individual approval.
Testing of the construction products by a testing laboratory prior to submitting the declaration of conformity can be stipulated in the technical rules according to article 20, para. 2, in Construction Products List A, in the national technical approvals, in the national test certificates or in the individual approvals if this is necessary to guarantee proper manufacture.
In these cases it is the task of the testing laboratory to check whether the construction product complies with the relevant technical rules, the national technical approval, the national test certificate or the individual approval."

Article 24b Certificate of conformity
"A certificate of conformity is to be issued by a certification body according to article 24c when the construction product
1. complies with the relevant technical rules, the national technical approval, the national test certificate or the individual approval, and
2. is subjected to factory production control measures and third-party inspections.

The latter is to be carried out by an inspection body according to article 24c."

Article 24c Testing, certification and monitoring institutes
"The highest building authority can acknowledge a person, institute or inspection body as a
1. testing laboratory for the issuing of national test certificates,
2. testing laboratory for the testing of construction products prior to attestation of conformity,
3. certification body,
4. third-party inspection body,

if it or persons working for it can provide a guarantee through their training, specialist knowledge, personal reliability, impartiality and services that these tasks are realised in a manner appropriate to public-

1a

law instruments and that they have the necessary apparatus.
The DIBt publishes regular updates of its directory of testing, certification and monitoring bodies that comply with the federal state building codes; part I lists the bodies that should be appointed to attest the conformity of regulated construction products with technical rules according to Construction Products List A part 1."

Construction Products Lists A and B
The legal basis for the Construction Products Lists is specified in the aforementioned article 20 of the MBO. Lists A and B are relevant for insulating materials. Construction products that play only a subsidiary role in fulfilling the requirements of the MBO are published in List C by the DIBt in agreement with the highest building authority.

Construction Products List A
In agreement with the highest building authority, the DIBt publishes the technical rules for construction products in Construction Products List A which are necessary for satisfying the requirements placed on buildings and structures stipulated in this act and in the regulations based on this act.

Construction products for which technical rules have been published in Construction Products List A and which differ from these significantly or for which there are no technical rules or generally acknowledged technical rules (non-regulated construction products), must have
1. a national technical approval, or
2. a national test certificate , or
3. an individual approval.
Construction products in List C are excluded from this.

Such technical rules necessary for satisfying the requirements of the federal state building codes (LBOs) are specified in general in Construction Products List A part 1, and they define adequately the products concerned with respect to satisfying the requirements relevant to the intended purpose.

The technical rules according to Construction Products List A part 1 can be rules for products that are not yet harmonised at European level. The traditional technical rules according to the hitherto customary national system then apply. These may also be non-harmonised European standards. However, the list can also contain the national standards that are still valid. The rules would then be applied, for example, together with a standard listed in Construction Products List B part 1.

Construction Products List B
In agreement with the highest building authority, the DIBt can use Construction Products List B to specify the classes and performance levels construction products have to satisfy which are contained in standards, guidelines or European Technical Approvals according to the German Construction Products Act or in other instruments for implementing the directives of the European Communities.
Construction Products List B part 1 is not an exhaustive list of all harmonised construction products. It lists only those construction products for which there are harmonised specifications and where it is necessary to include further details of the product properties necessary with respect to certain uses.

The annexes to the Construction Products Lists specify particular national requirements regarding
- reaction to fire
- verification of the absence of health risks
- smouldering behaviour
- resistance to mould

Construction Products List A, part 1
- Polyurethane in situ foam with CO_2 as blowing agent
- Urea-formaldehyde resin in situ foam for thermal insulation
- Flammable plasterboard composite panels with polystyrene or polyurethane rigid foam as insulating material
- Not readily flammable plasterboard composite panels with polystyrene or polyurethane rigid foam as insulating material

Construction Products List B, part 1

Insulating materials within the scope of harmonised standards according to the CPD
- Factory-made insulating materials made from
  - mineral wool (MW)
  - expanded polystyrene (EPS)
  - extruded polystyrene foam (XPS)
  - polyurethane rigid foam (PUR)
  - phenolic foam (PF)
  - cellular glass (CG)
  - wood wool (WW)
  - expanded perlite board (EPB)
  - insulation cork board (ICB)
  - wood fibres (WF)
- Thermal insulation plaster/render
- Thermal insulation made in situ
  - lightweight expanded clay aggregate (LWA)
  - products with expanded perlite (EP)
  - products with exfoliated vermiculite (EV).

Insulating materials issued with an ETA without Guideline:
- loose fill insulating materials made from vegetable or animal fibres
- factory-made insulating materials made from vegetable or animal fibres
- insulating material fixing elements
- special anchors for thermal insulation composite systems
- thermal insulation boards made from mineral material

Building kits within the scope of Guidelines for ETAs:
- external thermal insulation composite systems with render finish
- non-loadbearing permanent formwork kits/systems consisting of formwork/outer units or elements made from thermal insulation materials and – sometimes – from concrete

Building kits issued with an ETA without Guideline:
- kit for a permanent formwork system made from thermal insulation materials for the whole building

2

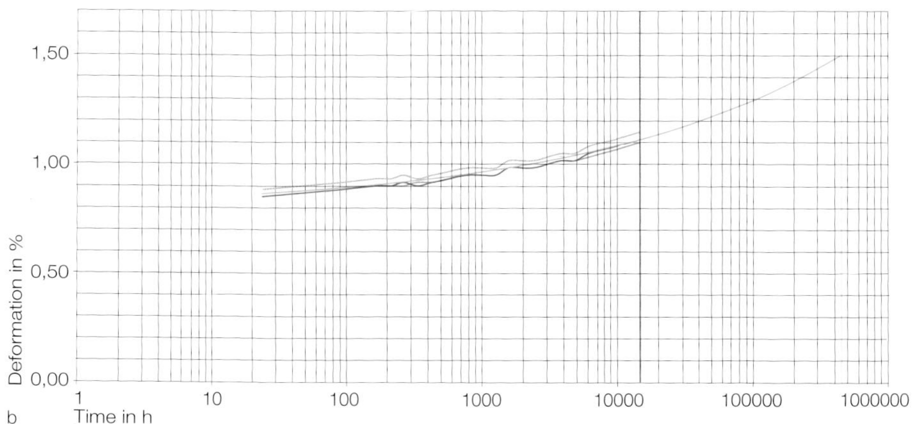

1 Measuring the creep behaviour of extruded polystyrene foam (XPS
a Testing apparatus
b Example of an evaluation curve with extrapolation to 50 years after Findley for the long-term creep behaviour caused by a permanent compression action effect

- settlement behaviour, and
- notes on satisfying the German Chemicals Act

separately for each insulating material.

Construction Products Lists A and B are amended with the involvement of the profession at large. Table 2 shows which insulating materials are currently listed in the Construction Products List (edition 2006/1).

European standards and approvals for thermal insulating materials

With mandate M/103 of 1995, the European Commission officially appointed the European Committee for Standardisation (CEN) to standardise products for the thermal performance of buildings. The aim of harmonised standards for insulating materials is to create the foundations for the free movement of goods in Europe. For this reason, the insulating materials should be uniformly

- tested (EN testing standards),
- described (EN product standards), and
- certified (EN conformity standards together with EN product standards).

The mandate specified a whole series of building physics characteristics that the standards had to cover. Due to the (legal) framework conditions of the Member States, the following aspects must be taken into account during the standardisation work, which are mentioned here in order to gain a better understanding of the structure of the finished standards:

- Separating the regulations for the product on the one hand and its uses on the other.
- Dividing the standards into harmonised and non-harmonised parts.
- Ensuring that the standard describes not the product, but rather its performance.
- Taking into account very different construction legislation traditions and, accordingly, the different structures of sets of rules to which the use of construction products are subjected at a national level.

The technical committee responsible, CEN/TC 88 “Insulating materials and products”, prepared the first package of product and associated testing standards. The German DIN organisation then published these standards in October 2001. Following a so-called coexistence period, during which insulating materials could be placed on the market in Germany with both the European CE marking and the national Ü-mark, the national standards that conflicted with the harmonised standards had to be withdrawn after 15 May 2003. However, national standards that do not conflict with the harmonised standards, and including the testing standards, continue to remain valid.
The following 10 harmonised standards are valid for the specification of thermal insulating materials for buildings:

- DIN EN 13162:
  Factory-made mineral wool (MW) products
- DIN EN 13163:
  Factory-made products of expanded polystyrene (EPS)
- DIN EN 13164:
  Factory-made products of extruded polystyrene foam (XPS)
- DIN EN 13165:
  Factory-made rigid polyurethane foam (PUR) products
- DIN EN 13166:
  Factory-made products of phenolic foam (PF)
- DIN EN 13167:
  Factory-made cellular glass (CG) products
- DIN EN 13168:
  Factory-made wood wool (WW) products
- DIN EN 13169:
  Factory-made products of expanded perlite (EPB)
- DIN EN 13170:
  Factory-made products of expanded cork (ICB)
- DIN EN 13171:
  Factory-made wood fibre (WF) products

Specification standards for a whole series of products (in situ insulating materials, insulating materials for building services) are still at the harmonisation stage; it is to be expected that the standards will be published by CEN in the course of 2007 and 2008. An up-to-date list of standards completed or still in progress can be viewed at www.cen.eu.

Determination of declared thermal conductivity to DIN EN 13162 to DIN EN 13171

The declared thermal conductivity λ_D is determined on the basis of statistically evaluated measurements ($\lambda_{90/90}$) and specified in steps of 0.010 W/mK. For example, a measurement $\lambda_{90/90}$ = 0.0291 W/mK equates to the declared value λ_D = 0.030 W/mK.

The $\lambda_{90/90}$ value means it can be assumed that there is a possibility of 90% that every measurement of thermal conductivity λ still to be determined will not exceed the $\lambda_{90/90}$ value.

The $\lambda_{90/90}$ value is calculated from the average value λ_m of, generally, at least 10 measurements, the standard deviation s_λ related to the measurements, and a factor k which takes into account the number of existing measurements ($\lambda_{90/90} = \lambda_m + k \cdot s_\lambda$).

From statistics tables it follows that folgt k = 2.07 for 10 measurements and k = 1.32 for 2000 measurements. This means that if there is a great scatter in the production, the λ_D value to be specified increases.

The thermal resistance $R_{90/90}$ is calculated from the nominal thickness d_N of the product and the $\lambda_{90/90}$ value using the equation $R_{90/90} = d_N / \lambda_{90/90}$.

2

Selected properties and their designations according to the European product standards

Property	Designation according to EN product standards
Thermal conductivity	λ_D
Thermal resistance	R_D
Reaction to fire (Euroclasses)	A1, A2, B, C, D, E, F
Compressive strength or compressive stress at 10% deformation	CS(10\Y)
Tensile strength perpendicular to plane of board	TR
Creep behaviour	$CC(i_1/i_2/y)\sigma_C$
Water absorption for short-term partial immersion	WS
Water absorption for long-term partial immersion	WL(P)
Water absorption for long-term full immersion	WL(T)
Freeze-thaw cycle stability	FT
Water vapour diffusion	MU
Point load for defined deformation	F_P
Dimensional stability in normal climate	DS(N)
Dimensional stability for defined temperature- and moisture load	DS(TH)
Deformation behaviour for defined compression and temperature load	DLT(i)
Width	b
Compressibility	c
Thickness	d
Stages of compressibility	CP
Practical sound absorption degree	α_p
Weighted sound a third party degree	α_w
Dynamic stiffness	SD
Bending strength	BS
Thickness tolerance class	T
Thickness under a load of 250 Pa	d_L
Thickness under a load of 2 kPa after removing an additional load of 48 kPa	d_B

1

Standards – structure and content

Due to the requirements of the European Commission and a "model standard", the standards all have an identical structure:

1. Scope
2. Normative references
3. Terms, definitions, symbols, units and abbreviated terms
4. Requirements
5. Test methods
6. Designation code
7. Attestation of conformity
8. Marking and labelling

Annex A (normative)
Determination of thermal resistance and thermal conductivity
Annex B (normative)
Factory production control measures
Annex ZA (informative)
Sections of this European standard that concern the provisions of the EU Construction Products Directive

Annex ZA is practically identical for all standards; it was prescribed by the European Commission. Further informative annexes containing explanations specific to the material can be added to the compulsory annexes A and B.

Chapter 4 of each standard ("Requirements") specifies the product performance in different levels and classes, with limiting values or with nominal values. The requirements are divided up as follows:

- for all applications – into thermal resistance (thermal conductivity), linear properties and handling properties,
- for certain applications – into mechanical and/or moisture-related properties[1] specifically for each product.

Table 1 provides an overview of the properties and their designations according to chapter 4 of the EN product standards. The latter are important for understanding the German codes of practice.

Two properties redefined at European level – thermal conductivity and the classification of reaction to fire – will be explained in detail below.

Thermal conductivity, thermal resistance

The thermal conductivity of an insulating material is specified by the manufacturer as a declared value or a design value. The declared thermal conductivity λ_D is determined on the basis of statistically evaluated measurements ($\lambda_{90/90}$), with λ_D specified in steps of 0.010 W/mK (table 2). This method of recording the quality scatter in the production of thermal insulating materials was not customary in Germany. In the past, the thermal conductivity was determined from a sample taken at random and was not permitted to exceed a certain limit. The method according to the European standards therefore represents a different statistical safeguard for the declared thermal conductivity value λ_D – or the design value of the thermal conductivity.

Reaction to fire

In line with European standard EN 13501, the following classifications with regard to the combustibility of building materials (reaction to fire) have been adopted:

A1 + A2	No contribution to a fire/ non-combustible
B	Very limited contribution to a fire • heat propagation • flame propagation • smoke propagation
C	Limited – but some – contribution to a fire
D	Not negligible contribution to a fire
E	Poor fire reaction properties • acceptable ignitability • limited flame propagation
F	No performance determined – no data available

3

Besides the above main criteria, the smoke intensity (s) and burning droplets (d) characteristics of building materials are graded in several classes. The smoke intensity classes are designated s1, s2 and s3, the burning droplets classes d0, d1 and d2 (see also p. 14 and p. 102). The implementation of the European classes in the German building authority requirements is described in the section "National codes of practice and technical approvals" (table 2, p. 70).

European Technical Approvals, Guidelines
A European Technical Approval (ETA) can only be granted for a construction product, not for a form of construction; the latter requires a national technical approval.
If neither harmonised nor acknowledged standards are published for a construction product, its fitness for use is to be verified by an ETA, especially if a European Technical Approval Guideline (ETAG) is to be adopted for this product (for terminology see pp. 59/60). If there is no ETAG available, the fitness for use can either be verified by means of a national technical approval as in the past or by a European Technical Approval without Guideline. This is then carried out on the basis of the agreement among the approval bodies (EOTA[2]) that issue ETAs, if this is permitted by the European Commission.
Upon receipt of a written application from the manufacturer or his agent in the European Union, an ETA is generally issued, without prejudice to third-party rights, for a period of five years by a European approval body. It is then valid throughout the EU and the contracting states to the agreement on the European Economic Area (EEA), but may be revoked at any time.

The European Commission issues mandates to the EOTA for the preparation of Guidelines for ETAs according to the constitution of the EU's Standing Committee on Construction.
Guidelines must include, in particular,
- a list of the relevant Interpretative Documents,
- the specific requirements for the products within the meaning of the Essential Requirements,
- the test procedures,
- the methods of assessing and judging the results of the tests,
- the procedures related to the Attestation of Conformity, and
- the period of validity of the approval.

The European Commission's mandates to the EOTA include specifications for
- drawing up the Guideline for a certain product, which may also be a complete kit or a family of products,
- describing the necessary content of the technical rules (field of application, description of product, definition of product properties, methods to describe product properties, classes and levels),
- the implementation of the prescribed Attestation of Conformity procedure, and
- adhering to the regulations regarding dangerous substances.

If Attestation of Conformity procedure 3 (initial type-testing of the product by an acknowledged approval body, manufacturer's declaration) or 4 (initial type-testing of the product by the manufacturer, manufacturer's declaration) is stipulated and the product differs only insignificantly from the corresponding standards or ETAs, then initial type-testing of the product based on the given technical rules by a testing laboratory within the scope of the conformity procedure (see pp. 71-72) is sufficient as proof of fitness for use; an EOTA approval body is therefore not involved in this procedure, not even if the difference from an ETA is to be assessed. This applies to thermal insulating products, provided they are not used for fire protection purposes.

According to building legislation, verification of applicability only serves to avoid hazards, in particular to protect the health and safety of users. So-called minimum requirements to be placed on products or forms of construction in the approval procedure can only be derived from this, and not from higher (private) quality demands, e.g. in terms of precautions.
By way of example, ETAG 004 will be briefly explained here:
The Guideline for European Technical Approval 004 "External thermal insulation composite systems with rendering" was published by the EOTA in March 2000 and announced by the German ministry responsible in the Federal Law Gazette on 19 May 2001. The Guideline provides very detailed information concerning the assessment of fitness for use (section 2) and the attestation of conformity (section 3). The Guideline forms the basis for issuing national approvals and a reference to it is included in Construction Products List B for building kits, and it is therefore legally binding.

[1] Properties in connection with the effects of moisture and water.
[2] European Organisation for Technical Approvals, EOTA; the approval body for Germany is the DIBt.

3 Measuring the thermal conductivity using the guarded hot-plate method

Insulating material standards of the second generation
The harmonised product standards for insulating materials valid since 2003 (the so-called first-generation standards) essentially highlight certain product characteristics that reflect the technical performance related to mechanical strength, fire protection, sound insulation and thermal insulation.

Essential requirement 3 "Hygiene, health and the environment" (CPD) assigned to interpretive document No. 3 places the requirement on the construction works that they should not endanger the users through the following effects:

- "the giving-off of toxic gas,
- the presence of dangerous particles or gases in the air,
- the emission of dangerous radiation,
- the pollution or poisoning of the water or soil,
- the faulty elimination of waste water, smoke, solid or liquid wastes,
- the presence of damp in parts of the works or on surfaces within the works." (CPD)

These aspects are also considered for the construction products that are to be used in conjunction with corresponding pollutants or dangerous substances. These requirements can be designated generally as the harmlessness of a construction product in health terms. It should be pointed out that all considerations regarding dangerous substances relate to the period of use of construction works, i.e. only a certain phase of its life cycle.

Recently, the European Commission, following on from the publication of Guidance Paper H on dangerous substances, has made great efforts to promote technical harmonisation in terms of the avoidance of health risks. In the meantime, standardisation mandate M/366 "Development of horizontal standardised assessment methods for harmonised approaches relating to dangerous substances under the construction products directive (CPD)" has been published. It contains details of the following:

- specifications of substances to be covered but no specification of limit values,
- development of release scenarios,
- development of the basics of testing methods.

The technical committee set up to handle this, CEN/TC 351 "Construction Products: Assessment of the release of dangerous substances", started its work in 2007. Once the committee has completed its work in 2010, the respective product standards can then be amended in a second step. Manufacturers will then know which environmental compatibility requirements their products will have to satisfy in order to carry out the CE marking correctly.

National codes of practice and technical approvals

Based on the European technical harmonisation, the EU Member States are responsible for developing rules for the specific use of insulating materials in construction works, e.g. in roofs or walls. In this respect, the Member States can exert their sovereignty because – as laid down expressly in the Construction Products Directive – they are responsible for construction works erected within their territories owing to the different geographical and climatic conditions and ways of life. On the other hand, all national codes of practice should refer to the harmonised European product, testing and conformity standards. Such an approach leads to transparency and comparability on a European level, and to planning security for manufacturers, who can then adjust their products exactly to the respective markets of the Member States. In Germany, the usability of insulating materials is regulated by the building legislation in general, and specifically via Construction Products List B and the technical building regulations, which in turn refer to certain DIN standards. When choosing products, users in Germany must become familiar with the new set of rules in order to exploit the advantages of the wider spectrum of products on offer in the European single market. In this respect, the most important issues are the fields of application, the design values for thermal conductivity and the reliability of the details regarding the performance of the materials.

As laid down by the MBO, Construction Products List B part 1 contains the corresponding regulations of the federal state building codes regarding the classes and performance levels that insulating materials have to comply with in order to guarantee their use. The classes and performance levels required are given in standards, guidelines, in European Technical Approvals according to the Construction Products Act (BauPG) or in other regulations for implementing directives of the European Communities. The following procedure is valid in Germany:

1. Construction Products List B part 1 also contains details of further classes, performance levels and application conditions that exceed the CPD provisions where this is deemed appropriate.
2. Construction Products List B part 1 therefore contains columns for "Consecutive No.", "Construction product", "Standard/Guideline/ETA", "Purpose" and "Classes & performance levels"
3. Further classes, performance levels and application conditions contained in the technical building regulations for

Applications for thermal insulation and application examples to DIN V 4108-10:2004-06

Floor, roof

External insulation to suspended floor or roof, protected from the weather, insulation below roof covering

External insulation to suspended floor or roof, protected from the weather, insulation below waterproofing

External insulation to roof, exposed to the weather (upside-down roof)

Insulation between rafters, double-skin roof, accessible but non-trafficked topmost suspended floor

Internal insulation to suspended floor (underside) or roof, insulation below rafters/structure, suspended ceiling, etc.

Internal insulation to suspended or ground floor (top side) below screed, without sound insulation requirements

Internal insulation to suspended or ground floor (top side) below screed, with sound insulation requirements

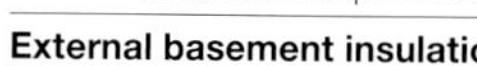

External basement insulation

External thermal insulation to walls in contact with the soil (on outside of waterproofing)

External thermal insulation below ground floor slab in contact with the soil (below waterproofing)

Wall

External insulation to wall, behind cladding

External insulation to wall, behind waterproofing

External insulation to wall, behind render (plinth insulation, thermal bridge insulation)

Cavity insulation to double-leaf walls

Insulation to timber-frame and timber-panel forms of construction

Internal insulation to wall

Insulation between party walls with sound insulation requirements

Insulation to separating walls

1

the use of the products are specified for every product standard/guideline/technical approval in a new product-related part in the existing list of technical building regulations.

4. "Adapted" codes of practice and approvals are to be produced by DIN to cover these requirements such that the harmonised product standards can be used with and are compatible with the technical building regulations. The same applies to the revision of approvals already issued.
5. When drawing up the "adapted" codes of practice and approvals, only those regulations should be included that are justified to achieve the protection aims of public-law instruments.

Differentiation of certain insulating material properties – extract from DIN V 4108-10:2004-06

Product property	Abbreviation	Description	Examples
Compressive strength	dk	No compressive strength	Insulation to cavities and voids, between rafters
	dg	Low compressive strength	Residential and office areas below screed
	dm	Moderate compressive strength	Non-habitable roof space with waterproofing
	dh	High compressive strength	Trafficked roofs and terraces
	ds	Very high compressive strength	Industrial floors, parking decks
	dx	Extremely high compressive strength	Heavily loaded industrial floors, parking decks
Water absorption	wk	No requirements regarding water absorption	Internal insulation to residential and office areas
	wf	Absorption of water as liquid	External insulation to external walls and roofs
	wd	Absorption of water as liquid and/or through diffusion	External basement insulation, upside-down roof
Tensile strength	zk	No requirements regarding tensile strength	Insulation to cavities and voids, between rafters
	zg	Low tensile strength	External insulation to wall behind cladding
	zh	High tensile strength	External insulation to wall behind render, roof with bonded waterproofing
Sound insulation properties	sk	No requirements regarding sound insulation properties	All applications without sound insulation requirements
	sh	Impact sound insulation, high compressibility	Floating screed, party walls
	sm	moderate compressibility	
	sg	low compressibility	
Deformation	tk	No requirements regarding deformation	Internal insulation
	tf	Dimensional stability when subjected to moisture and temperature loads	External insulation to wall behind render, roof with waterproofing
	ti	Deformation under loads and thermal effects	Roof with waterproofing

2

However, no changes may be made to the regulatory scope of the harmonised technical specification. The national application rules may not have any effects on products with CE-marking (according to European law). The CE-marked product has to be accepted as such; only its use can be regulated on a national level and, for example, restricted to certain types of application. If applicable, this can be carried out independently of the levels, classes and nominal values possible according to the harmonised specification and specified for the CE marking.

The following applies to codes of practice and technical approvals:

- They must be restricted essentially to satisfying the building authority requirements regarding the construction works while maintaining existing or new levels of safety and taking into account durability and economic requirements plus, if applicable, construction rules (they can, however, also comply with the requirements of interested groups, e.g. requiring a clearer, comprehensive compilation of application classes).
- They must be restricted to specifying the levels, classes and conditions of use to be maintained plus the methods for determining the design values of product properties from the nominal values.
- The methods for determining the design values of product properties from the nominal values should be specified such that the levels of safety of construction works attained hitherto when using products with a Ü-mark or new levels of safety can also be attained when using products with a CE marking. To do this, it may be necessary, for example, to apply a correction factor; this could be specified in Construction Products List B part 1 or in the Model List of the technical building regulations. It could also mean that a national technical approval is necessary to verify certain levels of safety in conjunction with a use.

If the application rules are available in the form of standards, then these should be comprehensive. DIN publishes codes of practice in the DIN V 20000 series "Application of construction products in structures". Codes of practice are referenced in the annexes to the Model List of the technical building regulations[1]. Technical approvals should also include all possible uses of the product or those specified by the manufacturer.

DIN V 4108-10 "minimum requirements"
As already mentioned, the harmonised European product standards do not provide any information on the uses of the individual insulating materials. This takes place in Germany according to pre-standard DIN V 4108-10 "Thermal insulation and energy economy in buildings – Application-related requirements for thermal insulation materials – Part 10: Factory-made products". This standard contains the minimum requirements to be satisfied by thermal insulating materials in buildings depending on the type of application. DIN V 4108-10 specifies the individual field of application and presents these in tabular form by means of abbreviations and pictograms (table 1, p. 67).
The differentiation of certain properties within the fields of application is also achieved by way of abbreviations (table 2, p. 67).

Matching up the minimum requirements placed on the insulating material for a specific field of application with the respective product properties is achieved by way of a matrix – every insulating material described in the harmonised standards DIN EN 13162 to DIN EN 13171 has its own matrix in DIN V 4108-10. As an example, table 1 shows the combination of the use of rigid polyurethane foam (PUR) for roofs and suspended floors and the associated product standard DIN EN 13165.

As the designations are codes, the details must be "deciphered" with the help of the respective product standard. And vice versa: owing to the classification according to products, the standard does not permit all insulating materials that can be used for a certain application, e.g. DAA, to be placed "next to one another"; a comparison of all application-related minimum requirements is only possible by comparing all the tables in DIN V 4108-10.

DIN V 4108-4 "thermal conductivity"
The planning, design and construction rules listed as technical building regulations are for the most part – as mentioned above – DIN standards. For example, pre-standard DIN V 4108-4 "Thermal insulation and energy economy in buildings – Part 4: Hygrothermal design values" is also recognised by the building authorities. This standard, the latest edition of which appeared in June 2007, contains the corresponding design values for standardised construction products, also for insulating materials according to the harmonised standards DIN EN 13162 to DIN EN 13171. The design values for these insulating materials – in contrast to the values of the European product standards – are the performance values of the products adjusted by safety factors which can be used in calculations for components and structures. The design

[1] The Model List of the technical building regulations contains technical rules for the planning, design and construction of buildings and structures and their parts. Section 4 "Technical rules for thermal and sound insulation" are taken into account for thermal performance in the various parts of DIN 4108.

Extract from DIN V 4108-10, table 6
Minimum requirements for PUR insulating materials to DIN EN 131651 for applications in roofs and floors

Applications	Abbre-viation		Designation code[2]				
			Thickness tolerance	Dim. stability under defined temperature and moisture conditions	Compressive stress or compressive strength at 10% deformation	Tensile strength perpendicular to plane of board	Flatness after one-sided wetting
			Ti	DS(TH)i	CS(10\Y)i	TRi	FWi
Roof, floor	DAD		T2	DS(TH)2	CS(10\Y) 100	–	–
	DAA	dh	T2	DS(TH)2	CS(10\Y) 100	TR40	FW2[3]
		ds	T2	DS(TH)2	CS(10\Y) 150	TR40	FW2[3]
	DUK		Not a standardised application				
	DZ		T2	DS(TH)2	–	–	–
	DI		T2	DS(TH)2	CS(10\Y) 100	TR40	–
	DEO	dh	T2	DS(TH)2	CS(10\Y) 100	–	–
		ds	T2	DS(TH)2	CS(10\Y) 150	–	–
	DES		Not a standardised application				

[1] PUR also includes polyisocyanurate rigid foam (PIR).
[2] See also table 1 (p. 64) and table 5 (p. 75).
1 [3] Only applicable in conjunction when laminated with paper.

Design values for thermal conductivity and guidance value for the water vapour diffusion resistance index of PUR rigid foam – extract from DIN V 4108-4:2007-06, table 2

Line	Material	Category I		Category II		Guidance value of water vapour diffusion resist. index[1]
		Nominal value [W/mK] λ_D	Design value [W/mK] λ^2	Limit value [W/mK] $\lambda_{limit}{}^3$	Design value [W/mK] λ^4	μ
5.4	Polyurethane rigid foam (PUR) to DIN EN 13165[5]	0.020	0.024	0.0195	0.020	40/200
		0.021	0.025	0.0204	0.021	
		0.022	0.026	0.0214	0.022	
		[illegible]	[illegible]	[illegible]	[illegible]	
		0.024	0.029	0.0233	0.024	
		0.025	0.030	0.0242	0.025	
		–	–	–	–	
		–	–	–	–	
		–	–	–	–	
		0.040	0.048	0.0428	0.045	

[1] The less favourable value should be used for the design in each case. See DIN 4108-3 for the use of the μ-value.
[2] $\lambda = \lambda_D \times 1.2$
[3] The λ_{limit} value is to be specified within the scope of the technical specification of the respective insulating material.
[4] $\lambda = \lambda_{limit} \times 1.05$
2 [5] The alternative determination of λ is possible according to appendix C.

values for thermal conductivity of insulating materials are divided into categories I and II (table 2).

Category I
The declared value for the thermal conductivity ĐD according to the respective harmonised product standard (see p. 64) is allocated to category I in DIN V 4108-4 and assigned a design value λ, which includes a safety factor of 1.2. This safety factor is intended to guarantee that the structure really does achieve a certain insulating value and the corresponding energy-savings.

Category II:
DIN V 4108-4 category II lists the limit value λ_{limit}, which is multiplied by a safety factor of 1.05 in order to reach the design value. The European product standards do not contain such a limit value for thermal conductivity. It is established within the scope of a national technical approval (abZ), which the manufacturer can apply for if he wishes to use a safety factor of 1.05 in the design of a structure. The certification body specifies this limit value in conjunction with the manufacturer within the scope of the certification and states this on the certificate. The wording in section 2.2.1 of the approval is as follows: "In the scope of production, the thermal conductivity Đi to DIN EN 131xx may not exceed a thermal conductivity limit value λ_{limit}." In addition, the manufacturer agrees to regular third-party inspections by an acknowledged inspection body. After the approval has been issued and after the initial type-testing carried out, the manufacturer receives the certificate of conformity from the certification body, and this permits him to label his product with the Ü-mark.

1

Classified for reaction to fire properties
On a national level, the requirements with respect to a material's reaction to fire can be specified by the individual countries according to their own discretion, although the European system of classification must be employed. The implementation of the European classes in the building authority requirements envisaged in Germany is specified in the annex to the Construction Products List (table 2).

This differentiated assessment of the building materials also results in different assessments with respect to fire protection requirements. In contrast to the DIN 4102-1 classification employed hitherto, not every building material in the new class A satisfies the requirements for incombustible materials; for example, classification A2-s2, d0 or A2-s1, d1 represents a not readily flammable building material (s = smoke; d = droplets).

Pipe lagging
The German Energy Conservation Act (EnEV), in addition to optimising the building envelope, also calls for the HVAC systems to be included in the planning. Taking the old Heating Systems Act of 1994 as its starting point, in the new Act the legislators have specified limits for the heat losses of space-heating and hot-water pipes and their fittings – to be achieved by way of appropriate thermal insulation. A minimum thickness of insulation is specified according to type of pipe and fitting, their locations and, in particular, their diameter, related to a thermal conductivity of λ = 0.035 W/mK.

The minimum thickness of insulation should be adjusted accordingly for materials with a thermal conductivity other than 0.035 W/mK. The methods of calculation and values contained in the technical rules are to be used for converting and measuring the thermal conductivity of the insulating material.

Building authority approvals for pipe lagging materials have been issued according to the Heating Systems Act since 1995. The following properties are assessed when verifying their suitability:

- Thermal conductivity to DIN 52613 at 40°C average temperature at the test pipe with different thicknesses of insulation according to the internal diameters of the pipes.
- The dimensions of the pipe lagging materials, their densities and thicknesses.
- Reaction to fire according to building materials class B1 (not readily flammable) to DIN 4102 and in the future to DIN EN 13501-1 (see table 2)

Correspondence between German building authority requirements and European classification for – reaction to fire extract from Construction Products List A part 1

Building authority requirement	**Additional requirements**		**Euroclass to DIN EN 13501-1**[1]	
	No smoke	No burning droplets	Construction products, excluding pipe lagging	Pipe lagging[2]
Incombustible	x	x	A1	$A1_L$
	x	x	A2 – s1, d0	$A2_L$ – s1, d0
Not readily flammable	x	x	B – s1, d0 C – s1, d0	B_L – s1, d0 C_L – s1, d0
		x	A2 – s2,d0 A2 – s3, d0 B – s2, d0 B – s3, d0 C – s2, d0 C – s3, d0	$A2_L$ – s2, d0 $A2_L$ – s3, d0 B_L – s2, d0 B_L – s3, d0 C_L – s2, d0 C_L – s3, d0
	x		A2 – s1, d1 A2 – s1, d2 B – s1, d1 B – s1, d2 C – s1, d1 C – s1, d2	$A2_L$ – s1, d1 $A2_L$ – s1, d2 B_L – s1, d1 B_L – s1, d2 C_L – s1, d1 C_L – s1, d2
			A2 – s3, d2 B – s3. d2 C – s3, d2	$A2_L$ – s3, d2 B_L – s3, d2 C_L – s3, d2
Flammable		x	D – s1, d0 D – s2, d0 D – s3, d0 E	D_L – s1, d0 D_L – s2, d0 D_L – s3, d0 E_L
			D – s1, d1 D – s2, d1 D – s3, d1 D – s1, d2 D – s2, d2 D – s3, d2 E – d2	D_L – s1, d1 D_L – s2, d1 D_L – s3, d1 D_L – s1, d2 D_L – s2, d2 D_L – s3, d2 E_L – d2
Highly flammable			F	F_L

[1] The smouldering behaviour of building materials is not covered in the European testing and classification specifications. For applications in which the smouldering behaviour is necessary, the national rules should be used.
[2] Can be used according to a supplement to DIN EN 13501-1;
the index L is a recent edition for identifying the fire behaviour classes for pipe lagging.

2

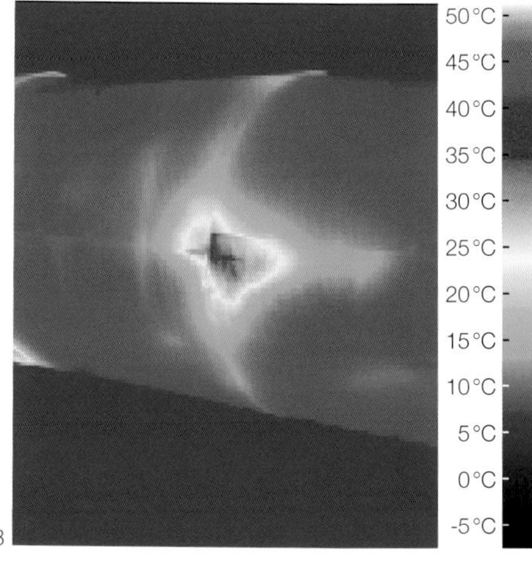

3

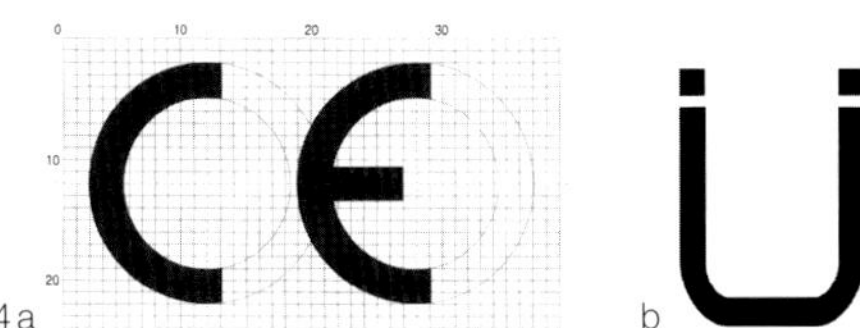

4 a b

- The cell gas composition in the case of closed-cell plastic foams (provided the cell gas is not air) depending on method of manufacture and blowing agent.

The characteristic value is specified according to the Heating Systems Act on the basis of measured thermal conductivity values and is published in the Federal Law Gazette.
No requirements for the minimum thickness of insulation are placed on the pipes of central heating systems in heated rooms or in components between the heated rooms of one and the same user and where their heat output can be influenced by readily accessible controls. This also applies to hot-water pipes in apartments up to an internal diameter of 22 mm that are neither included in the circulation circuit nor fitted with electrical trace heating.

Common synthetic insulating materials for pipe lagging are polyethylene and synthetic rubber, but products made from foam insulating materials (PUR, XPS, EPS, phenolic and melamine foams) are also available for this market segment, either in the form of semi-finished products or ready-to-use products with external coating and internal lamination.
Certificates of conformity based on building authority approvals are issued on a national basis for these materials. On a European level, the drafts of standards for insulating materials for building services (in CEN/TC 88 "Thermal insulating materials and products") have already been drawn up ready for harmonisation by the Member States.

1 Small burner test for determining flammability
3 Thermographic image of defective pipe lagging
4 a CE marking
  b Ü-mark

Attestation of conformity

Article 8 of the German Construction Products Act (BauPG) – which is based on the European Construction Products Directive (CPD) – calls for attestation of conformity of building products:
"A construction product whose fitness for use is based on published harmonised or acknowledge standards or according to European Technical Approvals requires attestation of its conformity with such standards or approvals according to paragraphs 2 to 7" (see below).

Attestation of conformity procedure
According to article 8, the procedure for attesting conformity can consist of:
1. initial type-testing of the product by the manufacturer,
2. initial type-testing of the product by an approved body,
3. testing of samples taken at the factory in accordance with a prescribed test plan by the manufacturer or an approved body,
4. audit-testing of samples taken at the factory, on the open market or on a construction site by the manufacturer or an approved body,
5. testing of samples from a batch which is ready for delivery, or has been delivered, by the manufacturer or an approved body,
6. factory production control,
7. initial inspection of factory and of factory production control by an approved body, or
8. continuous surveillance, judgement and assessment of factory production control by an approved body.

The procedures can be combined according to the requirements placed on the construction product and its properties. The activities of the testing and monitoring bodies plus the assessment of their results can be checked by a certification body. Attestation of conformity is provided by way of
- a certificate of conformity, or
- a declaration of conformity by the manufacturer.

The different procedures for attesting conformity lead in every case to the *CE marking*, the EU symbol of conformity.
In addition, the following must be specified:
- name or designation of the manufacturer and, if applicable,
- details of the product characteristics,
- the last two digits of the year of manufacture,
- the symbol of the inspection body involved, and
- the number of the EU certificate of conformity.

According to article 12 of the German Construction Products Act, for an insulating material with the CE marking it can be assumed that it is fit for use and that conformity has been verified, but, however, that this can be revoked.

Systems of conformity attestation
The following attestation of conformity (AoC) systems in annex ZA, the content of which is identical for all harmonised product standards, have been specified by the European Commission and are in accordance with the CPD.
- System for factory-made insulating materials for any of the proposed purposes: system 3
- Systems for factory-made products required to satisfy reaction to fire requirements:
  Euroclasses A1, A2, B, C system 1
  Euroclasses D, E system 3
  Euroclass F system 4

1 

1 Compressive stress test

System 1
Attestation of conformity of the product by an approved certification body on the basis of:
(Tasks for the manufacturer)
1. Factory production control
2. Further testing of samples taken at the factory by the manufacturer in accordance with a prescribed test plan
(Tasks for the approved body)
3. Initial type-testing of the product,
4. Initial inspection of factory and of factory production control,
5. Continuous surveillance, assessment and approval of factory production control
(testing by means of random samples is not envisaged)

System 3
Manufacturer's declaration of conformity for the product on the basis of:
1. Initial type-testing of the product by an approved laboratory
2. Factory production control

System 4
Manufacturer's declaration of conformity for the product on the basis of:
1. Initial type-testing by the manufacturer
2. Factory production control

EU certificate of conformity
A certificate of conformity (system 1) is issued by the certification body following an application by the manufacturer or his agent once the prescribed procedures for attestation of conformity of the construction product have been carried out and its conformity has been verified. A certificate of conformity in the German language is to be submitted according to BauPG article 10 and must contain, in particular, "details regarding
1. name/address of the certification body,
2. name and address of the manufacturer or his agent,
3. description of the construction product,
4. published harmonised or acknowledged standards or European Technical Approvals that are relevant for assessing the construction product,
5. special instructions for use,
6. number of the certificate, details of secondary provisions if applicable, and the period of validity of the certificate,
7. name and function of the person signing the certificate."

EU declaration of conformity
By providing a declaration of conformity (systems 3 and 4), the manufacturer or his agent confirms that the procedures prescribed for attestation of conformity have been carried out and have verified the conformity of the construction product. A declaration of conformity in the German language is to be submitted and as specified in BauPG article 9, and in contrast to a certificate (BauPG article 10), only needs to contain details of the manufacturer, the construction product, the harmonised or acknowledged standard or the European Technical Approval issued to the manufacturer plus any special instructions for use as well as the names and addresses of the testing, inspection and certification bodies plus a description of the function of the person or his representative signing the declaration.

If an attestation procedure with initial type-testing and permanent factory production control is prescribed, the manufacturer or his agent may only submit a declaration of conformity if he has guaranteed – through initial type-testing of the construction product and through factory production control – that the construction product manufactured by him complies with the published harmonised or acknowledged standards or European Technical Approvals.

Important for the manufacturer of an insulating material is that according to annex ZA the scope of work of the approval body for his products, which fall under the remit of system 3 for initial type-testing, is limited to a maximum of four properties:
- thermal resistance
- release of dangerous substances
- compressive strength (for loadbearing applications only)
- water permeability

The manufacturer is responsible for the other properties.

DIN EN 13172 "conformity"
To help manufacturers, approval bodies and users understand which procedure for attestation of conformity should be used, a (non-harmonised) standard was drawn up and published in parallel with the insulating material standards: EN 13172 "Thermal insulating products – Evaluation of conformity", which in the meantime is available in a revised DIN edition of September 2005. The contents specifies the elements specific to insulating materials mentioned in the CPD and in the ZA annexes.

Content of the standard:
1. Scope
2. Normative references
3. Terms, definitions, symbols, units and abbreviated terms
4. General requirements
5. Requirements placed on factory production control – tasks for the manufacturer
6. Initial type-testing

Annex A (informative)
Attestation of conformity (not for the case of CE marking)
Annex B (informative)
Manufacturer's declaration of conformity (according to system 1)
Annex C (informative)
Manufacturer's declaration of conformity (according to system 3)

Annex D (informative)
Manufacturer's declaration of conformity (according to system 4)
Annex E (informative)
Guidelines for using the annexes
Annex F (informative)
Criteria for assessing non-conformity – procedure in the case of a complaint

DIN EN 13172 can therefore be used for insulating materials as a reference standard for

- attestation of conformity,
- voluntary product certification, and
- possible complaints procedures.

Identification and labelling

The difference between placing construction products on the market and the actual use of such products, i.e. their use in construction works in the individual Member States, as envisaged by the Construction Products Directive leads to thermal insulating materials generally being subjected to two conformity procedures in Germany. The CE marking, as the sole legally required attestation of conformity, safeguards the placing of construction products on the market, whereas the Ü-mark, a superior system of quality assurance, regulates the use of such products, albeit only on a national and only on a voluntary basis.

CE marking (compulsory)
The CE marking is a legal requirement for construction products complying with EN standards and indicates that the insulating material product has passed through the prescribed testing and attestation procedures. Without a CE marking or details regarding the prescribed product properties, the product may not be placed on the market. However, the CE marking says nothing about the applications for which the thermal insulating material may be used. It is found on the respective insulating product, on a label on the packaging (Fig. 1, p. 74) or on the accompanying commercial documents. Table 3 (p. 74) contains all the details according to section 8 of the respective product standard – DIN EN 13165 in the case of PUR– that must be included on the label.

An essential component of the CE marking is the designation code. Besides the abbreviation for the insulating material and the number of the relevant standard, it contains all the details about the properties mentioned in section 4.2 of the respective product standard for "all applications", and apart from that, minimum requirements for "specific applications" according to section 4.3.
In order to make it possible for (national) users to check whether an insulating material complies with the minimum requirements according to DIN V 4108-10 for a certain application, the tested properties of the insulating material, with the designations according to the European product standard according to table 1 (p. 64), must be specified on the label.

The example of the designation code for PUR (table 5, p. 75) makes it clear that it cannot be "deciphered" without referring to the respective material standard, in this case DIN EN 13165 (see table 1, p. 64, and table 1, p. 69).

Ü-mark (voluntary)
In Germany manufacturers signify conformity of their insulating products to the respective technical application rules by printing the Ü-mark plus additional details on the product itself, the accompanying leaflets or the packaging. For example, the number of the national technical approval, details of the types of application according to DIN V 4108-10 and the design value for thermal conductivity according to the national technical approval, which is required for the verification of thermal performance to EnEV. The other information shown on the typical label (Fig. 1, p. 74) is therefore not part of the CE marking requirements, but instead is a national requirement. With the CE details alone, the product could be traded throughout Europe, but not necessarily used in Germany.
The details of use can be found in the upper part of the label: "PUR 024 DAD" indicates an insulating material for use above the rafters according to the designation code of DIN V 4108-10 (abbreviation: DAD); comparing table 6 of DIN V 4108-10 (here reproduced as table 1, p. 69) with the designation code shows that the minimum requirements for this application are fulfilled. The design value λ = 0.024 W/mK to DIN V 4108-4, category II, was derived from the manufacturer's limit value λ_{limit}. This product therefore requires an approval (Z-23.15-1431).

The ÜGPU quality logo printed within the Ü-mark shows that this PUR/PIR insulating product complies with the ÜGPU [1] quality guidelines and is checked at regular intervals. The ÜGPU quality logo is a meaningful, voluntary designation for PUR/PIR rigid foam insulating products. It eases the selection of products and gives users a sense of security that the product will satisfy all the requirements necessary for a certain application.

[1] Überwachungsgemeinschaft Polyurethan-Hartschaum e.V. – a trade association for polyurethane rigid foam

1 Sample label for an insulating material made from polyurethane rigid foam (PUR/PIR)
Source: puren gmbh
2 Examples of (voluntary) quality marks:
a Güteschutzgemeinschaft Hartschaum e.V. GSH (EPS, PUR and bound EPS products)
b BFA QS EPS (EPS products)
c Güteschutzgemeinschaft Qualitätssicherung Holzwolle (reformed in 2001, wood wool products)
d Gütegemeinschaft Mineralwolle (issues an RAL mark for mineral wool products)
e Überwachungsgemeinschaft Polyurethan-Hartschaum e.V. (polyurethane rigid foam products)
3 CE marking using the example of a PUR/PIR insulating material
4 The Keymark symbol for voluntary European product certification
5 Designation code using the example of a PUR/PIR insulating material

2a

b

c

1

CE marking

Details according to section 8 of the product standard	Example: PUR (DIN EN 13165)
a) Product name or other identification	puren Standard
b) Name or trademark and address of the manufacturer or his agent	(Z-23.15-1431)
c) Year of manufacture (last two digits)	(see batch No.)
d) Shift or production time and place of production or traceable code	
e) Euroclass for reaction to fire	E (EN 13501-1)
f) Thermal resistance	R_D = 5.20 m²K/W
g) Thermal resistance	λ_D = 0.023 W/(m·K)
h) Nominal thickness	120 mm
i) Designation code according to section 6	PUR EN 13165-T2-CS(10\Y)100-DS(TH)9-TR40
j) Type of lamination, if applicable	aluminium foil
k) Nominal length and nominal width	2400 × 1020 mm
l) Number of pieces and total area in one packaging unit, if applicable	2 boards; 4.88 m²

3

Consumer protection, quality control and voluntary product certification

Fitness for use and consumer protection
The legal framework for the monitoring of the construction products market was reorganised with effect from 1 May 2004. The Construction Products Act (BauPG) now contains only the legal basis for prosecuting the misuse of the CE marking. By contrast, guaranteeing the safety of construction products is now finally and comprehensively regulated by the new German Equipment & Product Safety Act (GPSG). The BauPG therefore no longer contains the legal basis for instigating proceedings against manufacturers of construction products that were manufactured according to harmonised technical specifications but whose use nevertheless could represent a danger for users.

For practical purposes, it is important to distinguish between two facts:

- the technical fitness for use of a construction product, which essentially depends on adhering to the relevant technical standards and monitoring the market according to the BauPG, and
- the consumer protection aspect, which depends on whether a danger can ensue from the predictable use of the construction product, despite correct technical properties; this is checked within the scope of the market surveillance according to the GPSG.

Depending on the jurisdiction arrangements in Germany's federal states, the responsibilities here could be divided between two different authorities.

Quality assurance and voluntary product certification
For insulating materials, third party certification is envisaged only for some of the compulsory product properties and then – apart from reaction to fire – only certified initial type-testing of the product with-

d

e

4

Designation code

PUR EN 13165-T2-CS(10\Y)100-DS(TH)9-TR40	
PUR	Polyurethane rigid foam
EN 13165	Product standard
T2	Tolerance class T2, i.e. for nominal thickness > 75 mm, the permissible deviation is +5/-2 mm
CS(10\Y)100	Compressive stress or compressive strength at 10% deformation ≥ 100 kPa
DS(TH)9	Dimensional stability level 9: relative change in length ≤ 2% (length and width) and ≤ 6% (thickness) under testing condition 1 (48 h at 70°C and 90 ± 5% relative humidity), also relative change in length ≤ 0.5% (length and width) and ≤ 2% (thickness) under testing condition 2 (48 h at -20°C)
TR40	Tensile strength perpendicular to plane of board ≥ 40 kPa

5

out further third-party inspections as attestation of conformity or quality assurance. In order to express a superior system of quality assurance, voluntary product certifications are necessary.

Voluntary product certification is based on sets of rules that specify the procedure within the scope of a symbol programme with which attestation of conformity can be carried out. Thereupon, a registered symbol is issued to the manufacturer according to the rules of a certification programme by certain authorised organisations. Such organisations can be quality assurance groups, associations, testing laboratories, etc. Voluntary product certification has a long tradition in Germany. There are various organisations or certification bodies responsible for insulating materials which have issued such a symbol in combination with the third-party inspections prescribed by the building authorities hitherto and an attestation of conformity procedure (Figs. 2 a–2 e).

KEYMARK

A European system for voluntary product certification was developed under the umbrella of CEN, the European Committee for Standardisation, which adheres to general principles not related to specific products, sets up clear requirements for a symbol programme for specific products and leads to transparent organisation.

The rules for KEYMARK for thermal insulating materials have been in place since December 2001. The main characteristics for the certification system are:

- KEYMARK certifies all the product properties contained in product standards EN 13162 to 13171 and not only the compulsory ones.
- KEYMARK goes beyond the requirements prescribed by the European Commission for attestation of conformity and carries out certification according to CPD system 1+ (see also DIN EN 13172, appendix A).

The tasks resulting from this for the KEYMARK certification bodies are:

- Initial inspection of the factory and the factory production control
- Initial testing of the product with respect to all product properties
- Constant monitoring of the factory production control
- Testing of random samples taken from the factory or the market

The KEYMARK certification body in Germany, DIN CERTCO in Berlin, in turn appoints accredited testing laboratories to carry out the testing and monitoring tasks. However, to date, there are hardly any products available in Europe that carry the KEYMARK symbol.

Summary

Every insulating material that has a European product standard must be provided with CE marking. Generally, an insulating material with CE marking is suitable for the thermal insulation of buildings. Further details of the product performance and the applications can be derived from the designation code. The CE marking embodies a different degree of reliability to the German Ü-mark because the details are essentially based on a declaration of the manufacturer – a product test by a third party is required for only a few product properties and constant monitoring by a third party is only prescribed and carried out for reaction to fire.
Adding a design value for the thermal conductivity to DIN V 4108-4 category II within the scope of the Ü-mark to the nominal value for thermal resistance in the CE marking is only possible by obtaining a national technical approval (abZ) from the DIBt. The design value is determined on the basis of a limit value monitored by a third party.
As the details of the design value are only sensible in conjunction with certain applications or types of construction, the national technical approval also prescribes third-party inspections of those product properties for which DIN V 4108-10 contains minimum requirements.
The national technical approval itself is not a requirement of the building authorities, but merely a possibility for the manufacturer to reduce the safety factor for his product via third-party inspections, i.e. it is an option, not a mandatory requirement. For the user, the Ü-mark associated with this is a signal of better performance reliability for an insulating material product and compliance with building authority stipulations.

Applications for insulating materials

Martin H. Spitzner
Christoph Sprengard
Wolfgang Albrecht

In order to safeguard against mould growth and ensure a good level of hygiene, buildings must be designed and built so that the minimal thermal performance is achieved for planar building components and thermal bridges according to DIN 4108-2:2003-07. The German Energy Conservation Act (EnEV) stipulates requirements for the thermal performance of building envelopes that go well beyond the basic requirements of DIN 4108-2, and in the case of opaque building components such requirements are usually realised in the form of insulating materials. Added to these are the higher living standards and levels of thermal comfort expected these days, in both residential and non-residential work.

The type of application, its aims and purpose, the climatic boundary conditions and the building physics loads give rise to different demands being placed on insulating materials, and these are explained below. In the case of external layers of insulation (upside-down roof and external basement insulation), each material characteristic must be considered separately. The elimination or at least minimisation of thermal bridges by means of insulating materials is covered in a separate section which examines the demands placed on the material and the thickness and position of the layer of insulation.
Following that, the use of air as an insulating medium is explained. Separate layers of air contribute to the total thermal resistance of building components differently depending on form, position, ventilation and surface characteristics. Multi-foil thermal insulation and low E coatings are discussed in this context.
The influence of thermal insulation on the thermal comfort in habitable rooms in summer and the use of thermal insulation in special climatic conditions are the subjects dealt with in the final sections of this chapter.

Fields of application

The principal uses of thermal insulation materials can be divided into three general areas according to the part of the building:
- suspended floor and roof,
- wall,
- basement (external, in contact with the soil).

DIN V 4108-10 breaks down insulating materials into a further 17 types of application which are indicated by way of pictograms and abbreviations (see p. 67):
- Roof and/or suspended floor: DAD, DAA, DUK, DZ, DI
- Suspended floor and top side of ground floor: DEO, DES
- External wall: WAB, WAA, WAP, WZ, WH, WI
- Internal wall: WTH, WTR
- Basement (outside of wall and underside of floor slab): PW, PB.

The properties insulating materials require as a minimum for uses in Germany, depending on material and type of application, are listed in the "code of practice" DIN V 4108-10.
This standard takes into account many of the forms of construction and uses of building materials customary in Germany. However, it refers only to this selection of uses and is valid only for the following insulating materials according to the harmonised European standards (in Germany DIN EN 13162 to DIN EN 13171:
- mineral wool (MW)
- expanded polystyrene (EPS)
- extruded polystyrene foam (XPS)
- polyurethane rigid foam (PUR; also valid for PIR, polyisocyanurate rigid foam)
- phenolic foam (PF)
- cellular glass (CG)
- wood-wool (WW)
- wood-wool composites (WW-C)
- expanded perlite board (EPB)
- insulation cork board (ICB)
- wood fibres (WF)

Further insulating materials, other fields of application for insulating materials, e.g. thermal insulation composite systems, or even other properties profiles, e.g. higher compressive strengths, are regulated in European technical approvals, in German national technical approvals or in German individual approvals (see pp. 59–72).

DIN V 4108-10 is not arranged according to fields of application, but rather according to products, with each insulating material having its own table. In order to compare the requirements for all insulating materials that could be employed for a certain application, all the tables must first be placed alongside each other.
If you do this, you will notice that, for the same application, instead of identical requirements, different requirements are placed on the insulating materials. The minimum requirements are therefore specific to material and application. For instance, the minimum compressive strength for application DAD (external insulation to suspended floor or roof, protected from the weather, insulation below roof covering) is 0 or 40 kPa for mineral wool (DAD-dk or DADdh), 10, 20 or 100 kPa for wood fibres (DAD-dg, DADdm or DAD-ds), 100 kPa for PUR and EPS, 150 kPa for PF, 200 kPa for XPS, and 400 kPa for cellular glass, depending on the compressive strength requirement (see table 2, p. 67, for explanation of abbreviations). This is partly for material technology reasons (e.g. guaranteeing the degree of welding between EPS beads), but it also reflects the typical uses of the respective product (e.g. cellular glass is frequently heavily loaded). If only one compressive strength

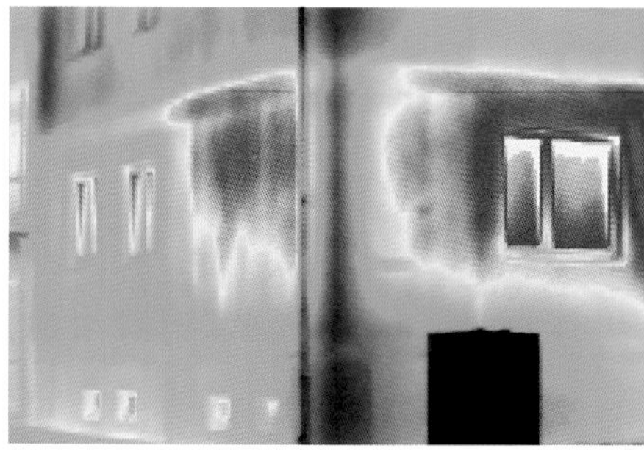

1

2

4,5 °C
4 °C
3,5 °C
3 °C
2,5 °C
2 °C
1,5 °C
1 °C
0,5 °C
0 °C

1, 2 Thermographic images of the corner of a building prior to (1) and after (2) refurbishment (thermal insulation composite system, plinth not insulated)
Thermographic images reveal the distribution of the surface temperature. Red colours correspond to higher temperatures (i.e. poorer thermal insulation), blue colours to lower temperatures (i.e. better thermal insulation).

requirement is standardised, the various supplementary abbreviations are omitted.

No details are given for properties that:

- are "automatically" linked with the material concerned,
- are irrelevant for this insulating material because of the nature of the product (e.g. the width of mineral wool batts for insulation between rafters – the batts are ordered with oversize anyway and are forced between the rafters),
- do not apply to this insulating material because of the nature of the material (e.g. insulation in cavities and voids required to improve sound insulation is only possible with fibrous insulating materials, not rigid foams, and consequently only mineral wool has to satisfy the requirement for sound impedance per unit length).

Generally, insulating materials – corresponding to their use in construction works and the stresses and strains to which they are subjected during transport and installation – must also exhibit certain minimum mechanical properties in addition to thermal and moisture-related qualities. The tensile, compressive, transverse tensile, bending and/or shear loads must therefore be examined. The tensile strength perpendicular to the plane of the board (tearing strength) plays a role for insulating materials in thermal insulation composite systems (wind suction). The bending strength is important for the handling of the insulating boards and, for example, when using insulating boards as a background for plaster/render in timber structures. The long-term (creep) behaviour under a constant compressive stress is important for insulation below loadbearing ground floor slabs or in the case of high imposed loads on impact sound insulation. In the case of applications with combined mechanical, moisture and/or thermal loads, such as in a roof, or a thermal insulation composite system, the permissible deformations under these combinations of actions should be regulated, and verified in tests. The compressibility of a product is important in the case of impact sound insulation.
Acoustic requirements can be placed on the sound attenuation (insulation to voids in lightweight stud walls) and the dynamic stiffness (impact sound insulating materials and insulating materials for party walls).
The short- and long-term water absorption is important for applications involving liquid water and water vapour diffusion, e.g. thermal insulation composite systems (driving rain) or external basement insulation (moisture in the soil and groundwater).
The reaction to fire must be verified for all building and insulating materials. Apart from that, adequate bending strength is required for all applications involving EPS, cellular glass and expanded perlite boards in order to avoid causing damage to the boards during handling. This property is intrinsic to boards made from XPS, PUR and wood-wool and therefore does not need to be specially verified. Wood-wool boards and the wood-wool layer in composite boards must be checked for their chloride content, which may not exceed 0.35% in any application.

EPS insulating boards must always achieve a certain minimum dimensional stability in a normal climate, PUR boards in defined temperature and moisture conditions. This requirement ensures that only those materials that have been stored for a sufficient length of time are installed; otherwise, the shrinkage of materials that are too new could result in gaps between the individual boards.
For reasons of space, the maintenance requirements for insulating materials are not given here for all insulating materials and all applications, but only as required for selected cases. Exact information can be found in the standards quoted or the respective approvals.

For the designer, the great advantage of the DIN V 4108-10 classification is that, for standardised insulating materials and fields of application, he does not need to specify the properties required for the desired insulating material individually, but instead only needs to refer to the type of application in the specification: "... insulating material X with type of application Y to DIN V 4108-10 or according to national technical approval". Upon delivery, the label or documents must be checked, first and foremost, for the correct type of application or approval number, the thermal conductivity value, the CE marking and the conformity symbol (Ü-mark).

Whether a form of construction is suitable with respect to thermal performance, climate-related moisture control, fire protection, loadbearing capacity, durability, etc., depends not only on the choice of a suitable insulating material, but is essentially determined by the sequence and interaction of all the layers in the building component. Corresponding component analyses are, for example, checking the climate-related moisture control (diffusion analysis, Glaser method) to DIN 4108-3, sound insulation to DIN 4109 and the fire resistance class to DIN 4102.

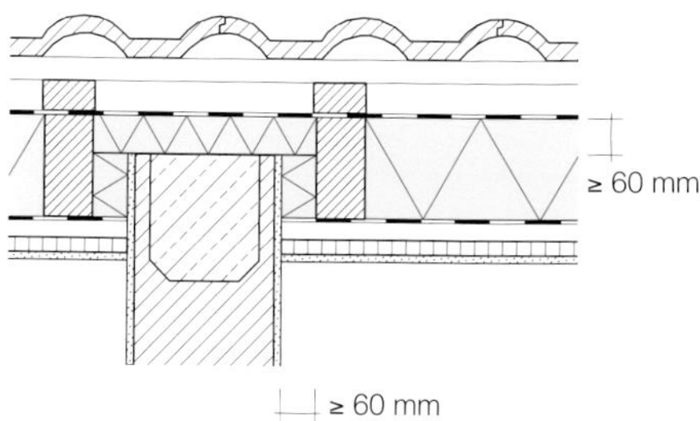

3

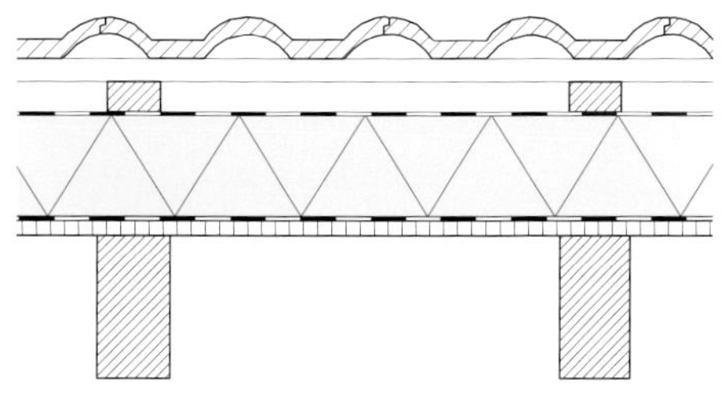

4

3 Insulation between the rafters (this example also shows an insulated connection to the incoming internal wall to minimise the thermal bridge at this point, in accordance with DIN 4108 supp. 2:2006-03)
4 Insulation above the rafters (in this case PUR/PIR insulation with aluminium facing both sides)

Insulation in floors and roofs

In a pitched roof and in the topmost suspended floor (insofar as this represents a component of the thermal envelope), the thermal insulation is in principle provided in the form of insulation between, above or below the rafters/joists, or as a combination of these options. It is always placed below the roof waterproofing, protected against the wind and weather by the roof covering and secondary waterproofing/covering layer. For flat roofs, there is also the possibility of placing the thermal insulation outside the waterproofing (upside-down roof).

Insulation between the rafters/joists in roofs and floors (application type DZ)
The majority of the insulating materials described in this book can be placed between the rafters of a pitched roof or the joists of a suspended floor. Fibrous insulating materials are easily pressed into the spaces between the structural members; rigid insulating materials are cut exactly to size.
Blown insulating materials, loose fill insulating materials or in situ foams can be installed in enclosed voids and cavities either at the factory or on the building site, e.g. in the voids between the roof and wall members, or in "inflatable" plastic cushions. In suspended floors, these materials are placed loose between the joists and are generally protected by boards or panels laid afterwards.
Essentially, insulating materials between the rafters support only their own weight and may not sag under this weight. Their properties and method of installation should enable them to be either clamped tight between the rafters prevented from slipping and dropping out of position by adding a soffit to the underside of the rafters. Accordingly, standardised application-related minimum requirements for application type DZ are mainly concerned with the dimensional stability of boards in a normal climate or under defined temperature and moisture conditions. This requirement is irrelevant for insulating material batts (MW and WF). In the case of mineral wool, adequate sound impedance is called for as well in order to attenuate the void.

Insulation above the rafters (application type DAD)
Insulation above the rafters is a continuous layer of insulation laid over the entire area of the roof, on top of the rafters. In new building work, insulation thicknesses from 140 to 200 mm are installed, which achieves very good thermal transmittance values (U-values) while at the same time permitting the rafters to remain exposed inside the building. The airtightness over the surface can be achieved with sheeting laid on the inside of the sheathing; tried-and-tested methods and products are available for ensuring airtight connections to the adjoining building components.

When using insulation above the rafters, the roof loads are either carried by the insulating material itself or transferred through the insulating material into the rafters, usually by means of special fixings for the counter battens.
If the insulation above the rafters is to carry the loads, then insulating materials with adequate compressive, tensile and shear strength must be used in order to accommodate the loads from roof covering, wind and snow. PUR/PIR, XPS and EPS inhibit diffusion, PUR/PIR with a facing of aluminium foil and cellular glass are virtually diffusion-tight. Rigid, diffusion-permeable insulation made from mineral wool and wood fibres has been available for use above the rafters for some time, which means that a suitable insulating material can be selected to suit the requirements and sequence of layers.

Rooftop elements made from rigid foams such as PUR/PIR, faced both sides with diffusion-tight aluminium foil, are frequently used. Self-adhesive overlaps of the external foil at the joints between the boards or bonding with durable, self-adhesive aluminium tape results in a rainproof secondary waterproofing/covering layer; joggle joints between the boards can achieve adequate airtightness and diffusion-tightness (verified by a test certificate) so that further sealing measures across the main area of the roof are superfluous. Junctions with adjoining components are sealed with the prescribed self-adhesive aluminium tape.

In terms of resistance to thermal and moisture loads in the roof, insulation above the rafters must satisfy similar stipulations as insulation between the rafters, but in addition it must also withstand a combination of thermal load plus compressive load (roof loads).

The standard minimum compressive strengths for insulating materials below waterproofing materials have already been given on p. 77. Approved versions of EPS, XPS and cellular glass, in some cases with much higher compressive strengths, are intended for such roof applications where the insulation is placed directly below the waterproofing (application type DAA, see p. 80).

If the roof loads are not carried via the insulating material itself, but instead via special structural fixings that pass through the layer of insulation and fix the counter battens directly to the rafters, the insulating material has, in principle, to comply only with the same requirements as insulation between the rafters. Such configurations are not covered by any standards; the requirements placed on the system setup (spacing and angle of screws, screw properties) are laid down in the respective approval.

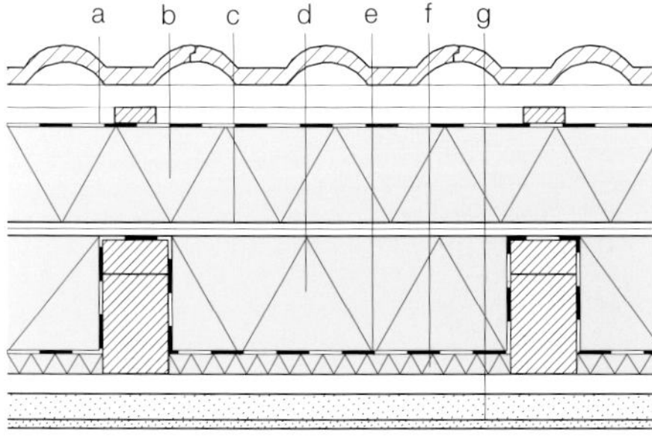

1

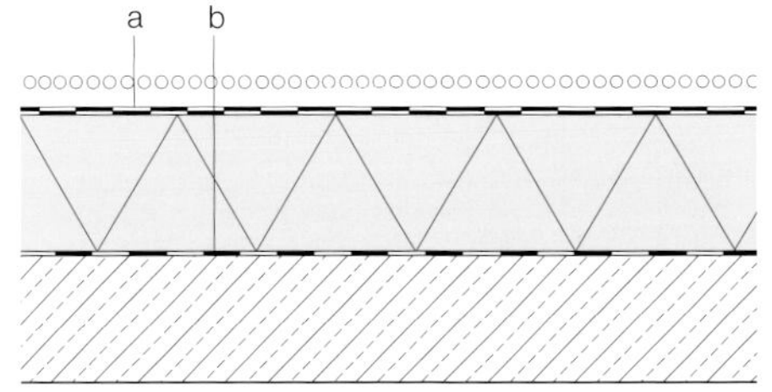

2

1 Refurbishment from outside with insulation between the rafters and diffusion-permeable insulation above the rafters (example)
a Diffusion-permeable secondary waterproofing/covering layer
b Diffusion-permeable insulation above the rafters
c Timber sheathing with open joints (boards max. 100 mm wide, joints 5–10 mm)
d Insulation between the rafters
e Vapour barrier with variable permeability
f Thin insulating board to protect vapour barrier
g Inner lining (here: plaster on background, laths)

Energy-efficiency upgrades for pitched roofs
When planning energy-efficiency upgrades for old pitched roofs, the rafters are often not deep enough to accommodate the thickness of insulation required. Doubling up the rafters can create the necessary depth required.

Combining the existing or new insulation between the rafters with an additional layer above the rafters represents an alternative solution. In such arrangements, the former ventilation space above the existing thermal insulation should be filled completely with insulating material so that no voids ensue within the layers of insulation. If the old insulation between the rafters is removed, the entire space between the rafters can be used for insulation anyway. The former ventilation openings at eaves and ridge should be closed off carefully so that no outside air can infiltrate the layer(s) of insulation.

In cases where the inner lining may not be removed or renewed and therefore the roof has to be upgraded from the outside, special attention must be paid to achieving the necessary airtightness and diffusion behaviour of the roof construction over the surface of the roof and at the junctions with adjoining components. A vapour barrier with variable permeability is then required, laid (from the outside) between the rafters (as close to the inside as possible) and around them. The diffusion resistance of such vapour barrier materials varies depending on the temperature and moisture conditions of the surrounding layers: in winter the resistance is high and hinders diffusion, in summer it is much lower and permits any moisture to dry out.

In order that a combination of insulation between and over the rafters guarantees no moisture problems in the roof construction with respect to water vapour diffusion to DIN 4108-3,

- diffusion-retardant or diffusion-tight insulating elements above the rafters should either account for at least 80% of the total thermal resistance of the roof construction, or
- the diffusion behaviour of the planned roof construction should be verified using the Glaser method to DIN 4108-3 or dynamic calculations,
- diffusion-permeable insulation above the rafters should not be laid on continuous timber sheathing, but instead on open planking with the joints left open 5–10 mm.

Flat roof insulation and roof insulation below waterproofing (application type DAA)
On a flat roof, the insulating material must support the loads due to the roof finishes, any gravel or chippings, wind, snow and rooftop structures permanently and reliably. In addition, the insulating material must also be suitable for traffic loads, either constant or for maintenance purposes only.
In terms of the compressive strength, the tensile strength perpendicular to the plane of the board (wind suction), the dimensional stability, or deformation caused by temperature loads, or a combination of temperature and compression (both short- and long-term), this application type has to satisfy more rigorous minimum requirements than application type DAD. Those applications with higher roof loads must also satisfy requirements regarding point loads (cellular glass and expanded perlite boards) and long-term creep behaviour (XPS and cellular glass on parking decks).

Upside-down roof (application type DUK)
In the upside-down or inverted roof, the insulating material is not placed below the waterproofing like on a conventional flat roof, but instead on top. This protects the waterproofing material against severe temperature fluctuations, ultraviolet radiation and mechanical actions. But the insulating material is exposed to precipitation.

Normally, we distinguish between three main types of upside-down roof:

- with gravel,
- with planting (extensive or intensive),
- for traffic (rooftop parking, parking deck).

The sequence of layers in the construction is, in principle, as follows:

- gravel, green roof make-up, or wearing course on base
- diffusion-permeable filter of non-woven material
- thermal insulation (XPS), one layer
- waterproofing
- loadbearing roof construction

According to DIN 4108-2:2003-07, only layers of thermal insulation that lie below the waterproofing may be taken into account when determining the thermal resistance of a construction. Excluded from this rule are upside-down roofs with gravel or concrete flag finishes and extruded polystyrene foam as the insulating material. These are covered in DIN V 4108-10. For the other types of upside-down roof (with rooftop planting or parking), the application should be covered by a national technical approval issued by the German Institute for Building Technology (DIBt) as in the past.

Upside-down roof with gravel finish
Long-term studies of upside-down roofs with a gravel finish show that in this diffusion-permeable form of construction (the water absorbed in the thermal insulation can escape again via diffusion in periods of dry weather, via the diffusion-permeable filter of non-woven material and the layer of gravel) the moisture absorption

3

remains below 1–2% by vol. over decades. Such low quantities of moisture fall within the ageing and statistics allowances according to DIN EN 13164:2001-10 and the rounding-off rules of DIN EN 10456, which means that apart from the German 5% safety allowance to DIN V 4108-4, no further moisture allowance has to be taken into account in the insulating material. The situation is different in the case of heat losses due to precipitation seeping beneath the layer of XPS rigid foam. In Germany DIN 4108-2:2003-07 stipulates that 0.05 W/m²K should be added to the U-value for upside-down roofs with water-permeable non-woven fabric plus gravel topping. Upside-down roofs in the form of a so-called duo-roof (with a further layer of thermal insulation below the waterproofing) require the U-value to be increased by 0.03 or 0 W/m²K.
The addition to the U-value can be omitted according to a national technical approval if the water-permeable non-woven fabric above the layer of XPS insulation is replaced by a diffusion-permeable separating layer so that precipitation can be drained away to roof outlets above the layer of insulation. Only very small amounts of precipitation then seep below the insulation.

Upside-down roof with rooftop planting
Field tests on green upside-down roofs have revealed average moisture contents of 0.3–4.6% by vol. for roofs 7–18 years old, with the moisture content decreasing as the thickness of insulation increased. This higher moisture content is taken into account in Germany by classing the XPS insulation in the next higher thermal conductivity group (older approvals) or by adding a moisture allowance of 0.002 W/mK (newer approvals). No distinction is made between extensive and intensive planting.
Upside-down roof for traffic
(rooftop parking, parking deck)
The wearing course can be one of the following:

- paving bricks, ≥ 100 mm thick, on a base of chippings 30–50 mm thick
- precast concrete flags, on bearing pads or laid in gravel
- in situ concrete

Both the wearing course and the base should be laid very carefully because otherwise considerable problems can be expected. For instance, the joints between paving bricks must be re-sanded and the elastic joints for absorbing the horizontal forces of vehicular traffic maintained at regular intervals. A lifetime exceeding 15 years can be expected for carefully constructed and regularly maintained parking decks.
The absorption of moisture in a parking deck is also taken into account in the approvals by adding 0.002 W/mK to the design value for thermal conductivity. In practice, long-term moisture contents of 1.3–4.6% by vol. have been found in parking decks with a wearing course of paving bricks, and values about half that for in situ concrete.

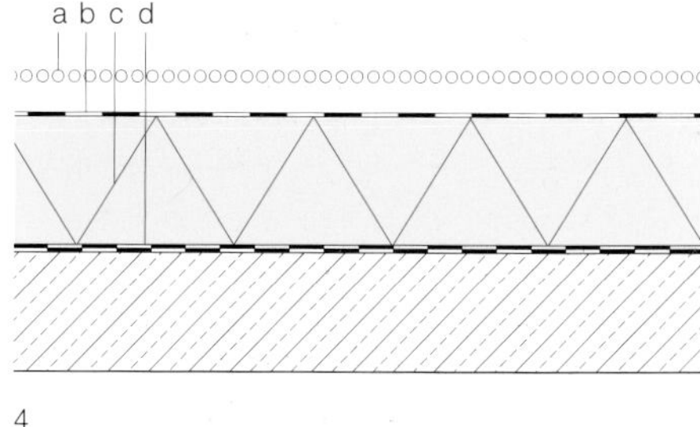

4

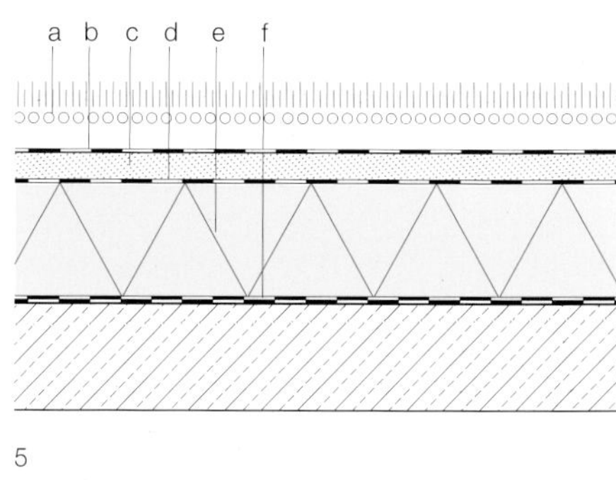

5

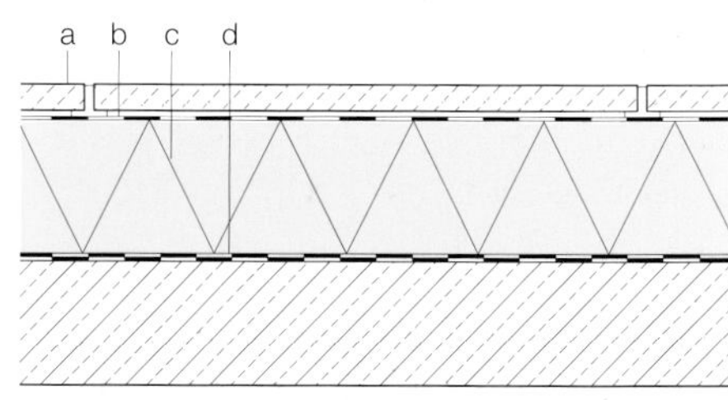

6

2 Single-skin flat roof
  a Waterproofing
  b Vapour barrier
3 Single-skin flat roof with PUR insulating boards
4 Upside-down roof with gravel topping
  a Layer of gravel at least 50 mm thick as ballast and to satisfy the stipulation of the federal state building codes for a covering resistant to flying sparks and radiant heat
  b Diffusion-permeable non-woven fabric
  c Thermal insulation made from extruded polystyrene foam (XPS), one layer
  d Waterproofing
5 Upside-down roof with extensive planting
  a Substrate
  b Filter (non-woven fabric)
  c Drainage layer (expanded clay or gravel)
  d Filter (non-woven fabric), diffusion-permeable
  e Extruded polystyrene foam (XPS), one layer
  f Root-resistant waterproofing, two layers
6 Upside-down roof with wearing course for rooftop parking
  a Precast concrete flags on bearing pads or gravel bed
  b Filter (polypropylene), diffusion-permeable
  c Extruded polystyrene foam (XPS), one layer, loadbearing
  d Bitumen waterproofing, min. two layers

Insulation in walls

Insulation to the walls of panel and frame construction in timber (application type WH)
The majority of insulating materials can be fitted between the timber members of panel and frame walls just like they are fitted between the timber rafters in a roof. The loads due to heat, cold and moisture in the walls are lower than those in the roof, partly because of the reduced heating of the surface by solar radiation. Accordingly, DIN V 4108-10 does not stipulate any requirements for the dimensional stability of factory-made insulating boards used in walls under defined thermal or thermal plus moisture loads. Used vertically, such insulation fitted between the timber members may not sag under the weight of the "stack of insulating material" up to the next horizontal rail. Batts made from fibrous insulating materials are ordered oversize for clamping between the timber studs. Board-type insulating materials made from plastic foams or fibres are cut exactly to size or with minimal oversize and likewise clamped between the studs. No settlement is to be expected in either case.

When using loose insulating materials (blown and loose fill materials), settlement can lead to voids (and hence undesirable thermal bridges) caused by vibration during the transport and installation of factory-filled wall panels, or by vibrations during the use of the building (wind, doors and windows slamming). It is not possible to "top up" the filling without damaging the component.

Settlement tests involving transport in goods vehicles, a specially devised "slamming door" test and a vibrating table have shown that cellulose fibres, wood fibres and wood chippings do not suffer from any unacceptable settlement. When using wood chippings, several hardboard bulkheads within each compartment carry the load of the chippings, which is why such walls should be filled by the manufacturer. Fillings of expanded perlite tend to settle, but this can be readily compensated for by including strips of mineral fibre at the top of each compartment. The permissible settlement and bulk density of the filling are specified in the product approvals.

Polyurethane in situ foam is frequently used, e.g. in North America, for insulating the timber stud walls of houses. The cavities in the wall should be filled from the inside before the inner lining is attached. No products are available for this application in Germany.

If a degree of acoustic attenuation is also required, mineral wool and wood fibre insulating materials are a good choice because they exhibit adequate sound impedance characteristics for separating walls (application type WTR).

Insulation behind render (application type WAP)
Various insulating materials and composite boards are used in the facade as, for instance, (small-format) backgrounds for render around thermal bridges, for covering over the ends of suspended floors and concrete columns in masonry walls with good thermal insulation qualities. These applications are grouped together under application type WAP (excluding thermal insulation composite systems) and fall within the scope of DIN V 4108-10.

Thermal insulation composite systems
Insulating materials for composite systems consisting of insulating boards attached to large wall areas and then covered with a render finish are regulated by national technical approvals for thermal insulation composite systems.
In such systems, the insulating material is affixed to the external wall with adhesive and/or mechanical fasteners or a system of rails and subsequently finished with one or more coats of render. The system concept is crucial here: adhesive, insulating material, reinforcing mesh and render system must be coordinated with each other and different products may not be combined at random. They may only be used as a complete system according to the respective national technical approval. On substrates suitable for adhesive, the use of adhesive to attach the insulating material is adequate for all the approved systems on the market. However, above a certain height, the higher wind suction loads generally call for the use of (additional) mechanical fasteners.

The requirements placed on the insulating material are primarily concerned with its mechanical qualities:

- compressive strength (self-weight, wind pressure),
- transverse tensile strength (tensile strength perpendicular to plane of board; wind suction, adhesion of render),
- shear strength and shear modulus (stability, self-weight).

But the hygrothermal behaviour is also important, e.g.

- dimensional stability,
- short- or long-term water absorption, and
- reaction to freeze-thaw cycles.

In addition, a coordinated expansion behaviour between render system and insulating material is essential in order to avoid cracks. The render system itself must be water-repellent and should not inhibit diffusion.

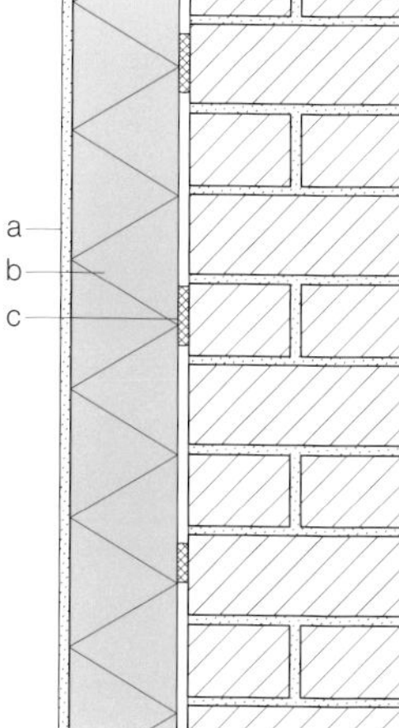

1 Thermal insulation composite system, principles
a Render system with reinforcing mesh
b Insulation boards
c Adhesive

Expanded polystyrene (EPS) is the most popular insulating material for this application; the grey version of this product with reduced heat transport via radiation, lower thermal conductivity and hence a reduced thickness for the same insulating performance is also frequently used. To improve the sound insulation against noise from outside and sound transmissions from adjoining areas, elasticised EPS insulating boards are available. Mineral wool for thermal insulation composite systems is given a permanent hydrophobic treatment to limit the water absorption. If the fibres are mainly aligned parallel with the wall surface, mechanical fasteners will be required in addition to adhesive. But when the fibres are mainly aligned perpendicular to the wall surface (lamella products), the mechanical fasteners will not be required, provided the substrate is suitable for adhesive and the building does not exceed a certain height. Owing to the favourable dynamic stiffness of mineral wool, thermal insulation composite systems with mineral wool insulation generally offer sound insulation benefits. Besides EPS and mineral wool, polyurethane rigid foam, mineral foam, expanded cork and phenolic foam products are available for this application. Thermal insulation composite systems using straw as the thermal insulation are also on the market. Furthermore, the use of vacuum insulation panels bonded between layers of conventional insulation, so that they can be used for thermal insulation composite systems, is currently undergoing trials.

The thickness of a thermal insulation composite system should not be less than about 140 mm, especially since greater thicknesses of insulation involve hardly any extra costs but offer better thermal performance. Insulation thicknesses of about 200 mm and in the case of passive-energy houses (new buildings and energy-efficiency upgrades) up to about 300 mm are certainly advisable, in each case related to a thermal conductivity of 0.035 W/mK. Wherever possible, the windows should be positioned within the depth of the insulation. A retrofitted thermal insulation composite system where the windows are retained in their original position will require external insulation to the window reveals as well in order to reduce thermal bridges (the old render in the reveals can be removed first if necessary).

Internal insulation to external walls (application type WI)
Practically all conventional insulating materials can be employed for internal thermal insulation to walls, provided these are placed in the compartments of a timber construction which are then covered with an inner lining. EPS, XPS, PUR, cellular glass and plasterboard composite panels can be bonded directly to the inside of the external wall without the need for any supporting framework.

As a rule, insulating materials that are permeable to diffusion require a vapour barrier on the room side so that moisture from the interior air cannot infiltrate the cold wall construction and cause interstitial condensation. Vapour barriers are not usually necessary with XPS and cellular glass, also EPS or PUR with a covering of plasterboard, and plastered wood-wool composite boards with EPS insulation. In specific cases, verification by means of a dynamic calculation can be carried out; or laboratory and field tests can be carried out to verify the practical viability of the internal insulation.

Owing to their special moisture behaviour, calcium silicate foam boards are interesting for internal insulation to external walls. They are used without a vapour barrier, are finished with a diffusion-permeable plaster and are themselves diffusion-permeable, absorbing any interstitial condensation between internal insulation and wall and distributing it over the insulation by means of capillary action. This reduces the total amount of condensation. Calcium silicate foam boards may only be used in moderate, appropriate thicknesses so that the quantity of condensation does not exceed a certain level and can dry out again.

Retrofitting of internal insulation to basement walls
In basements with a low moisture level (heated storage rooms, workrooms not in constant use, etc.), adding internal insulation to basement walls in contact with the soil is not critical, irrespective of the groundwater level. When using insulating materials with a sufficiently high diffusion resistance, e.g. EPS, XPS and PUR, an additional vapour barrier is superfluous. When using mineral wool, a simple vapour barrier with a low diffusion resistance (s_d > 1 m) should be installed.

Internal insulation to basement walls with continuous but not excessive moisture levels (e.g. living rooms) presents no moisture problems if the groundwater level is sufficiently deep (> 10 m) and the basement wall affected is deeper than 1 m below ground level at every point or external insulation extends to about 1 m below ground level. Moreover, the interior must be adequately ventilated.
If the groundwater is less than 10 m below the ground floor or if the basement room has a high moisture level, each case must be checked to see whether more moisture can evaporate than can condense within the wall cross-section.
Walls to wet areas such as kitchens and bathrooms must be insulated against the soil, generally with vapour-tight internal insulation.

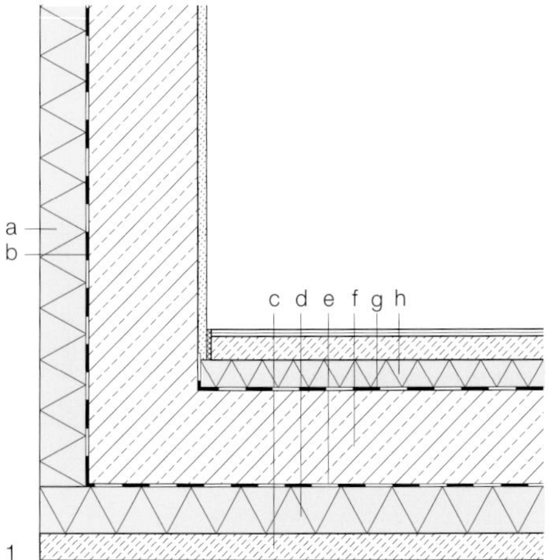

1 External basement insulation beneath basement slab with XPS, wall–floor slab junction
a External basement insulation, wall
b Waterproofing
c Blinding layer
d External basement insulation, floor slab
e PE sheeting to prevent cement slurry infiltrating into the butt joints
f Loadbearing basement floor slab
g Vapour barrier if required
h Thermal insulation

3 Insulation arranged to protect against frost (approx. 500 mm horizontal)

4 Insulation to sides of strip footing

External basement insulation

Examples of components in contact with the soil that require thermal insulation are basement walls and basement floors. In this arrangement, the thermal insulating material is affixed to the outside of the basement, and external to the waterproofing. The insulating material is permanently in contact with the soil, precipitation, earth pressure and in some applications groundwater, too.
The demands placed on the insulating materials regarding water absorption, compressive strength, rotting resistance and the durability of these characteristics are therefore high in connection with external basement insulation.

The advantages of external basement insulation are that it prevents condensation on the inside of the basement wall and basement floor, it protects the external waterproofing, it prevents thermal bridges and, above all, it saves energy.

External basement insulation, wall
The following insulating materials have been included in the standard for external basement insulation up to now (application type PW) or have been issued with a national technical approval:

- cellular glass (CG)
- extruded polystyrene foam (XPS)
- expanded polystyrene (EPS)

For the sake of completeness, it should be mentioned that polyurethane rigid foam (PUR) and cellular glass loose fill are also available but represent only a small market share.

The standardised or approved thermal insulating materials used for external basement insulation differ very distinctly in terms of their structure, compressive strength, thermal conductivity, water absorption and processing. Significant here is whether the insulating material may also be used under hydrostatic pressure conditions (groundwater) and whether the moisture has to be taken into account when measuring the thermal conductivity (table 2).

Technical rules for external basement insulation

Insulating material	Cellular glass (CG)	XPS	EPS	PUR
Product standard DIN EN	13167	13164	13163	13165
External basement insulation, wall and floor (no compressive loads)				
Technical rule				
DIN V 4108-10 in conjunction with DIN 4108-2	+	+	–	–
National technical approval	+[1]	+[1]	+	+
External basement insulation beneath loadbearing floor slab				
Technical rule				
National technical approval	+	+	+	–
Perm. constant compressive stress	160–380 kPA	100–250 kPa	100–140 kPa	–
Application in hydrostatic pressure conditions (approved products only)	approval regulates installation depths down to 12 m	approval regulates installation depths down to 3.5 or 7 m	–	–
Moisture allowance				
ΔU, without hydrostatic pressure[2]	–	–	0.04 W/m²K	0.04 W/m²K
$\Delta\lambda$, with hydrostatic pressure	–	0.002–0.005 W/(mK) depending on product	–	–

[1] For applications in hydrostatic pressure conditions.
[2] Exception: with particularly thick EPS external basement insulation, the influence of moisture is taken into account using an allowance of $\Delta\lambda$ = 0.003 W/mK.

2

The respective construction requirements of the approvals with respect to waterproofing the construction works, arrangement, laying and fixing, backfilling and junction details must all be taken into account.
If the soil's permeability to water is inhibited by cohesive or stratified soils, and a build-up of water or aquifer conditions can occur, drainage to DIN 4095:1990-06 must be provided.

External basement insulation, floor
In this type of application we distinguish between the non-loadbearing case and the use below loadbearing elements.

Typical examples of external basement insulation beneath non-loadbearing components are the insulation between the foundations of a building and insulation provided to prevent freezing (application type PB, Figs. 3 and 4).

Insulating structural components against the soil has become more widespread in recent years. Raft foundations are on the increase for residential and office buildings in particular. The principles of this form of construction can be seen in Fig. 1. In such an application, the insulating material is subjected to a permanent static load perpendicular to the plane of the board. Horizontal loads are not permitted apart from one exception. The design values of the insulating material for permanent compressive stress are determined from the short-term compressive strength or the short-term compressive stress at 10% deformation and long-time creep tests with appropriate safety factors.

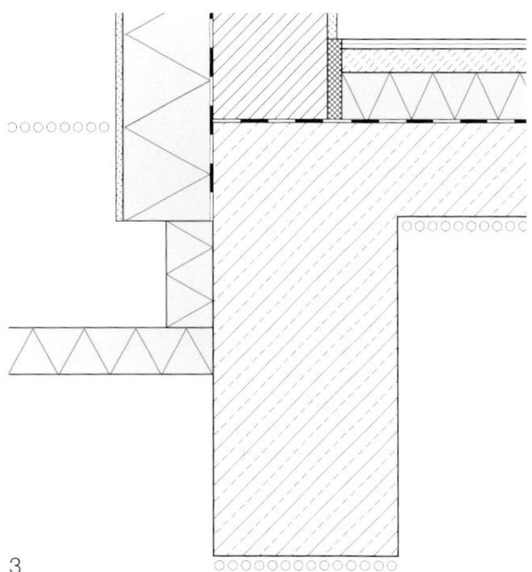

3

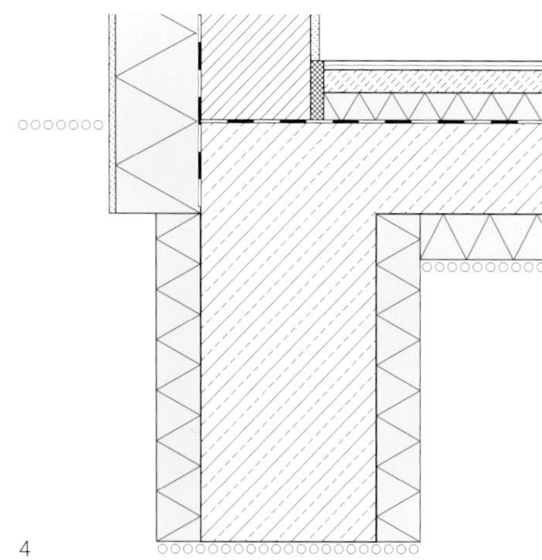

4

Over a period of 50 years, the deformation of a loadbearing insulating material due to structural and thermal effects may not exceed 2–4%. In structures that react sensitively to settlement, this deformation should be taken into account in settlement calculations.

Normally, only suitable products with a national technical approval may be used beneath loadbearing ground slabs (table 2), or an individual approval must be obtained from the building authority prior to installation. No insulation may be specified beneath strip footings because the insulating materials available do not have adequate compressive strength.

The vertical insulation around the wall to the basement and the horizontal insulation beneath a loadbearing basement floor slab can be easily joined together so that the principle of an "uninterrupted layer of insulation" can be achieved to avoid thermal bridges (Fig. 1). The heat losses through such "seamless" junctions are much lower than for insulated ground slabs in conjunction with strip footings, where the strip footing interrupts the layer of insulation.
Further information on energy-efficient junctions between ground slabs and external walls, also with insulation beneath the ground slab, can be found on p. 86.

Avoiding thermal bridges

Thermal bridges are places in the building envelope where a local, higher heat transfer takes place through the construction. This is coupled with local differences in the temperatures of the internal and external surfaces of the construction.
In winter, thermal bridges lead to higher heat losses. This is often linked with very low internal surface temperatures and, as a result, condensation and mould growth. So, in addition to the energy aspects, thermal bridges should therefore be avoided, or at least their effects limited, in order to maintain the quality of the construction and levels of hygiene. This is guaranteed in Germany by applying the Energy Conservation Act (EnEV) and by adhering to the recommendations of DIN 4108 supplement 2 "Thermal insulation and energy economy in buildings – Thermal bridges – Examples for planning and performance", or by applying for an individual approval.
Thermal bridges can be caused by
- a change in building materials (e.g. concrete column in masonry wall),
- building geometry (e.g. corner, window reveal),
- built-in items (e.g. roller-shutter housing, facade anchors), or by a
- combination of these causes (e.g. eaves detail, suspended floor support).

Depending on their nature, we distinguish between linear or point thermal bridges. The heat transfer through planar components without thermal bridges is specified by the U-value (thermal transmittance per unit area in W/m²K). The higher heat transport in the vicinity of linear thermal bridges is designated with the ψ-value (thermal transmittance per unit length in W/mK), and in the case of point thermal bridges, we use the χ-value (thermal transmittance through one point in W/K).

As the standard of insulation has increased, so the significance of thermal bridges has also risen, both in the planning process and in the energy-efficiency evaluation of a building. Generally, the strategy for avoiding thermal bridges is to minimise interruptions to the layer of thermal insulation and to keep its thickness constant right around the heated volume. This principle applies to monolithic forms of construction (in which the loadbearing walls at the same time have an insulating effect) and also to forms of heavyweight or lightweight construction that require additional layers of insulation.

Eaves detail, new building and refurbishment work
Prudent planning usually allows the design principle of the uninterrupted layer of insulation to be maintained in new construction works.
However, in the refurbishment of existing structures the continuous insulation concept is frequently only possible at extra cost or in some cases is no longer an option.
The example of a ring beam around a purlin roof with insulation between the rafters, which is to be upgraded to a high energy-efficiency level by adding new insulation above the rafters, shows the uninterrupted thermal insulation around the eaves purlin (Fig. 1a, p. 86). The refurbishment work can also be carried out from outside: the old thermal insulation is removed, a vapour barrier with variable permeability (which also serves as the airtight membrane) is laid between and around the rafters and the roof then insulated anew. Fig. 1b, p. 86, shows that the internal surface temperature in the vicinity of the eaves purlin is only marginally below that of the other internal components. The surface temperatures at the rafters are marginally lower, but owing to the generous layer of insulation over the rafters they are still well above the critical point.

The joints between vapour barrier and adjoining building components must be airtight (e.g. top and inside faces of ring beam), which, however, is very difficult to achieve when carrying out the refurbishment work from outside. "Wrapping" rafters and purlins in insulating material is only to be recommended for old, dry timbers and

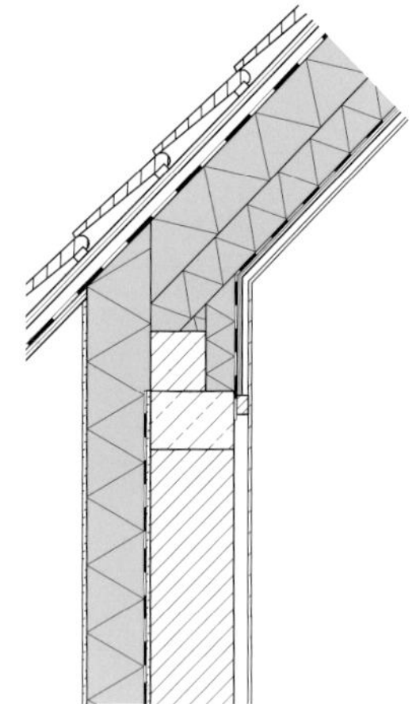
1a

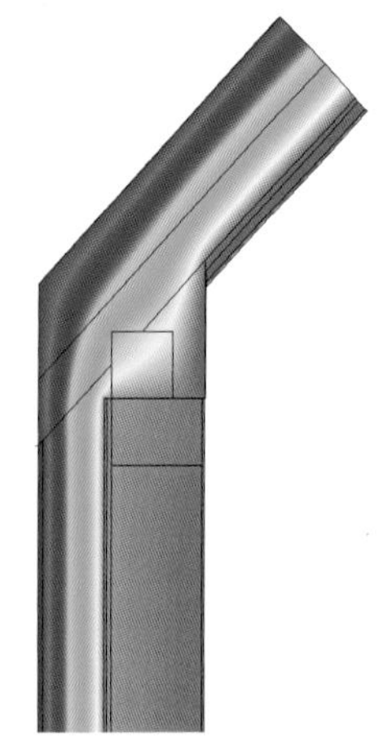
b

when using a vapour barrier with variable permeability. New timber members dry out only very slowly in such circumstances and would then be at risk of mould growth. The moisture content of the timber should be determined beforehand if necessary. It is also necessary to check whether the roof structure can carry the additional load of the insulation above the rafters.

Ground floor slab – external wall junction
A design with only minimal thermal bridges – adhering to the principle of an uninterrupted layer of insulation – is also important for the junction between ground/basement floor slab and external/basement wall.
The difficulty and diversity of this detail quickly becomes obvious from the number of examples of this junction given in DIN 4108 supplement 2: the first 24 in a total of 95 sketches showing the principles of how to overcome thermal bridge problems deal with the junction between base of wall and ground floor slab in all its various forms. The next 17 sketches cover the junction between the external wall and a suspended floor over the basement – clear evidence of the importance and diversity of this junction, but perhaps also an indication of thermal bridges frequently ignored.

The following information applies to the junction between ground floor and external wall in the case of buildings with and without basements, and also to the junction between external wall and suspended floor over an unheated basement.
In the case of a ground floor junction, we distinguish between ground floor slabs insulated internally and externally, and between raft and strip foundations.
The use of masonry with good insulating qualities and a layer of insulation below the screed upholds the principle of the continuous layer of insulation. It is more difficult when the thermal conductivity of the masonry wall is high (e.g. slender masonry with a high compressive strength) and the insulation is on the outside. The layer of insulation is then interrupted by the masonry, which causes the heat losses to rise steeply. Even though Figs. 3 and 4 differ only marginally, the heat losses are very different. In such cases, the uninterrupted layer of insulation can be realised with the help of a levelling course with better thermal values instead of the bottommost course of masonry units (Fig. 5). The levelling course can be made up of special levelling course units and "normal" masonry units, insulating elements or an insulating material with a high compressive strength; the thermal conductivity must be lower than that of the wall and may not exceed 0.33 W/mK.

Suspended floor over basement
Solutions with a levelling course instead of the bottommost course of masonry units can be used in a similar way for the walls rising from a suspended floor over an unheated basement. This of course also applies to internal basement walls and internal walls at ground floor level. In this detail it is recommended to construct a plinth for the wall using levelling courses if there is thermal insulation on the ground floor or the suspended floor over the basement, also for walls between a heated staircase and an unheated basement. Beneath the suspended floor over the basement as well, the last course of masonry units could be replaced by a levelling course with better thermal performance values if the basement is un-heated and the underside of the suspended floor is insulated. This also applies to internal basement walls.
If the principle of the uninterrupted layer of insulation cannot be maintained, especially for energy-efficiency upgrades to existing buildings, there is still the possibility of adding insulation to the sides of the vertical components.

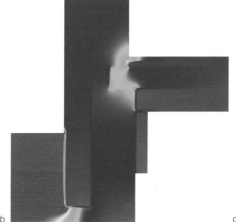

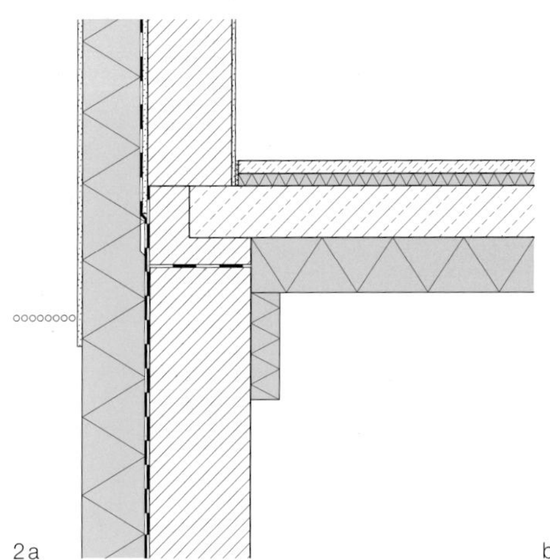
2a

b

c

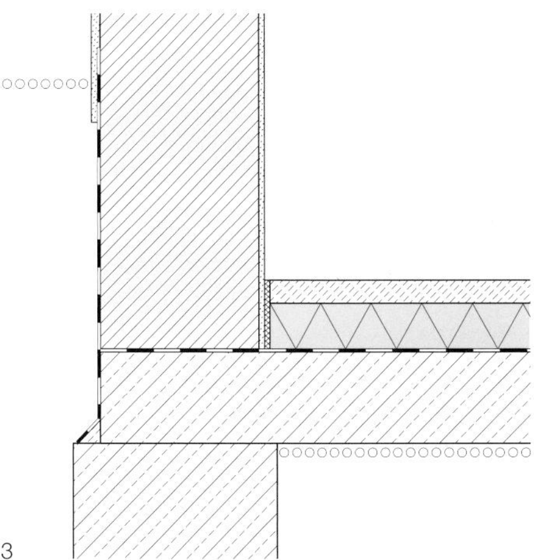

3

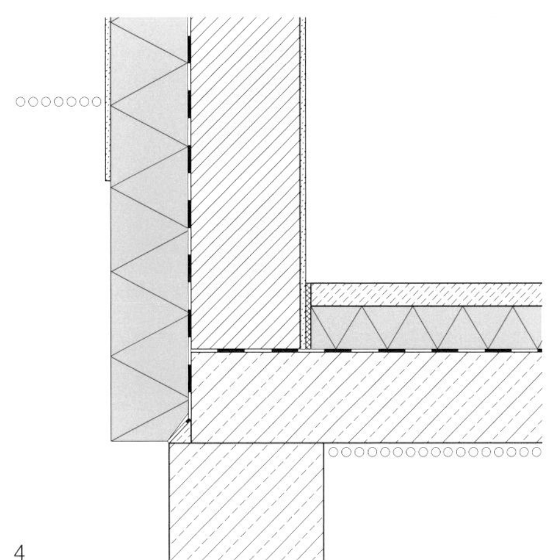

4

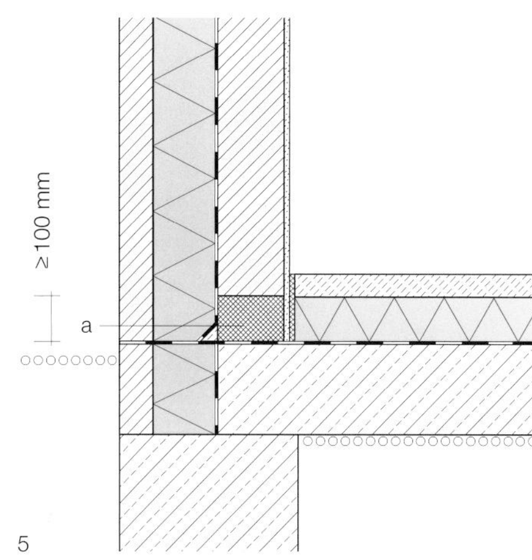

5

Figs. 2a–c show solutions with and without strips of insulation along the inside of the external basement wall. In this detail the external wall is insulated for about 1 m below ground level. This design principle would also be possible with a moderate reduction in the thickness of the insulation in contact with the soil. Instead of the vertical external basement insulation, insulation laid horizontally or at an angle in the soil would also be conceivable if the cost of excavating around the external wall were unreasonably high (similar to Fig. 3, p. 85). Placing insulation on the inside of the basement wall almost halves the thermal bridge losses compared to Fig. 2c. Furthermore, this detail results in higher surface temperatures in the corner of the floor finishes at ground floor level and hence a reduction in the risk of mould growth.

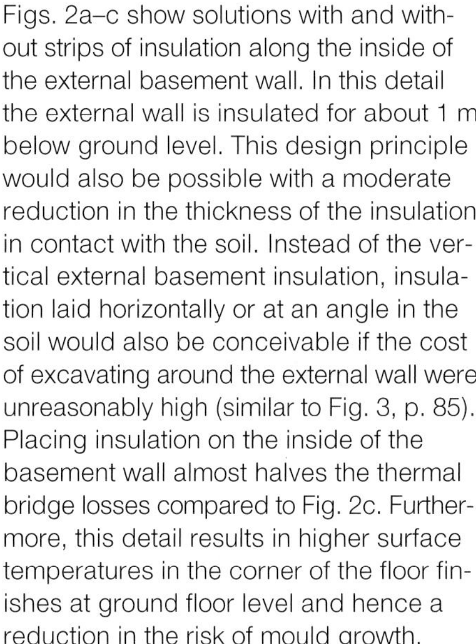

Cantilevering balcony slab, parapet
Cantilevering balcony slabs and similar constructions, e.g. concrete canopies, are only permitted in new building work when they include a thermal break. Fully developed prefabricated components are available for these details which reduce the thermal bridge effect considerably. Most solutions consist of bearing pads with optimum thermal performance properties and ties of stainless steel (lower thermal conductivity than normal steel). Similar assemblies and systems with even more favourable thermal performance properties, made from cellular glass with a high compressive strength, are available for parapet junctions in order to maintain the principle of the uninterrupted layer of insulation around the edge of the roof.

When refurbishing existing buildings, cutting off any existing, cantilevering balcony slabs should be considered in order to improve the energy efficiency, especially if the refurbishment is designed to reduce energy levels considerably.
If, for example, an existing external wall is to be provided with a thermal insulation composite system 140 mm thick and the balcony slab is not insulated, the result is a ψ-value exceeding 0.7 W/mK at the junction with the balcony slab. In this case it is necessary to investigate the risk of mould growth due to an excessively low surface temperature on the inside at the junction between external wall and suspended floor. If the balcony slab is completely "wrapped" in insulating material (top, bottom and sides), the ψ-value is reduced to about one-third of the above value for 80 mm thick insulation. But this is still a far inferior solution to a new balcony separated from the existing building, with minimal thermal bridges.
When deciding on the type of refurbishment, however, the cost of the measures should always be compared with the energy-savings expected. As long as the construction is in accordance with the standards and is not damaged, an isolated, remaining thermal bridge is certainly acceptable.

Bottom rail in thermal insulation composite system
One detail often neglected is the bottom rail fitted to external walls as part of a thermal insulation composite system.
The conventional aluminium bottom rail at the transition from thermal insulation composite system to external basement insulation passes right through from the warm to the cold side of the insulation. It consists of an aluminium channel approx. 1.5 mm thick and represents a flagrant thermal bridge. In the meantime, several manufactures have added plastic rails and rails with thermal breaks to their product ranges.
The difference in thermal terms becomes abundantly clear in the isotherm diagrams of Figs. 1a and 1b (p. 88): whereas the continuous aluminium rail enables the

1 a Eaves detail for refurbishment to achieve a low-energy house standard (example):
The thermal insulation on the external wall (200 mm, thermal conductivity group 035) and on the roof (300 mm between and over rafters) continues uninterrupted around eaves purlin and ring beam.
b Isotherms showing the temperature distribution in °C in the building components. Red colours correspond to higher temperatures (i.e. poorer thermal insulation), blue colours to lower temperatures (i.e. better thermal insulation).
An uninterrupted layer of insulation produces continuous isotherms. The thermal bridge effect of the ring beam or eaves purlin is more than compensated for by the amount of thick insulation over a large area.

2 a Junction between external wall and suspended floor over basement, with thermal insulation composite system, external basement insulation (down to approx. 1 m below underside of floor over basement), insulation to soffit and strip of insulation at top of wall internally (thermal conductivity group 035, 500 mm wide, 100 mm thick)
b Isotherms with strip of insulation at top of wall internally
c Isotherms without strip of insulation at top of wall internally. The green and, above all, the red colours show a high local heat flow, whereas the blue and violet colours indicate insignificant heat flows.
The strip of insulation improves the thermal bridge situation considerably. The surface temperature in the corner of the floor finishes at ground floor level is raised, which reduces the risk of mould growth.

3 Junction between monolithic, well-insulated masonry wall and basement floor with internal insulation (heated basement, strip footing) – a detail that reduces the thermal bridge effect. The low thermal conductivity of the insulating masonry maintains the principle of the uninterrupted layer of insulation.

4 Junction between masonry wall with a low insulating value plus external insulation and basement floor with internal insulation (heated basement, strip footing). Heat is lost to the outside through the route "base of wall – concrete slab – foundation – soil"; this is a substantial thermal bridge.

5 Junction between external wall plus cavity insulation and levelling course with better insulation values to ensure an uninterrupted layer of insulation and ground floor slab with internal insulation, on strip footing.
a Levelling course (special levelling units, insulating element or insulating material with high compressive strength and $\lambda \leq 0.33$ W/mK)

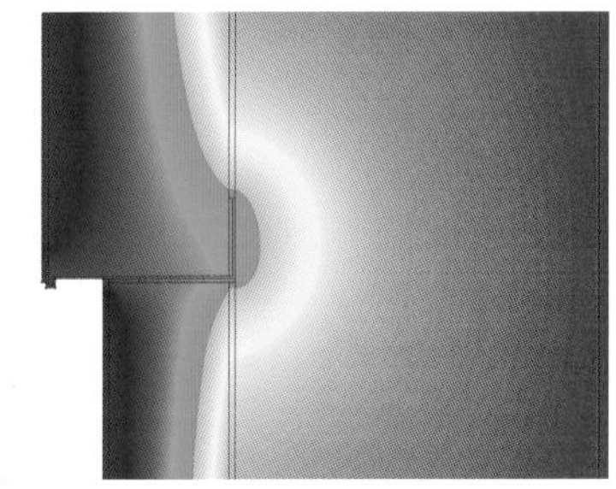
1a

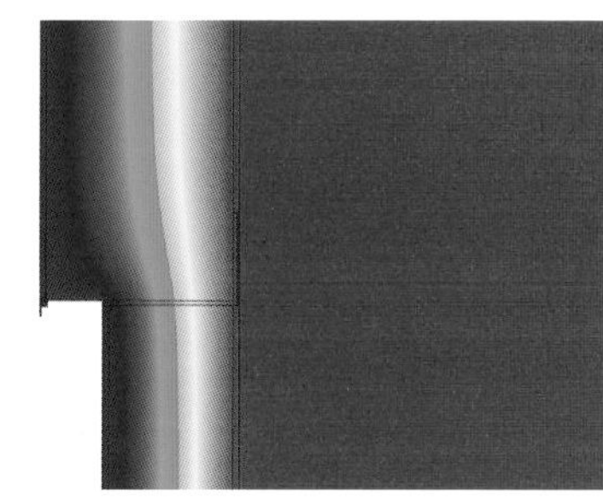
b

1 Temperature distribution (isotherms) for the bottom rails of thermal insulation composite systems
a Continuous aluminium bottom rail
b Plastic bottom rail, with better insulation values, supported on separate mounting brackets
The isotherms show the different temperature distributions in the building components. Red colours correspond to higher temperatures (i.e. poorer thermal insulation), blue colours to lower temperatures (i.e. better thermal insulation)

cold to "penetrate" into the masonry, the temperature distribution for the version with thermal break is practically unaffected by the rail.
The difference in energy terms is similarly obvious: the heat loss through the version with thermal break is only about 1/100 that of the heat loss through the conventional rail. The amount of heat lost through the aluminium section is equivalent to an uninsulated section of wall 160 mm wide; the transmission heat loss of the external wall surface at ground floor level is effectively increased by about one-third. Expressed in another way: the rail "negates" the insulating effect of a 45 mm thickness of insulation across the entire ground floor!

Fixings for thermal insulation composite systems
Fixings for thermal insulation composite systems represent point thermal bridges, the effect of which on the insulating properties of the entire system must be taken into account numerically in the form of the thermal transmittance through one point χ. This value is not a product constant, but instead depends on the installation situation, the substrate and the thickness of the thermal insulation composite system. The influence of the fixings can rise or fall as the thickness of insulation increases, depending on the type of fastener. Fasteners with plastic expansion parts, recessed fixing systems with caps and very deeply recessed screws achieve very low values.
In accordance with Technical Rule TR025, fasteners are divided into classes depending on the substrate, from which additions to the U-values of a wall without fixings can be derived based on the number of fixings. Table 2 shows that the number of fixings per square metre for which the influence of the fixings can be ignored decreases as the thickness of insulation increases.

Air as an insulator

A good part of the insulating effect of insulating materials is based on the effect of the trapped gases (mostly air, but blowing agents in the case of some foamed materials). The gases are contained either in the porous foamed plastics, cellular glass, etc. or in the spaces between the fibres and particles of fibrous, loose fill and blown materials. Heat is transported in air by way of convection (movement of the air particles), by conduction in stationary air, and by radiation from the warmer to the colder boundary surfaces.

The vacuum insulation panel (VIP) also exploits the insulating effect of air and gases. The almost total vacuum and the very fine powder of the filling makes the transport across the trapped residual air between the particles of powder so difficult that thermal conductivities, including the framework of solid materials, lower than air itself can be achieved.

Layers of air to DIN EN ISO 6946
DIN EN ISO 6946 distinguishes the insulating effect of air gaps according to the following criteria:

- A stationary layer of air is separated from its surroundings such that any openings present do not constitute an area exceeding 0.5 cm^2 per metre length and an airflow through the layer is not possible. Vertical open joints serving as weepholes in leaves of facing brickwork are to be disregarded; such layers of air are also considered to be stationary. The thermal resistance of a stationary layer of air varies depending on width of gap, inclination and direction of heat flow. Air gaps with inclinations exceeding 60° to the horizontal count as vertical gaps, those at lower angles as horizontal gaps (table 3).
- Poorly ventilated layers of air have openings with areas amounting to 0.5–1.5 cm^2 per metre length. The thermal resistance is half that of a stationary layer of air of equal width.
- Well-ventilated layers of air have openings with areas amounting to more than 1.5 cm^2 per metre length, e.g. ventilation spaces in roofs with an uninterrupted cross-section at least 20 mm deep throughout the roof. Such layers of air and all the subsequent layers of building components on the outside are ignored when calculating the U-value. Instead, the surface resistance on the inside boundary of the ventilation space, for stationary air, is taken to be the external surface resistance, i.e. the same surface resistance as for the inside of the component.

Multi-foil thermal insulation and other low E coatings
So-called multi-foil thermal insulation products, increasing numbers of which have been appearing on the market recently, generally combine several layers of special foils with intermediate layers of insulation which also act as spacers between the foil layers. Aluminium or plastic sheets with a vapour-deposited aluminium coating are used for the foil, with the separating layers being made from polyester fibre fabric or bubble wrap. Similar special foils are used as facings to conventional insulating materials such as PUR boards, or as a facing to secondary waterproofing and/or covering layers in roofs in order to reflect the heat radiated from the roof covering in the air gap and hence reduce the heat gains through the roof.
The insulating effect of multi-foil thermal insulation is primarily based on reducing the transport of heat via radiation within the group of foils and from the outermost foil of the group to the respective adjacent air gap. This is achieved with special foils with a very low emissivity. Whereas the

Influence of fixings for thermal insulation composite system

(example for fixings class 0.002)		
U-value of wall [W/m²K]	Fixings class (χ-value of fixing) [W/K]	max. No. of fixings per m² of wall that need not be included in the U-value calculation
0.50	0.002	8
0.32	0.002	5
0.22	0.002	3
0.095	0.002	1

2

Thermal resistances R [m²K/W] of non-ventilated (stationary) layers of air
to DIN EN ISO 6946 for layers of air that are narrow compared to their length and width (depth less than1/10 x length and width), for 10°C average temperature; intermediate values may be obtained through linear interpolation.

Depth of layer of air [mm]	Horizontal layer of air (up to 60° inclination), upward heat flow			Vertical layer of air (60° to 90° inclination), horizontal heat flow			Horizontal layer of air (up to 60° inclination), downward heat flow		
d	a	b	c	a	b	c	a	b	c
5	0.11	0.17	0.19	0.11	0.17	0.19	0.11	0.17	0.19
10	0.15	0.29	0.36	0.15	0.29	0.36	0.15	0.29	0.36
15	0.16	0.34	0.45	0.17	0.37	0.52	0.17	0.37	0.52
24	0.16	0.34	0.45	0.18	0.44	0.66	0.19	0.49	0.77
30	0.16	0.34	0.45	0.18	0.44	0.66	0.20	0.54	0.92
48	0.16	0.34	0.45	0.18	0.44	0.66	0.21	0.65	1.29
100	0.16	0.34	0.45	0.18	0.44	0.66	0.22	0.75	1.71

3 a: "normal" building materials on both sides; b: foil with emissivity ε = 0.2 on one side; c: foil with ε = 0.05 on one side.

majority of conventional building materials exhibit emissivity (ε) values of about 0.9, these foils achieve values between ε = 0.05 and ε = 0.2 (the possible spectrum for ε ranges from 0 to 1).
Reducing the radiation from the surface only works if the surface is bounded by air, not when the surface is in direct contact with another building material. Any radiation-inhibiting effect of the surfaces in contact then remains unused; the effect is also no better than any other surface (an exception is the partly radiation-transparent spacer layers within the multi-foil thermal insulation itself).

There is not yet sufficient information available about how the emissivity increases over the long-term due to ageing, soiling, dust or corrosion. Therefore, in the case of multi-foil thermal insulation or facings in contact with the outside air (e.g. ventilation space), the outer foil is treated like a normal building material surface in the calculations. This means that on roofs with multi-foil thermal insulation serving as the secondary waterproofing and/or covering layer, the normal surface resistance as for other secondary layer materials is assumed in the ventilation space.

If on the other hand the low E surface is bounded by an enclosed, non-ventilated air gap (e.g. the layer of air within the multi-foil thermal insulation itself), its effect is included in the calculation of the effective thermal resistance of this air gap. DIN EN ISO 6946 contains the necessary equations; table 3 contains pre-calculated figures that can be entered directly into the U-value calculations.

Consequently, the U-values of roof and wall constructions with low E coatings or multi-foil thermal insulation can be calculated correctly:

- the design value for the thermal resistance of the group of foils or the faced insulating board is taken to be as stated in its national technical approval;
- the design values for the adjoining layers of air on one or both sides are taken from the above table or calculated according to the standard;
- all other building material layers are treated in the usual way;
- the normal surface resistance is assumed for low E surfaces in contact with the outside air – the low E property is ignored in this instance.

Owing to the different temperature levels and the different temperature gradients in building components in summer and winter, primarily in the roof, the effect of the reduction in radiation varies between summer and winter.

In summary, it can be said that a low E coating or foil on one side makes a contribution to the thermal resistance equal to about 10 mm of conventional insulating material. When using a low E multi-foil thermal insulation product on both sides of an enclosed air gap, the contribution is doubled.
When the roof construction is heated up from the outside in the summer and there is a heat flow from outside to inside, the effect of a low E surface is more significant, for flat roofs in particular. The effect during such periods may well be equivalent to about 20–30 mm of conventional insulating material.
Roof and wall constructions that are insulated exclusively with multi-foil thermal insulation exhibit unacceptably poor U-values, however.

Insulating materials and thermal performance in summer

In order to keep the interior climate comfortably "cool" during the hotter months of the year, the heat flow from outside and the heat gains in the rooms must be kept as low as possible and the (night-time) heat dissipation to the outside must be kept as high as possible. Insulating materials play an important role here because they limit the influx of heat from the warmer outside environment and from the component surfaces heated up by the sun into the cooler interior of the building via the opaque exterior components.

Paths for heat gains
The paths for heat input and output that are important for the summertime thermal performance of habitable rooms can be specified by the following influencing factors:

- windows (size, position, orientation)
- proportion of windows
- energy transmittance of glazing
- nature, effectiveness and use of sunshading
- usable heat storage capacity of enclosing components and internal components
- ventilation of the interior, especially at night
- internal heat loads
- thermal insulation properties of external components
- materials and types of roof covering and roof structure

Steady-state and non-steady-state analysis
Strictly speaking, describing heat transport through building components by way of U-values and thermal resistances applies only to the steady-state case, i.e. for temperature and surface boundary conditions that remain consistent or vary only slowly.

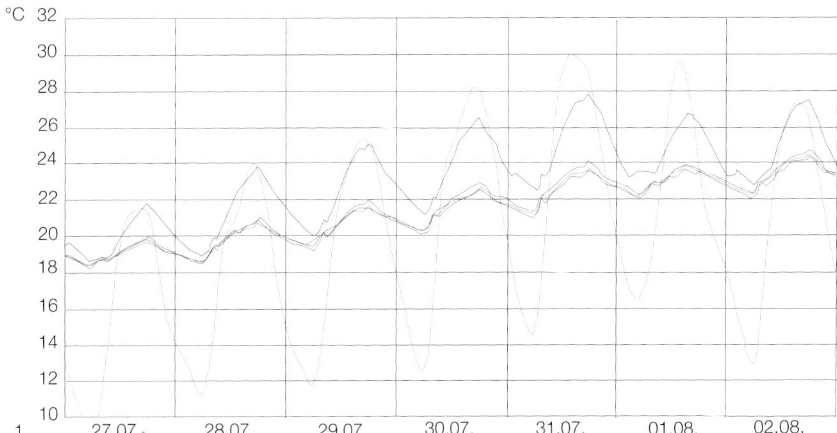

1 Summertime interior temperatures in habitable roof space
Example: masonry construction with different roof constructions (insulation above/between rafters) and insulating materials; the diagram shows the perceived interior temperature in the hottest week of the year.
External air temperature
30 mm wood-wool lightweight building board, plastered (existing building; U = 1.5)
80 mm foil-faced MW with overlapping joints between rafters (existing building; U = 0.43)
160 mm wood-fibre above rafters (new building; U = 0.23)
105 mm PUR/PIR above rafters (new building; U = 0.22)
220 mm MW between rafters (new building; U = 0.20)

But in reality, all factors are subjected to noticeable fluctuations over the course of each day, e.g. outside temperature and incident solar radiation, especially in summer. In addition, heat is stored in the building components.
The non-steady-state behaviour of building components can be described by the temperature amplitude ratio (TAR), the temperature amplitude damping (TAD) and the phase lag (or phase shift) φ. These variables depend on the thickness of the layer, the thermal conductivity, the specific heat capacity and the density of the material.

Temperature amplitude ratio and phase lag
The temperature of the external air fluctuates between maximum values during the day and minimum values at night. At the same time, the surfaces of building components are heated up on sunny days. This gives rise to a temperature wave on the outer surface which propagates in attenuated form in the building component and reaches the inner surface after a certain time. This damping effect means that the amplitude is considerably lower by the time the wave reaches the inner surface and arrives there with a time displacement (phase lag φ).

The ratio between the attenuated temperature amplitude on the inner surface and the larger amplitude on the outer surface forms the so-called temperature amplitude ratio TAR. The smaller the TAR, the better the attenuation by the building component and the smaller the temperature peaks (day/night) on the inner surface. The inverse of this ratio (the reciprocal of TAR) is called the temperature amplitude damping (TAD). A TAD of 5 means that the amplitude on the inside is one-fifth of that on the outside ("is damped by a factor of 5").

TAR, TAD and φ can only be calculated with theoretical, unrealistic boundary conditions. For example, it is assumed that the building component does not release any heat into the environment, neither inside nor outside; nor can it absorb any heat from its environments. TAR, TAD and φ do not describe the behaviour of the temperature of the interior air; they are also not a measure for the energy gains in the interior. The assumption that differences in the TAR, TAD and φ values reflect differences in the interior climate is erroneous.

We could attempt to make use of the phase lag by choosing suitable building materials and building material thicknesses so that the maximum internal temperature first occurs when the outside air has cooled down to an extent that it can be used for night-time ventilation. However, this is really only of benefit when at the maximum temperature a reasonable quantity of heat is available on the inner surface. In practice, the heat gains through the roof and walls are frequently not critical for the interior climate (but rather the heat gains through the windows) and therefore it is irrelevant when the heat arrives on the inside.

Influence of thermal insulation materials
The influencing factors for the interior temperature can be investigated numerically using dynamic building simulation programmes.

A comparison of various roof structures shows that in solid masonry and concrete construction (with an identical insulating effect for all building components), the choice of type of insulating material and the type of roof is virtually insignificant for temperature differences of just a few tenths of one Kelvin (Fig. 1). In lightweight construction, the choice of insulating material generally has a somewhat greater influence on the temperature gradient in summer for a difference in the perceived interior temperature up to about 1–1.5 K. A thicker inner lining can compensate for these differences effectively without raising the costs significantly over comparable forms of construction.

Heat storage
Rooms exposed to strong sunshine and which have little storage mass to buffer the incoming solar radiation are particularly at risk of overheating in summer (e.g. open-plan offices, lightweight structures). The storage masses must be left exposed so that they can act as a buffer for the heat in the room. Internal insulation, suspended ceilings, thick carpets and inner linings all have a "barrier" effect between the heat storage capacity of the structure and the interior.

A very interesting option for increasing the available heat storage capacity has only recently become available for buildings: building boards and plasters with the addition of micro-encapsulated waxes that act as phase change materials (PCM). These store heat as they change from the solid to the liquid state and initially prevent a further rise in the interior temperature. At night, increased night-time ventilation causes them to "discharge" so that they are ready to "buffer" the heat again the next day.

The most important aspect in terms of ensuring agreeable interior temperatures in the summer, however, is to prevent direct solar radiation from actually reaching the rooms. This task is primarily catered for in the basic concept of the building design and the specific sun-shading measures.

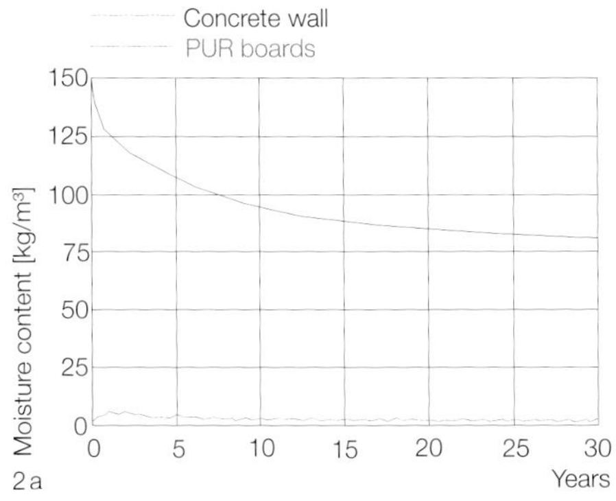

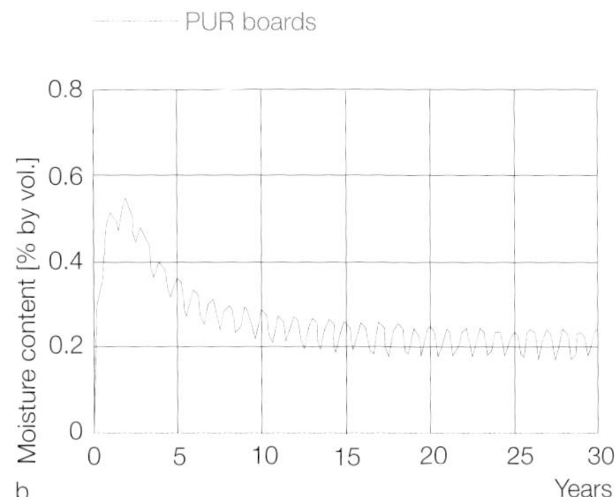

Insulating materials in other climate zones

Building in other climate zones calls for a detailed knowledge of the temperature and moisture conditions that prevail in those zones.
For instance, a moist, hot climate is characterised by predominantly high humidity and, at the same time, high exterior temperatures. Conditioned interior air is cooler and drier. This results in a vapour pressure drop from outside to inside over long periods of the year.
In terms of water vapour diffusion, thermal insulation composite systems, for example, are "on the wrong side" in such climate zones. A check should be carried out to establish whether such systems in such latitudes lead to a long-term accumulation of water between the layer of insulation and the loadbearing concrete wall and prevent the construction moisture of the concrete from drying out. The use of dynamic calculations for example, a thermal insulation composite system with polyurethane rigid foam boards without a diffusion-tight facing, revealed that the system remains dry and continues to function properly over the long-term (Fig. 2).
If it is necessary to convert the thermal performance values for insulating materials, which have been determined under standard tempered and moisture conditions, to suit the respective "local" conditions, then this should be carried out according to international standard DIN EN ISO 10456. This standard specifies the determination of the performance values of building materials and products that are homogeneous in terms of their thermal performance plus the methods for conversion to other temperature levels and moisture contents.
The conversions according to this standard are not normally necessary for Germany because the national design values have already been adjusted to suit the local boundary conditions.

When using insulating materials in other climates, the ageing behaviour of the materials must be considered. This depends on the type of material, its structure, the diffusion properties of any blowing agents that may be present, the temperature, the thickness and any facings. All these factors are already incorporated into the thermal conductivity value specified by the manufacturer for long-term practical conditions.

Depending on the field of application and the climatic and building physics conditions, thermal insulation may have to satisfy totally different requirements. An exact analysis of the respective situation, knowledge of the building physics relationships and the applicable statutory instruments and standards enable the right insulating material to be selected from the multitude of materials available on the market.

2 Moisture behaviour of PUR thermal insulation composite system in hot, moist climate
a Mass-related moisture content of concrete wall and PUR boards
b Volume-related water content of PUR boards
Wall construction:
plaster, concrete wall, PUR boards without diffusion-tight facing, render
Result:
The diffusion resistance of the PUR insulating material limits the diffusion of moisture from outside into the wall construction even without an additional vapour barrier or aluminium facing. The initial construction moisture in the concrete wall can dry out without any problems.

Insulating materials from the ecological viewpoint

Alexander Rudolphi

Sustainability – definition and assessment

The term "sustainability" was coined in 1987 by the World Commission on Environment and Development, the "Brundtland Commission". What this means is: "... to make development sustainable – to ensure that it meets the needs of the present without compromising the ability of future generations to meet their own needs."
The expression "sustainable development" became the motto of the United Nations Earth Summit in Rio de Janeiro in 1992, which formulated a concept for the future known as "Agenda 21". Unfortunately, the positive sound of this term quickly led to its overuse, particularly in the political arena. Nevertheless, sustainability gradually became a central theme of political and practical planning, and in Germany was first formulated on the political level in the "national sustainability strategy" of 17 April 2002.
Every human activity aimed at satisfying today's needs has an impact on the environment – mostly detrimental, unfortunately. Sustainable action therefore consists of, in the first place, questioning the necessity and sense of individual needs. In contrast to many consumption-focused needs, the need to live in a secure, reasonably agreeable and healthy environment is vital. Providing a reasonable interior climate in buildings inevitably leads to a temperature gradient between inside and outside, which has to be maintained by heating or cooling over longer periods. The energy and construction requirements for this are therefore subjected to an ecological optimisation strategy, the aim of which, first and foremost, is to minimise the quantity of energy required.

An ecological assessment of insulating materials taking into account their technical function within the scope of normal and economic applications almost always leads to a positive result. This is because the energy saved over a period of use lasting 20, 30 or more years exceeds the energy required for the acquisition of raw materials, production and processing to a greater or lesser degree – for all insulating products currently available. From the energy viewpoint, insulating buildings always pays off.
Nevertheless, the environmental risks linked with the production of various insulating materials mean that there is still potential for ecological optimisation in some areas. Furthermore, the insulating materials are still assessed with respect to the health and safety of users of course, plus their availability. For this reason, a comparative assessment of individual insulating materials is important and advisable.

A comparative ecological assessment of construction products in the name of sustainability first calls for a definition of what needs to be protected. This question has been addressed within the scope of the European terminology and standardisation discussion on sustainability in building by defining the following protection aims[1]:

- *Ecological dimension*
  Protection of the global environment
  Protection of natural resources
- *Social dimension*
  Protection of the residential environment and public facilities
  Protection of health, hygiene and safety
- *Economic dimension*
  Maintenance of capital and value

It is also necessary to define in detail which sustainable environmental impacts are to be included in each protection aim. In doing so, the respective causes and effects must be researched in order to be able to describe the underlying human activities.

For a comparative assessment of environmental impacts it is also essential that these impacts be provided with measurable, quantifiable indicators. And for practical actions, i.e. the desired ecological optimisation, the results must also be evaluated. To do this we need a scale of reference, which can be set up by the comparative assessment of numerous individual results. The scale can, however, also be defined by the optimum state of the art in each case (best practice), or by a defined target or limit value. The outcome of all this is assessment tools which should be used to guide and support practical construction activities.

Ecological dimension

Protection of the global environment
Over the past 20 years, the quantitative life cycle assessment (LCA) has been developed into the primary tool for describing and evaluating global environmental impacts. It has been standardised within the scope of the series of environmental management standards beginning with DIN EN ISO 14001:

- DIN EN ISO 14040:2006-10
  Environmental management – Life cycle assessment – Principles and framework
- DIN EN ISO 14044:2006-10
  Environmental management – Life cycle assessment – Requirements and guidelines (with a description of the steps involved) (replaces ISO standards 14041–14043)

[1] Classification of protection aims according to ISO TC 59/SC 17 (Sustainability in Building Construction) and CEN TC 350 (Sustainability of Construction Works), and on a national level via the "Round Table on Sustainable Construction" of the Federal Ministry of Transport, Building & Urban Affairs (2004). CEN TC (Comité Européen de Normalisation, Technical Committee) is responsible for devising voluntary methods for assessing the sustainability aspects of new and existing construction works plus the development of standards for the environmental declaration of construction products.

As the quantitative descriptive and evaluation method, the life cycle assessment (LCA) constitutes a key tool in the recording of global environmental impact that results from the production and use of products in general (see p. 97, "Using life cycle assessments"). The description covers the entire life cycle of a product – from obtaining all the raw materials involved, to the production and its use in construction, its use in the building, possible reuses (e.g. through recycling), right up to final disposal, plus all the transport requirements.
The prerequisite, however, is that the phases of the life cycle are known exactly in the form of process steps, or can be reasonably assumed. An input-output audit of all materials flows involved is carried out for each individual process step. Unknown processes cannot therefore be included, something that applies, above all, to the particularly long phases of use intrinsic to buildings and which at best can only be estimated within the scope of a forecast.
A typical comparison of several material or construction variations for a planned component with the help of a life cycle assessment can be broken down into four work phases:

1. Goal and scope definition
2. Inventory analysis
3. Impact assessment
4. Interpretation

These four phases are explained below.

1. Goal and scope definition
This is the description and definition of a functional unit. The desired technical functions of the building component are crucial here. For example, insulating materials may not be directly compared if they exhibit different thermal conductivities or – if relevant – different compressive strengths. In principle, equivalent functionality is called for, i.e. equivalent insulating performance. In a direct comparison, different insulation thicknesses and hence different material quantities must be assumed where different thermal conductivities apply. At the same time, various auxiliary products, e.g. special fixings or specific subsequent treatment, should be included in the assessment, depending on the material.

Another key element here is describing and defining the scope of the assessment. This step defines which auxiliary products during production and use should be included in the assessment. In order to keep the work within reasonable limits, cut-off criteria are necessary here. For example, fixings for thermal insulation can be omitted from the assessment if they are the same for all the variants examined. Likewise, individual auxiliary products may be left out of the calculation if only very small quantities are involved.

2. Inventory analysis
All the process steps and all the transport requirements in the scope defined beforehand are compiled for the functionally equivalent variants of a building component that are to be assessed. Every individual step is described in terms of energy consumption, energy type and all materials required on the "input side", and all emissions and waste or residue on the "output side". This inventory analysis is added up in the order of the process steps to give a final result. Of course, for the user, this part of the life cycle assessment is extremely difficult to carry out. For this reason, the most important elements in the inventory analysis have been worked out in advance and published in the form of ready-to-use databases for conventional materials, forms of energy or types of transport.
In Germany equivalent, consistent databases are currently being compiled in cooperation with research institutes and manufacturers of construction products[1]. Furthermore, European manufacturers of construction products will in future be required to compile appropriate databases for their products within the scope of the construction product declarations to ISO 14025 (see p. 97).

3. Impact assessment
One essential component of the life cycle assessment is defining the impact categories and their indicators. Only this allows the most important environmental effects to be defined and the materials flows listed in the inventory analysis placed in order, compiled with respect to their impacts and presented for assessment.

For an initial comparison of different insulation variants, we can use the energy requirement, which is calculated as primary energy from the various forms of energy consumed during their production:

- total primary energy input (PEI)
- proportion of renewable energies (RE) in primary energy input, and
- proportion of non-renewable energies (NRE).

In addition to these values, the energy requirement over the entire life cycle, including possible recycling potential, can be used – the "cumulative energy demand" to VDI 4600. The energy requirement during the use of the building is estimated by way of assumptions or scenarios here.

[1] "Updating and harmonising of basic data for sustainable building", Federal Ministry of Transport, Building & Urban Affairs (2007)

Factors for global warming potential in the form of CO_2-equivalent [kg] for emissions

Emissions of trace gases	Factor after 20 years	Factor after 100 years
CO_2 (carbon dioxide)	1	1
CH_4 (methane)	62	24.5
NO_2 (nitrogen oxide)	290	320
O_3 (ozone)	–	2000
H 1201 (halon)	6200	5600
R 134a (CFC)	3300	1300
R 22 (refrigerant)	4300	1700

1

When carrying out a comprehensive quantitative energy assessment, the environmental impacts linked with the generation of the energy used are also included:

- Global warming potential (GWP)
- CO_2 storage (in products made from renewable raw materials)
- Ozone depletion potential (ODP)
- Acidification potential (AP)
- Eutrophication potential (EP) or nutrification potential (NP) (excessive fertilisation)
- Photochemical ozone creation potential (POCP)
- Space requirements

Owing to the complex database, the indicators for the toxicity of processes, also defined for the life cycle assessment, are used only in the case of significant individual assessments. The following indicators have been defined for this:
- Aquatic ecotoxicity (ECA)
- Terrestrial ecotoxicity (ECT)
- Human toxicological classification (HC)

The individual environmental impacts are compiled in the inventory analysis and weighted similar to their effects in comparison with a known indicator substance. For instance, all the substances that contribute to the greenhouse effect are weighted and compiled in the indicator for global warming potential, the CO_2-equivalent [kg], e.g. methane (CH_4) with the factor 62 or the refrigerant R 134a (used in air-conditioning systems) with the factor 3300 (table 1).

4. Interpretation
If within the scope of a comparative life cycle assessment different durabilities of the variants are to be expected (e.g. for thermal insulation composite systems), the effects determined in the impact assessment must be adjusted with corresponding factors.
An assessment of the results by simply comparing the figures is possible only rarely. In the majority of cases there is a conflict of aims when a material variant has, for example, a high global warming potential but another variant a high ozone depletion potential. It is for this reason that appropriate priorities and targets must be established prior to the assessment. These can be based on:
- an estimate of the duration or reversibility of an impact,
- an estimate of the secondary or tertiary consequences of an impact,
- the relative relationship of an impact compared to the local or underlying loads,
- the safety margin between an impact and a defined limit value.

The result of a life cycle assessment must always be checked for additional aspects and risks that are not directly included. If the production of a material involves the use of environmental pollutants and hazardous substances, the infrastructure required to ensure safe transport and production processes may become a criterion. The same applies to problematic production waste.

Protection of natural resources
Besides the protection of the global environment, there is another ecological target to be achieved: the protection of natural resources. This protection primarily covers finite and non-renewable raw materials. The consumption of non-renewable energy generated from fossil fuels forms a large proportion. These resources are included and reflected in the life cycle assessment. But the use of renewable energy sources should also be investigated critically. For example, the associated technical requirements for obtaining renewable energies should be subjected to a life cycle assessment in order to check the ecological efficiency of the measures. There are certainly some photovoltaic, geothermal and heat recovery installations that consume considerably more energy in their production than they can be expected to save over a realistic period of time!

However, the natural resources also include impacts that are impossible to handle in a quantitative assessment. For example, the ongoing devastation of the variety of plant and animal species and the associated genetic resources cannot be described using a life cycle assessment. Generally, the effects that occur in several steps in nature can seldom be described in terms of causes, and are certainly not quantifiable. Qualitative individual ecological optimisation measures are therefore called for in the case of well-founded suspicions or detectable damage. One familiar example of this is the FSC (Forest Stewardship Council) environmental mark for timbers obtained from sustainable forest operations in the forest regions of the Earth at risk. Some manu-

1 As an indication of the global warming potential of gases, their effect is weighted in comparison with CO_2. The CO_2-equivalent determined in this way can vary depending on the period of observation. For example, 1 kg of the refrigerant R 134a has the same effect on the Earth's atmosphere after 20 years as 3300 kg of CO_2, after 100 years the same as 1300 kg of CO_2.

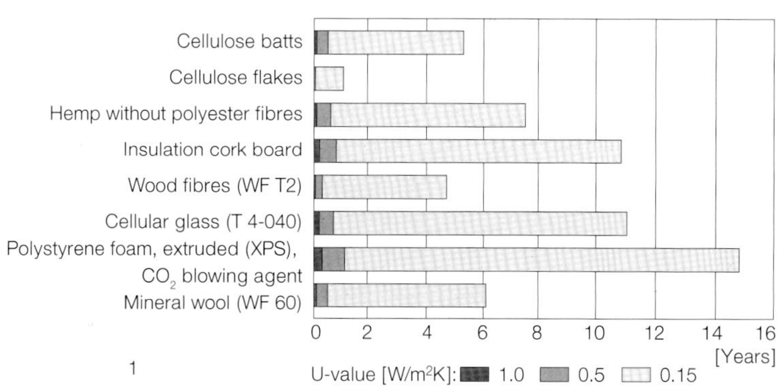

1

1 Energy-related payback times of insulating materials
A randomly chosen heavyweight component with a U-value of 2.0 W/m²K is insulated with three layers of insulation in succession. The first layer leads to a U-value von 1.0 W/m²K, the second to a U-value of 0.5 W/m²K, and the third layer is the additional insulation required to achieve a passive-house U-value of 0.15 W/m²K. The diagram shows a simplified energy-related payback calculation for each individual layer.
The payback times increase with the standard of insulation (U-value) of the component. The energy-related payback time of a layer of insulation therefore increases with the thickness.

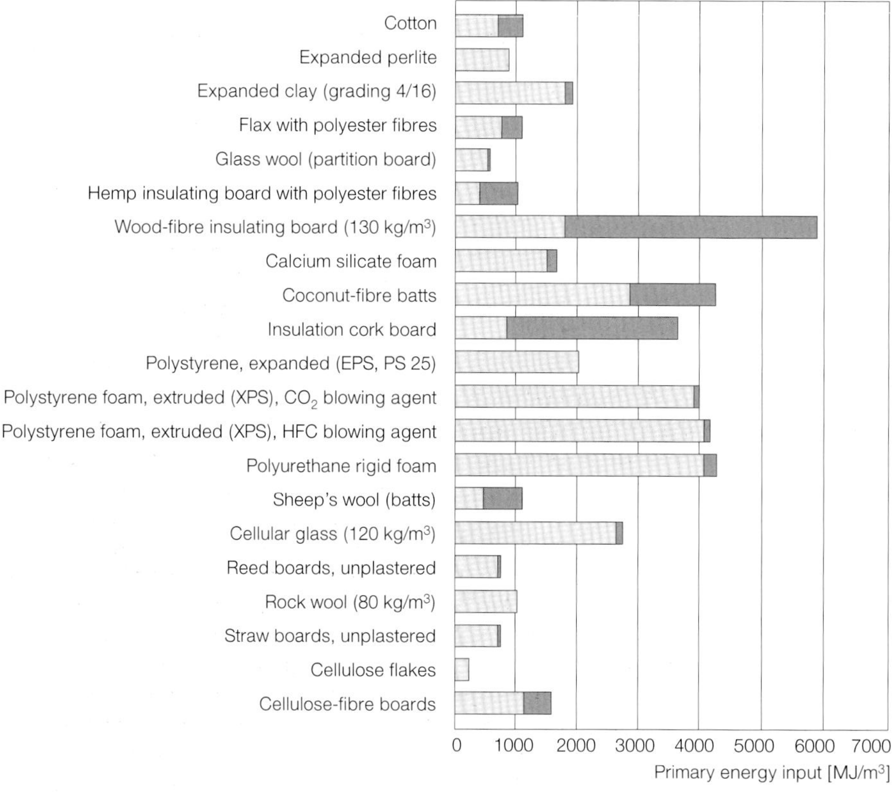

2

facturers of wood-fibre insulating boards use FSC-certified timbers as their raw materials.

When it goes beyond fossil fuels, an assessment of the availability of raw materials is not possible with a life cycle assessment, or at least not without additional appraisals. This applies primarily to various renewable raw materials. The term alone is not an ecological quality feature, but instead should always be considered in conjunction with the quantities consumed and the generation conditions. Good examples of this are sheep's wool and cotton for insulating products. The production of cotton requires vast quantities of water, fertilisers and pesticides, and is coupled with monocultures and soil erosion. The low prices on the world markets – without which it could not even be considered as an insulating material – can be attributed to child labour and poor working conditions. Sheep's wool should also be assessed critically. All the sheep in Germany would, theoretically, permit a market share for this insulating material of no more than 0.3%! Apart from the feed requirements and the use of the land, the wool has to be scoured and cleaned, and the insulating materials produced from wool also include polyester fibres plus diverse fire and moth protection additives.
On the other hand, there is a growing potential for using cellulose fibres produced from waste paper, and also wood, flax or hemp fibres.

Energy-related assessment of insulating materials
If insulating materials are to be investigated with respect to their energy efficiency, a comparison of the total embodied energy is insufficient. It is much more pertinent to carry out an energy payback calculation in which the energy use is compared with the energy saved by the insulating measures, although a lifetime on which to base the comparison will have to be estimated in this instance.
For conventional applications in timber structures, the energy payback of insulating materials is always positive. However, marked differences are possible depending on component, specific product features (thermal conductivity) and thickness of insulating material. The results range from a few weeks (mostly insulating materials made from plant fibres) to 10 years or more for energy-intensive insulating materials and very well-insulated components (U-value < 0.2 to 0.3 W/m²K) or

2 Primary energy input (PEI) of insulating materials
The values shown here are valid for the products described only, not for all the products in that material group. For an exact comparison, the thicknesses of the insulating materials had to be adjusted to suit a feasible U-value.
3 Energy values for insulating materials
Insulating materials for the flat roof of an office building with a high standard of insulation (passive-house standard) are compared with respect to their energy consumption.
Roof area: 900 m²
Usable floor space: 2500 m²
Average thickness of insulation (integral falls): 300 mm
(3.6 megajoule [MJ] = 1 kilowatt-hour [kWh])

Energy values for roof insulating materials

Material	Thermal conductivity [W/(mK)]	Thickness [cm] related to 0.035 W/(mK)	Density [kg/m³]	Renewable energy RE [MJ/m²]	Non-renewable energy NER [MJ/m²]	Total energy requirement [MJ/m²]
Cellular glass CG	0.040	35	110	47.65	897.86	945.51
Extruded polystyrene foam XPS, CO_2 blowing agent	0.035	30	30	11.87	1124.66	1136.53
Expanded polystyrene EPS	0.035	30	30	7.67	1041.71	1049.38
Mineral wool MW	0.035	30	50	7.76	364.98	372.74

3

reduced temperature differences (e.g. external basement insulation). A critical assessment of the insulating materials is therefore certainly advisable when planning buildings with thick layers of insulation (low-energy and passive-energy houses).
The proportion of the U-value attributable to the insulating material of a component is entered into the calculation for the payback period. The thickness of insulation required results from the respective thermal conductivity of the insulating material and the U-value specified. If we compare various insulating materials using identical boundary conditions, we can compare the payback periods. It should be remembered here that energy-savings do not increase linearly with the thickness of insulation. The payback of the insulation should therefore be considered in individual steps, similar to other planning decisions, e.g. for insulation 100, 150 or 200 mm thick.
Taking the example of insulation to a heavyweight component, it can be seen that the energy payback for normal insulation is no longer than one year, but that this period increases considerably with the thickness of insulation (Fig. 1). It is also clear that the choice of insulating material plays a role because the energy payback periods are all very different. Wood-fibre boards or cellulose, also mineral wool, should therefore be used for layers of insulation > 200 mm thick.

In the case of high insulation requirements for a component, a comparison of different insulating materials by way of the energy consumption alone can be helpful if the material variants with similar or identical thermal conductivity do not call for any significant constructional changes.
A comparison between expanded polystyrene (EPS) and mineral wool (MW) for insulation with integral falls on a flat roof with maintenance-only foot traffic is a good example. The same applies when comparing mineral wool, cellulose fibres or other fibrous materials for the sound insulation to lightweight partitions. The effect possible here is often underestimated.
Table 3 shows the energy-related assessment of insulating materials with integral falls for a flat roof. A comparison of expanded polystyrene (EPS) and mineral wool results in a primary energy input (PEI) of 608 985 MJ and 169 162 kWh respectively for a roof area of 900 m². Assuming a lifetime of 20 years and a usable floor space of 2500 m², that results in a value of approx. 3.4 kWh/m²a. The material prices for mineral wool products are, however, higher than those for EPS insulating materials. The extra cost of the insulating material with better energy figures could then be compared with the cost, for example, for other building or building services measures that reduce the annual primary energy requirement of the building by the same amount. When applying high insulation standards, this comparison usually ends in favour of the material. On the other hand, this approach is less advisable when considering energy-efficiency upgrade measures for an existing building. In such cases it is usually more effective to invest the extra money in upgrading the heating systems or windows.

Using life cycle assessments
Important conditions for the use of life cycle assessments are the provision of the necessary data and the standardisation of the terminology, steps and evaluations. Besides the series of standards covering environmental management, a second set of standards covering sustainable building is currently in preparation:
- ISO/CD 21929
  Buildings and constructed assets – General principles for sustainability
- ISO/DIS 21930
  Environmental declaration of building products
- ISO/CD 21931
  Assessment of environmental impacts of buildings
- ISO/CD 21932 Sustainability indicators

ISO 21930 will have a special role to play. The aim of this standard is to introduce manufacturers' declarations for the environmental impacts of their products, which are determined on the basis of life cycle assessments. All the information the planner needs for comparative assessments of components could therefore be integrated into the planning work.
The use of life cycle assessments as a planning aid has been stipulated in Germany since March 2002, within the scope of the "Guidelines for Sustainable Construction" published by the Federal Ministry of Transport, Building & Urban Affairs. The results of life cycle assessments, building component costs and socio-cultural factors are to be brought together in a three-stage assessment and then evaluated for the planning decisions. At present, the guidelines are only mandatory for German government buildings to which the public has access.

The degree of difficulty in applying LCA data depends on the component under consideration. For simple constructional functions, a number of suitable materials are selected first, which could be, for example, fibres or fibrous batts of light to medium weight for insulating lightweight partitions, or closed-cell, rigid insulating boards for external basement insulation below ground slabs. This preliminary selection means that the most important technical functions have already been dealt with. The functional equivalent to be examined (see p. 94) now refers only to the main function required and must be

1 

2 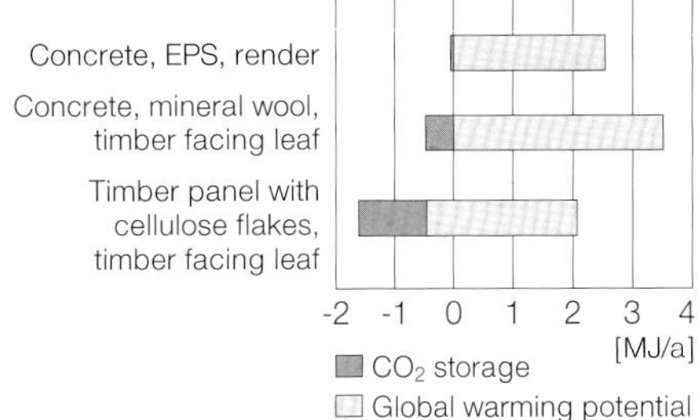

3 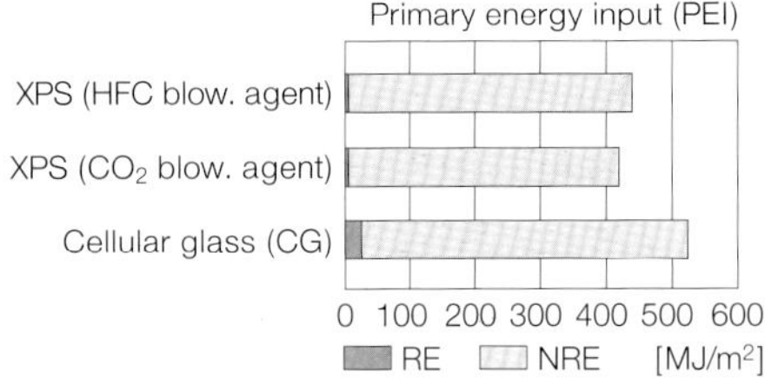

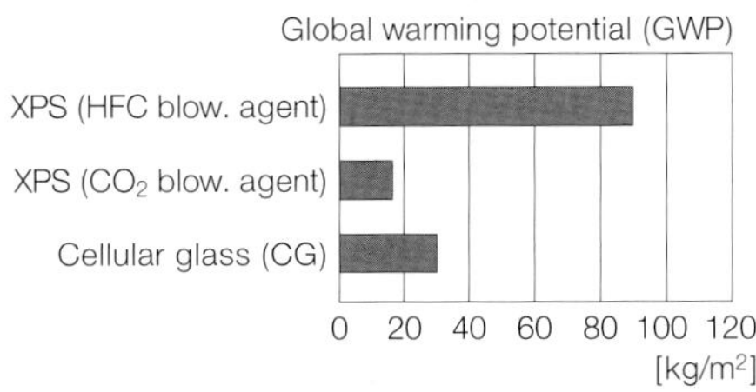

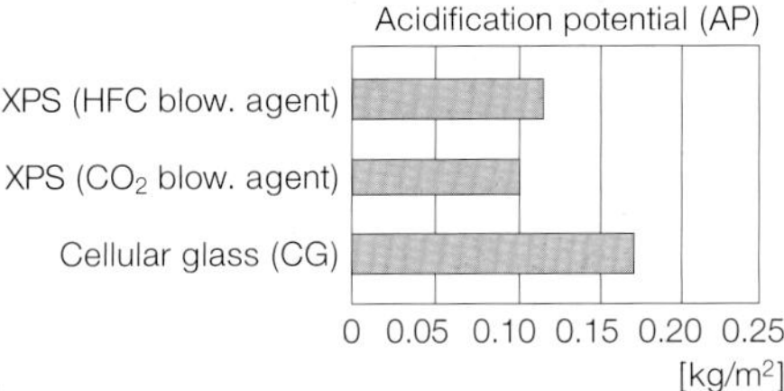

1 Prefabricated timber panel element factory-filled with cellulose insulation. A facing leaf (with ventilation cavity) will be erected on the outside.

2 Life cycle assessment for facade insulation (CO audit)
Three variations with the same insulation properties were investigated for a loadbearing external wall in reinforced concrete:
a Thermal insulation composite system with EPS
b Mineral wool insulation with ventilation cavity and timber facing leaf
c Prefabricated timber panels factory-filled with celluose flakes plus ventilation cavity and timber facing leaf
The result of the CO_2 audit shows clear advantages for the cellulose flakes + timber panel solution. The CO_2 storage shown in the diagram must be subtracted from the global warming potential.

3 Life cycle assessment for external basement insulation
The primary energy input (PEI) is considered, differentiated according to renewable (RE) and non-renewable (NRE) energy sources, global warming potential (GWP) and acidification potential (AP).
Boundary conditions:
External basement insulation beneath ground slab, on blinding, no adhesive, butt joints, covering of PE sheeting. Founded clear of groundwater. Permanent compressive stress ≤ 18 N/mm² to prEN 1606.
Material variants:
- extruded polystyrene foam (XPS), with HFC blowing agent, λ = 0.040 W/mK, 100 mm thick
- extruded polystyrene foam (XPS), with CO_2 blowing agent, λ = 0.040 W/mK, 100 mm thick
- cellular glass, λ = 0.055 W/mK, 140 mm thick

adjusted accordingly to suit the material properties (thickness of insulation matched to thermal conductivity λ).
Fig. 3 shows several aspects of a life cycle assessment using the example of external basement insulation: the primary energy input (PEI) of the insulating materials being investigated, their global warming potential (GWP) and their acidification potential (AP). Besides cellular glass, two XPS products with different blowing agents (HFC, CO_2) are considered in order to investigate the environmental relevance of the blowing agent. The evaluation of the results reveals contrary effects. The ozone-depleting GWP is much lower with cellular glass insulation, but the energy requirement is somewhat higher. Higher priorities therefore have to be applied for the final assessment. For example, the greenhouse effect has a very high priority at the moment and can serve as a reason for a certain choice of material. In addition, aspects such as the work involved with industrial production and costs can be employed as decision-making criteria.

The comparison becomes complicated when different materials call for different types of construction. For example, the insulation to a facade could be carried out with expanded polystyrene (EPS) or mineral wool as a thermal insulation composite system on masonry or in situ concrete. If a version with cellulose fibres is to be considered as well, this is only possible if constructional changes are accepted, e.g. in the form of prefabricated timber panels with factory-applied insulation. In this case all the respective types of construction should be included in the comparison with all their material constituents.
Fig. 2 shows just such a life cycle assessment for facade insulation: owing to the very different variations with a large number of associated materials, the assessment becomes correspondingly involved. The result of the CO_2 assessment shows clear advantages for the cellulose/ timber panel solution, partly because of the CO_2 storage in the materials used, which reduces the low ozone-depleting GWP yet further.

Data for life cycle assessments
Several materials usually have to be included in a comparative assessment of building components. Besides the insulating materials involved, different cladding, render, plaster, coatings, paint, fixings and supporting constructions will be necessary. When comparing the assessments, the data used should be consistent with respect to its suitability, accuracy and reliability (~ realistic) in order to enable a faithful evaluation. This problem can be illustrated by means of a simple example: if when comparing two cars we consider the petrol consumption of one of them when driving in town and the petrol consumption of the other when driving on the motorway, each measurement would itself be correct, but comparing the two would lead to a wrong conclusion.
Up until now there was no appropriate, consistent data for use in life cycle assessments, but intensive work has been going on since about 2005 to obtain such data – within the scope of the environmental product declarations (EPD) manufacturers will require in the future. Older and more general data has been published or is available in computer programs (LEGEP, GaBi). Current LCA data that can be used as a database for insulating materials is listed on page 99. As limited EPD data was available at the time of going to press, the reader is recommended to obtain information about the respective state of progress and expected publication dates from the Internet (see sources, p. 99, table 4).

4 LCA data for insulating materials
The LCA data is related to 1 kg of material. The primary energy figures are stated in MJ (1 kWh = 3.6 MJ). In practice they are to be multiplied by the actual product weight.
Example: The non-renewable primary energy for a mineral-fibre insulating board, 200 mm thick, density 120 kg/m³, is calculated as follows: 120 kg/m³ x 0.2 m x 12.9 MJ/kg = 309.6 MJ/m² = 86 kWh/m².
Data from different sources should only be compared for approximate analyses. Generally, insulating materials should only be compared for the same function and the same components (see "Goal and scope definition", p. 94, functional unit). The data is heavily dependent on the respective production conditions and methods plus the type of compilation. It should therefore be as up to date as possible. New data for construction products based on a uniform calculation principle has been collated since 2005. Thanks to the introduction of the European construction product declaration according to ISO 14025, this data can in future be obtained directly from the manufacturers of the respective products. The first construction product declarations can be found under www.bau-umwelt.de[1].

LCA data for insulating materials

Insulating material	**Density** [kg/m³]	**Thermal conductivity** [W/(mK)]	**Global warming potential** [kg CO_2 eq.]	**Photochem. ozone creation potential** [kg C_2H_2]	**Acidification potential** [kg SO_2 eq.]	**Eutrophication potential** [kg PO_4 eq.]	**Primary energy, non-renewable** [MJ]	**Primary energy renewable** [MJ]
Inorganic insulating materials								
Expanded perlite board (EPB)[3]	85	0.042	0.52	0.00014	0.00236	0.00030	10.2	0.2
Expanded perlite board (EPB), with hydrophobic treatment3	145	0.053	0.52	0.00014	0.00236	0.00030	10.2	0.2
Expanded clay (grading 4/16)[3]	400	0.800–1.000	0.31	0.00016	0.00194	0.00009	4.4	0.4
Glass wool (MW, cavity insulation board)[2]	13	0.036	2.81	0.00124	0.00603	0.00072	40.4	2.4
Glass wool (MW, clamped in place)[2]	17	0.036	2.52	0.00105	0.00537	0.00066	36.3	1.6
Glass wool (MW, partition board)[2]	14	0.040	2.62	0.00110	0.00560	0.00068	39.7	2.7
Calcium silicate foam[1]	115	0.045	1.10	0.00028	0.00200	0.00026	12.3	1.7
Autoclaved aerated concrete[1]	400	0.100	0.45	0.00009	0.00066	0.00011	3.57	0.2
Cellular glass (CG)[1]	105–160	0.041–0.050	1.26	0.00008	0.00768	0.00034	21.8	1.1
Rock wool (MW)[1]	20–200	0.035–0.040	1.16	0.00052	0.00750	0.00083	12.9	0.1
Organic insulating materials								
Cotton[3]	20–50	0.040	0.02	0.00082	0.01047	0.00054	18.1	13.6
Flax with polyester fibres[3]	20	0.040	0.41	0.00031	0.01100	0.00076	38.8	16.2
Flax without polyester fibres[3]	20	0.040	0.22	0.00027	0.00764	0.00071	33.2	17.3
Hemp with polyester fibres (boards)[3]	30	0.045	-0.55	0.00087	0.00672	0.00077	14.9	18.9
Wood-fibre insulating board (WF)[3]	130–200	0.040–0.045	-0.45	0.00044	0.00478	0.00037	13.59	31.6
Wood-fibre insulating board (WF), bitumenised[3]	270	0.060	-0.21	0.03479	0.01048	0.00035	15.16	23.3
Coconut-fibre batts[3]	70–90	0.045	0.56	0.00019	0.03630	0.00094	34.9	19.2
Insulation corkboard (ICB)[3]	100–120	0.040	-1.46	0.0001	0.00290	0.00025	7.19	23.3
Natural granulated cork[3]	160	0.060	-1.81	0	0	0	0	20.3
Polystyrene, expanded (EPS)[2]	15	0.040	2.76	0.00095	0.00590	0.00061	83.0	0.4
Polystyrol, expanded (EPS)[2]	20	0.038	2.68	0.00094	0.00579	0.00060	81.6	0.4
Polystyrene, expanded (EPS)[2]	25	0.035	2.64	0.00094	0.00575	0.00059	81.0	0.4
Polystyrene, expanded (EPS)[2]	30	0.035	2.62	0.00094	0.00572	0.00059	80.7	0.4
Polystyrene insulation render, cement-bonded[2]	600	0.060–0.100	1.53	0.00038	0.00280	0.00037	30.4	0.7
Polystyrene foam, extruded (XPS), CO_2 blowing agent[3]	37	0.038	3.73	0.00271	0.02515	0.00178	107.1	1.3
Polystyrene foam, extruded (XPS), HFC blowing agent[3]	37	0.032	21.97	0.00278	0.02854	0.00181	110.2	1.3
Polyurethane rigid foam (PUR)[3]	40	0.030	13.7	0.00048	0.06680	0.00160	102.1	4.4
Sheep's wool (batts)[3]	30	0.035	0.24	0.00066	0.00548	0.00034	16.4	20.6
Reed boards, unplastered[3]	190	0.056	-1.45	0.00006	0.00133	0.00011	3.9	0.19
Straw boards, unplastered[3]	190	0.056	-1.45	0.00006	0.00133	0.00011	3.9	0.19
Cellulose flakes[3]	30–70	0.040–0.045	0.23	0.00003	0.00264	0.00013	4.2	0.4
Cellulose-fibre boards[3]	70–80	0.040	1.61	0.00127	0.01230	0.00047	15.4	5.8

Sources:
[1] Manufacturer's environmental product declaration (EPD) to ISO 14025, www.bau-umwelt.de, since 2005
[2] LCA data, GaBi-4, www.gabi-software.de
4 [3] IBO, Austrian Institute for Building Biology & Ecology, Vienna, 2000

1

Social dimension

The insulation of buildings usually involves concealed, very durable components. The protection aims regarding the residential environment and public facilities are seldom affected. Exceptions can be found in solutions that become necessary for reasons of the preservation of monuments or an existing facade planting. Crucial to the life cycle assessment of insulating materials is, on the other hand, the protection of health, hygiene and safety. Here, the design and construction targets can be divided into:

- requirements regarding interior comfort,
- requirements regarding healthy interior conditions, and
- special consideration of direct and indirect fire hazards caused by the materials employed.

Interior comfort

In recent years, the regulations covering the boundary conditions responsible for a healthy and agreeable interior climate have been made more precise, and target values have been included. Important aspects that have been affected are the airtightness of buildings (measured using the blower door method to DIN EN 13829), the minimum air change rate (which should be 0.6 to 0.7 times the volume of the room per hour in order to remove hazardous substances and CO_2 from the interior air), and the avoidance of thermal bridges and mould growth with the help of the methods of calculation given in DIN EN ISO 10211. The perceived comfort in rooms also depends on the air velocity, the "cold radiation" from the walls and ceiling, and the thermal stratification. The interaction of all individual factors and their physical effect and individual perception cannot be recorded with simple physical calculations. To do this, DIN EN ISO 7730 makes use of the subjective perceptions of test persons for determining the thermal comfort. The predicted mean vote (PMV) index represents an assessment of the thermal comfort and is made up of several physical interior conditions.
The predicted percentage of dissatisfied (PPD) index is a statistical function of the PMV and describes a prognosis value for dissatisfied persons as a percentage.
We distinguish here between three quality categories: A (highest), B and C.
Like DIN EN ISO 7730, the Swiss standard SIA 180 also specifies the climatic requirements that should be employed when planning air-conditioned buildings. For example, maximum and minimum values are specified for the design of heat storage masses, for summertime heat dissipation concepts, for ventilation installations or the design of thermal insulating components and their internal surfaces. The requirements regarding comfort are building physics factors and dictate the scope of the chosen insulating measures. However, they are not ecological assessment criteria for selecting a particular insulating material, whose basic functionality within the component must essentially be presumed.

Healthy interiors

The situation is different with regard to the requirements regarding a healthy interior. This protection aim has also seen an increase in the measurable indicators and targets in recent years. The interior air is contaminated by numerous pollutants and odours caused by the construction itself. These can be divided into:

- emissions of volatile organic compounds (VOC) from building materials,
- contamination due to spores from mould,
- emissions of fibres and dusts from building materials, and
- odours from building materials.

Volatile organic compounds

The group of volatile organic compounds comprises approx. 160–180 individual substances ranging from highly to not readily volatile that can be given off by construction products. Besides their principal constituents, synthetic materials can also contain a multitude of organic and inorganic additives designed to improve product characteristics, e.g. plasticisers, flame retardants or binders. Natural materials such as wood, cork or animal and vegetable fibres can also contain volatile compounds and may include additives to protect against moths or increase fire resistance. The measurements and checks are carried out on a sample of air taken from the room. The air passes over a collector in which the substances are

1 Cellulose fibres
2 Laboratory measurement of products for VOC emissions. Product samples are placed in the chamber for measurement.
3 In situ measurement of VOC emissions of products already installed. The apparatus is placed over the sample.
4 Limit values for volatile organic compounds (VOC) in the interior air as emitted from building materials, measured after 28 days in the chamber according to standards of the DIN EN 16000 series. Source: Interior Air Hygiene Commission, Federal Environment Agency

2

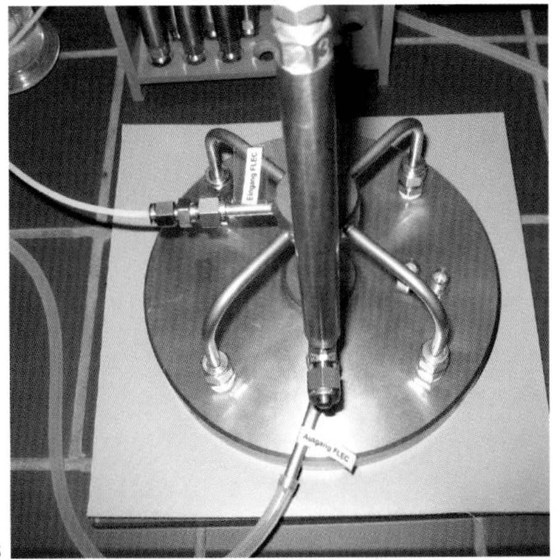

3

deposited before being evaluated by means of gas chromatography (Fig. 3). The result can be expressed as the sum of all the substances in the interior air, the TVOC (total volatile organic compounds) value in mg/m^3. There is no mandatory value for this figure. The Federal Environment Agency in Berlin recommends a target figure that has been incorporated in the "Guidelines for Sustainable Construction". According to that document, the load should not exceed the following values:

- 1– 2 months after completion of the building works: approx. 1.5 – 2.0 mg/m^3
- 1– 2 years after completion of the building works: approx. 0.25 – 0.3 mg/m^3

As the measured substances have varying effects on the human body, the results are also evaluated with respect to the concentration of the individual substances. More or less mandatory figures are specified by the Interior Air Hygiene Commission of the Federal Environment Agency. Guide value I (RW I) specifies the concentration of a substance for which no health hazards are to be expected. Guide value II (RW II) specifies a concentration that, if exceeded, requires action, e.g. in the form of replacing a material or modifying a form of construction. These values can be obtained from the website of the Federal Environment Agency.
In order to limit the total emissions in the interior, it is necessary to know something about the materials used. It was for this reason that the "Committee for Health-related Evaluation of Building Products" at the Federal Environment Agency devised an evaluation scheme with which products could be measured and assessed separately. In the scheme, product samples are measured in a chamber according to a defined procedure in accordance with standards of the DIN EN 16000 series. The VOC value is determined just as for measuring the interior air. After 28 days in the chamber the total of normally volatile substances may not exceed 1 mg/m^3, the total of not readily volatile substances 0.1 mg/m^3. In addition, the total of all carcinogenic substances may not be higher than 0.001 mg/m^3. If the product satisfies these requirements, it is regarded as "suitable for interior use". This verification forms part of the DIBt approval conditions and up until now applied only to floor coverings requiring an approval.
These requirements can be transferred to insulating materials if they are to be used indoors. That would affect all sound insulation measures (floors, partitions, suspended ceilings) if volatile substances are to be expected, namely blowing agents, binders and resin constituents in vegetable fibres, or flame retardants. Hitherto, emissions of terpenes from binders for granulated cork and naphthaline from impact sound insulation have been found in isolated instances.

Limit values for volatile organic compounds (VOC) in the interior air and emitted from building materials

Total VOC, normally volatile	≤	1 mg/m^3
Total VOC, not readily volatile	≤	0.1 mg/m^3
Total of active carcinogenic substances	≤	0.001 mg/m^3

4

Spores

Contamination caused by mould spores has been increasing in recent years. The causes are frequently improperly insulated external components where the surface temperatures on the inside of heated rooms drop below approx. 10–14°C, which allows condensation to form. Situations that are particularly critical are those in which mould forms within the external components and leads to emissions into the interior without actually being visible itself. This is often the result of constructional defects allowing insulation to become too wet or not allowing it to dry out. The ability of vegetable fibres to absorb more moisture than mineral fibres and foamed plastics, a hygroscopic behaviour characteristic that is often regarded as advantageous, should be looked at more critically in this context.
Concealed mould growth is generally detected through the odours given off because moulds emit microbial volatile organic compounds (MVOC) with a typical musty, earthy smell. If hidden mould is suspected, measurements of the interior air should be carried out in which the extracted air is passed over a culture medium. After that, the germinative spores (nucleating units) are measured by cultivating the samples in an incubator. The moulds most frequently encountered are *Aspergillus* varieties, *Penicillium spp.*, *Cladosporium spp.* and numerous other less common species. It is primarily *Aspergillus versicolor* together with some types from the *Aspergillus restrictus* group and *Aspergillus sydowii* that are regarded as indicators of moisture damage in buildings. If inhaled, mould spores can lead to allergic reactions (e.g. asthma, colds, irritation of the eyes) in some people, or indeed cause an allergy in predisposed, atopic persons.

Fibres and dusts

When it comes to fibre contamination, it is primarily the carcinogenic effects of certain ultra-fine mineral fibres that have captured the headlines. Besides asbestos fibres, the synthetic mineral fibres (mineral wool, MW) are also relevant here. According to the definition of the World Health Organisation (WHO), fibres with the following properties can be inhaled and are hence classed as a health hazard:

- length> 5 µm
- diameter < 3 µm
- length-diameter ratio > 3:1.

2

Constituents given off from natural raw materials in a fire depending on the phase of the fire

Raw material	Outbreak	Flashover	Fire-fighting	Cooling
Wood fibres, cellulose	CO, CO_2, H_2O	CO, CO_2, H_2O, aldehydes, aromatics, PAH, alcohols, acetic acid, HC	CO, CO_2, H_2O, aldehydes, aromatics, PAH, alcohols, acetic acid, HC	aldehydes, aromatics, PAH, alcohols, acetic acid, HC
Wool, hair	CO, CO_2, H_2O, HCN, SO_2	CO, CO_2, H_2O, HCN, SO_2, H_2S amines, aromatics, PAH	CO, CO_2, H_2O, HCN, SO_2, H_2S, amines, aromatics, PAH	amines, aromatics, PAH

HCN: hydrogen cyanide
PAH: polycyclic aromatic hydrocarbons, e.g. benzo[a]pyrene
HC: hydrocarbons
CO: carbon monoxide
SO_2: sulphur dioxide
H_2S: hydrogen sulphide

1

In addition, the resistance of the fibres in the lungs is crucial (bioresistance). Whereas the WHO and the IARC (International Association of Cancer Registries) carry out a global and formal classification of mineral wool in general owing to the lack of a classification method, the classification of the EU and the German Hazardous Substances Act adhere to the precautionary principle. According to this, hazardous fibres are divided into three categories, the first of which is for carcinogenic fibres and the third if "a suspicion cannot be ruled out".

Only mineral-fibre insulating materials that cannot be classified in any of the three categories may be used in Germany. This has to be verified and declared according to EU law[1]. Since about 1995, manufacturers have been changing their formulations to achieve higher biosolubility (see also p. 22). In order to safeguard the necessary ongoing tests regarding biosolubility, the quality assurance scheme in Germany is ensured by including a liability exclusion arrangement in the RAL quality mark RAL GZ 388; the quality scheme of course embraces all the important technical properties (Fig. 2). Almost all customary mineral-fibre insulating materials are labelled with this quality mark. Care should be taken with products imported from outside Europe.
Tests designed to establish hazards due to fibres are very involved and expensive. It is clear that although mineral fibres have been thoroughly investigated, the majority of organic fibres and dusts of synthetic or natural origin have not. For example, cellulose flakes made from waste paper can contain heavy metals, biocides, formaldehyde or boron compounds; cotton may be contaminated with pesticides and might have been "upgraded" with diverse chemicals. The same is true for insulating materials made from sheep's wool and coconut fibres.
In addition, even the coarser fibres in insulating materials can irritate and damage the respiratory tract and mucous membranes, which can lead to health problems in children or people with chronic ailments such as asthma. Therefore, just as a precaution, fibrous insulating materials should not be used in direct contact with the interior air. This precautionary measure affects fibrous insulating materials laid on suspended ceilings with open sides, and sound insulation in partitions and the underside of pitched roofs if uncovered installation openings, e.g. unguarded electric sockets, are present. Airtight arrangements are essential here. Besides the risk of fibres in the interior air, contamination with dust from insulating materials has been found, but only in isolated cases. The dust from cork processing is just one example of a health hazard that certainly could occur once the cork is installed in a building.

Odours
Odour problems are hard to define, but are increasingly becoming an issue, especially in buildings for the retail trade and offices. Permanent odour problems impair the comfort and well-being of users and occupants, but there is still no reliable means of technical verification ("artificial noses"). Verification is therefore carried out by suitably trained persons who first check a large sample of air (min. 300 l) for the intensity of odours according to a defined procedure. Afterwards, the samples are checked for their odour quality and designated using a scale that ranges from "very pleasant" to "very unpleasant". In order that the results have a practical use and can be compared, the influence on the air of a stationary person has been defined and is designated by the decipol (dp) unit of measurement. The majority of insulating materials – including all mineral wool products and synthetic foams – are essentially neutral in terms of smell. In contrast to this, odours can be expected with some plant-based insulating materials, and the resins in insulation cork board can sometimes be very unpleasant. The terpenes and phenols in wood fibres can also result in unpleasant odours.

Direct and indirect fire hazards due to insulating materials
As a rule, the approved uses of insulating materials are coupled with their reaction to fire, among other things. The require-

[1] European Council Directive 67/548/EEC of 27 June 1967 on the approximation of laws, regulations and administrative provisions relating to the classification, packaging and labelling of dangerous substances (OJ 196, 16 Aug 1967, pp. 1–98) last amended on 29 April 2004.

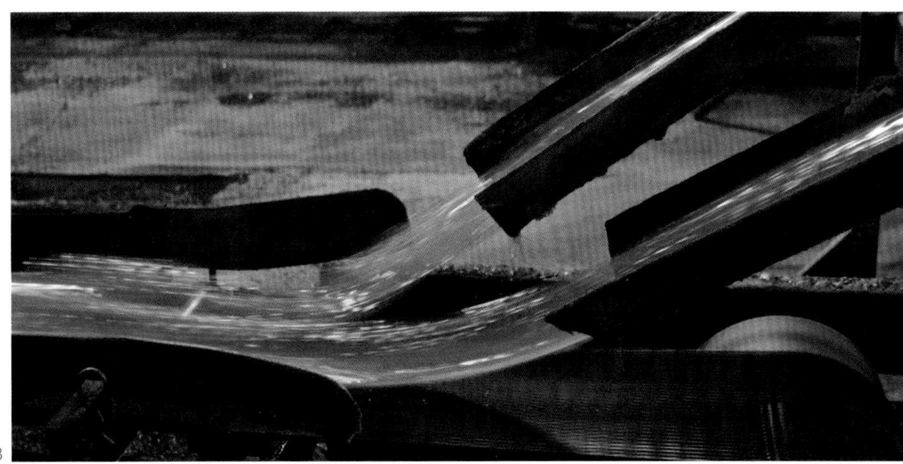

2 RAL quality mark RAL GZ 388
3 Molten glass prior to foaming to form foamed glass 3

ments are stipulated in building authority regulations and until complete harmonisation of the standards at European level, by the building materials classes of DIN 4102. A new European classification to DIN EN 13501, which comprises seven so-called Euroclasses (A1, A2, B, C, D, E and F) has been in place since 2002. Also linked to this is the need for uniform fire tests for building materials throughout Europe. The key value for classifying building materials is the time taken for a material to burn fully (flashover). There is no flashover in classes A1, A2 and B, whereas the combustible materials of classes C, D and E reach this condition in between 10 and 2 minutes.
The sub-classes for smoke development (s1, s2 and s3) and burning droplets (d0, d1 and d2) were introduced to improve precautionary measures. The sub-classes will have to be specified on the product packagings in the future (see also pp. 14, 64 and 73/74).
Not included in this assessment are indirect fire risks such as additional toxic constituents in smoke and fumes (in addition to carbon monoxide) and precipitation in the form of soot and ashes.

The problem in fires is often not the flames themselves but the density of the accompanying smoke and the constituents of the fumes. About 80% of the victims of fires die as a result of inhaling smoke and fumes. This is particularly true for certain groups of people in buildings who for reasons of age, illness, disability, etc. are unable to escape. Thick smoke prevents fire-fighters and rescuers from carrying out their work efficiently, and hazardous constituents in fumes shorten the time in which victims can be rescued. Insulating materials belonging to DIN EN 13501 classes C to E may therefore not be used in certain areas of buildings, or at least not before the fire load has been thoroughly investigated. Besides synthetic foams, it is primarily the various plant-based fibrous insulating materials that are relevant here. Insulation cork board (pressed cork board) more than any other material is associated with extreme fire propagation rates and smoke densities, sheep's wool (like all types of hair) gives rise to additional toxic fumes, likewise polyurethane insulating materials (hydrogen cyanide, HCN). The latter materials are, however, seldom used internally.

Another problem occurs if the insulating materials contain halogenated additives, i.e. chlorine, bromine or fluorine compounds (frequently used as flame retardants). Besides the corrosive effects of the fumes – mostly caused by the formation of hydrogen chloride (HCl) –, highly toxic polychlorinated dibenzodioxins or dibenzofurans (PCDD/PCDF) occur during a fire, which rain down as soot and ashes and therefore raise the cost of refurbishment substantially.
Various commercially produced synthetic foam pipe lagging products contain halogenated constituents, for example. For this reason, zero-halogen insulating materials should be used in buildings whenever possible. The products should carry corresponding declarations.

Economic dimension

The protection aim here is the long-term safeguarding of the capital invested. There is a close tie between the cost of building and maintenance on the one hand and the environmental impacts on the other because in both cases the same materials are behind the causes. Every product to be installed in a building can be described in terms of its material costs and – with the help of LCAs – the environmental impacts linked with its production. The quantity of material required is crucial in both cases. This organizational correlation is so obvious in construction processes that the costs and the ecological effects are already implemented side by side in software tools for planning, tenders and construction. With the help of the LCA data stored in such programs for each building material, it is possible to obtain information about the status of the overall life cycle situation of a building at any time of its life. The respective degree of accuracy is the same as that for the cost calculation. Looked at in this way, sustainable building is at the same time cost-effective building because in the long-term it saves material.

The interface between the ecological and the economic considerations is formed by the anticipated durability of a building component. Appropriate assumptions have always been necessary for this, whether for operating costs calculations, life cycle costs (LCC) or for the standardised times of the LCAs. Figures for this can be found in, for example, the commentary to the German Valuation Act (WertV) by Rössler, Langner and Simon, 8th edition, 2005. This publication mainly specifies anticipated lifetimes for building components, taking into account the materials used, in the form of average or "from-to" values. Owing to the ecological importance, the appendix to the "Guidelines for Sustainable Construction" published by the Federal Ministry of Transport, Building & Urban Affairs contains a list of durabilities that can be assumed. Similar tables for taking into account the renewal cycles of individual building components or layers have been prepared within the framework of estimates of operating costs.
In reality, the anticipated durability of a component depends on numerous factors and often exhibits a wide spectrum,

Selection of durabilities for insulating materials in building components

Cost group			Building component	Average value (in years)	Value optimised through quality assurance (in years)
332			**Non-loadbearing external walls**		
	332.3		Insulation		
		332.3.1	Cellulose fibres	35	50
		332.3.2	Mineral wool	40	50
335			**External wall cladding, outside**		
	335.5		Thermal insulation, with ventilation cavity		
		335.5.1	Wood fibres	30	50
		335.5.2	Insulation cork board	50	60
		335.5.3	Mineral wool	40	50
	335.6		Thermal insulation, composite system		
		335.6.1	Wood fibres	20	30
		335.6.2	Insulation cork board	40	40
		335.6.3	Calcium silicate foam	40	40
		335.6.4	Mineral wool	30	30
		335.6.5	Polystyrene, expanded (EPS)	30	30
363			**Roof coverings**		
	363.6		Roof insulation, warm deck		
		363.6.1	Cellulose fibres	30	50
		363.6.2	Mineral wool	40	60
		363.6.4	Polystyrene, expanded (EPS)	40	50
	363.7		Roof insulation, upside-down roof		
		363.7.1	Cellular glass	80	80
		363.7.2	Polystyrene, expanded (EPS)	30	30

1

2

which cannot be assessed realistically with simple average values. Important influences on durability that should be regarded as optimisation criteria are:

- quality assurance and sustainability of technical functions,
- ease of maintenance and repair,
- flexibility of the constructions in terms of usage,
- restricting the diversity of materials (material-saving forms of construction),
- detachable connections, the avoidance of composite assemblies and recyclability.

Owing to the great economic and ecological significance, trade associations for individual product groups have developed various prognosis methods for durability.
Besides the essentially empirical general estimates, there is one specific method described in ISO 15686 "Buildings and constructed assets – Service life planning". Parts 1 and 3 of this standard have already been published, parts 2, 4, 5 and 6 exist as drafts or are still in preparation. A research project organised by the Federal Office for Building & Regional Planning[1], drew up optimisation targets for building components in 2006. These take into account specific damage risks and a corresponding quality assurance for the detailed planning and construction. As expected, it was shown that fully concealed insulating components such as external basement insulation, cavity insulation in solid walls or impact sound insulation represent only minimal risks of damage and, consequently, demonstrate only minimal optimisation options. Exter-

[1] Research project of the Federal Office for Building & Regional Planning (project No. 03.125): "Tools for quality-related estimates of the durability of materials and forms of construction", Gesellschaft für ökologische Bautechnik mbH, Berlin, 2006

nal walls and roofs, on the other hand, present clear opportunities for optimisation, which depends on the particular form of construction.
The importance of such optimisation processes can be seen in the example of material group 363.6.1 "cellulose fibres in roof insulation" (table 1). Only prefabricated timber panel elements factory-filled with cellulose flakes were investigated here, which means that the risk of subsequent settlement can be avoided. In situ, blown cellulose fibre insulation was not investigated owing to the uncertainties involved with this type of installation. The fundamental damage potential for the layer of insulation is essentially based on the risk of saturation should the outer rainproof covering or the inner vapour barrier develop defects. This is where the main optimisation potential is to be found. Permanent protection against moisture from outside and inside (condensation) is a prerequisite for avoiding subsequent damage to the loadbearing timber construction caused by fungi and mould. The optimisation measures are to be found primarily in the quality assurance for the production processes. These aspects are, for example, the object of the RAL GZ 422 quality assurance scheme for timber houses. The prolonging of the expected durability by 20 years derived from observations of damage leads to considerable improvements in the calculation of the operating costs and the ecological impacts.

Sustainable use of insulating materials

In normal cases it can be assumed that approved insulating materials installed properly will not lead to any risks for occupants or the environment. As already shown, insulating measures generally result in a payoff in terms of energy and economics. As the impact on the environment and the available resources depends on the quantity of material installed, the main components, at least for large construction projects, should be subjected to a comparative impact assessment which includes the most important categories of the life cycle assessment.
The work involved is too great for small construction projects with small amounts of materials. In such instances, ecological and economic optimisation means comparing the desired functions of the building components carefully with the respective properties of the insulating materials and making sure that these match up. For example, the particular properties of insulation cork board are fully utilised – with respect to its resistance to moisture and infestation and the associated durability – when it is employed for insulating joist or beam bearings, as cavity insulation in masonry or as impact sound insulation. The high price is justifiable in such applications. Cellulose in its ecologically favourable application as flakes without any synthetic fibres is ideal for factory-filled timber panel elements. Due to their combination of strength, incombustibility, insulating performance, moisture properties and easily skim-coated surface, calcium silicate foam boards are particularly good for internal insulation where mechanical loads are to be expected. Despite their high price, they are therefore being used more and more in underground car parks. Insulating materials should always be chosen and specified carefully, even for small projects. During the selection process, besides investigating the respective technical approvals, a check can be carried out to establish whether the insulating material has any special properties that are irrelevant for the building component under consideration. In such cases, an ecologically optimised alternative material with a suitable properties profile can be considered. It is also advisable to question whether the insulating material selected requires special protective measures, e.g. against moisture, animal or plant pests or emission of fibres. If this is the case, the use of materials and energy should be questioned critically for these measures.

Even if the use of insulating materials is worthwhile in terms of energy and economics, the individual materials are very different in terms of the energy consumed during their production and the associated environmental risks.
The method shown here for the ecological assessment of building materials enables these differences to be identified and evaluated, and the intrinsic optimisation potential to be exploited.

1 A quality management system for improving the durability of building components has been drawn up in a research project of the Federal Office for Building & Regional Planning.For insulating materials in external walls and roofs, considering specific damage risks and a corresponding quality assurance system for the detailed planning and construction results in considerable opportunities for optimisation, which can prolong the lifetime of the materials by 10 to 20 years. This leads to marked improvements in the costs for building maintenance and in the life cycle assessment.
2 Board made from bitumenised polystyrene beads.

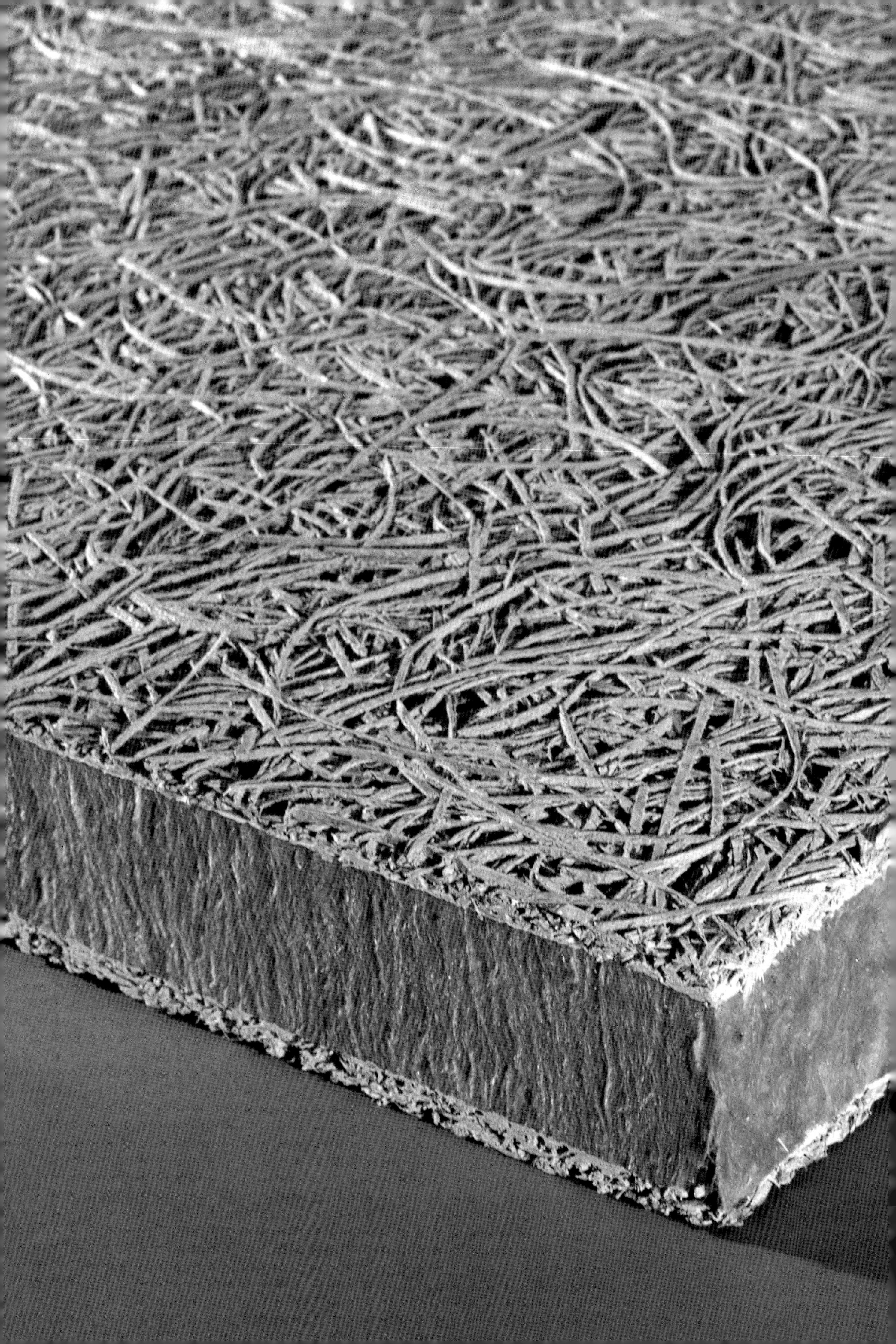

Trade associations (selection)

ADNR Arbeitsgemeinschaft für Dämmstoffe aus natürlichen Rohstoffen e.V. (natural insulating materials)
www.adnr.info

BLP Bundesverband der Leichtbauplattenindustrie e.V. (WW, WW-C)
www.leichtbauplatten.de

Fachverband Schaumstoffe (plastic foams)
www.fsk-vsv.de/en/index.html

Fachverband Strohballenbau (straw bales)
www.fasba.de

Fachverband Transparente Wärmedämmung (transparent insulation)
www.umwelt-wand.de

Fachverband Wärmedämmverbundsysteme (thermal insulation composite systems)
www.heizkosten-einsparen.de

FPX Fachvereinigung Polystyrol Extruderschaumstoff (XPS)
www.fpx-daemmstoffe.de

FMI Fachverband Mineralwolleindustrie e.V. (MW)
www.fmi-mineralfaser.de

FNR Fachagentur Nachwachsende Rohstoffe (renewable resources)
www.fnr.de

GDI Gesamtverband Dämmstoffindustrie (insulation umbrella organisation)
www.gdi-daemmstoffe.de

GSH Güteschutzgemeinschaft Hartschaum e.V. (EPS, PUR)
www.gsh.eu

IVH Industrieverband Hartschaum (PS)
www.ivh.de

Internationaler Verband der Naturtextilwirtschaft e.V. (natural textiles)
www.naturtextil.com

IVPU Industrieverband Polyurethan-Hartschaum e.V. (PUR)
www.ivpu.de

VDH Verband Holzfaserdämmstoffe (WF)
www.holzfaser.org

Directory of manufacturers and suppliers (selection)

aprithan Schaumstoff-GmbH (PUR/PIR)
www.aprithan.de

ARMACELL GMBH (PE, PP)
www.armacell.de

AUSTROTHERM GmbH (EPS, XPS)
www.austrotherm.com

AWA GmbH (PIR, EPS)
www.awa-dachbaustoffwerke.de

KARL BACHL GmbH & Co. KG (EPS, XPS, PUR, perlite)
www.bachl.de

BASF (EPS, XPS)
www.basf.de

Bauder (PUR/PIR)
www.bauder.de

Bayer MaterialScience AG (PUR/PIR, PUR in situ foam)
www.bayer.de

Biber Baustoffe GmbH (cellulose)
www.biber-online.de

Gebr. Brohlburg Kunststoffwerk (EPS)
www.brohlburg.de

Calsitherm Silikatbaustoffe GmbH & Co. KG (silicate foam)
www.calsitherm.de

Celotex Limited (PUR/PIR)
www.celotex.co.uk

Daemwool Naturdämmstoffe GmbH (sheep's wool)
www.daemwool.at

Doscha Wolle (sheep's wool)
www.doschawolle.de

Eiwa Lehm GmbH (reed)
www.eiwa-lehmbau.de

Elastogran GmbH (PUR/PIR, PUR in situ foam)
www.elastogran.de

Fibo Exclay (expanded clay)
www.fiboexclay.de

Fibrolith (WW, WW-C)
www.fibrolith.de

Flachshaus (flax)
www.flachshaus.de

Foamglas (cellular glass)
www.foamglas.de

GLAPOR Werk Mitterteich GmbH (cellular glass)
www.glapor.com

Gonon Isolation AG (EPS, PUR, PF, XPS)
www.gonon.ch

Gutex (WF)
www.gutex.de

Heraklith (MW, WF)
www.heraklith.de

Hock Vertriebs GmbH & Co. KG (hemp)
www.thermo-hanf.de

Homatherm (WF, cellulose)
www.homatherm.com

IsoBouw Dämmtechnik GmbH (EPS)
www.isobouw.de

Isocotton (cotton)
www.isocotton.de

Isofloc (cellulose)
www.isofloc.de

Isola (MW, vermiculite)
www.isola-mineralwolle.de

Isolahn GmbH (UF in situ foam)
www.isolahn.de

Isover (MW, EPS, XPS)
www.isover.de

Jackon Insulation GmbH (XPS)
www.jackon-insulation.com

JOMA-Dämmstoffwerk GmbH (EPS)
www.joma.de

Wilhelm Kaimann GmbH & Co. KG (PE, PUR)
www.kaimann.de

Kingspan Insulation (PIR, PF)
www.kingspan.com

Knauf (EPS, XPS, perlite)
www.knauf.de

KORFF & Co. KG Isolierbaustoffe
(MW, PUR, XPS, MF)
www.korff.com

Lackfa Isolierstoff GmbH & Co. (PUR/PIR, PUR in situ foam)
www.lackfa.com

Liapor (expanded clay, foamed glass)
www.liapor.com

Meha Dämmstoffe GmbH
(PF, perlite, WF)
www.meha.de

MISAPOR (cellular glass)
www.misapor.de

E. MISSEL GmbH & Co. KG (PE)
www.missel.de

Nestaan Holland B.V. (PUR/PIR, PUR in situ foam)
www.nestaan.nl

PAROC (MW)
www.paroc.de

Pavatex (WF)
www.pavatex.de

PHILIPPINE GmbH & Co. (EPS)
www.philippine.de

pinta acoustic (melamine resin, PUR, foamed glass)
www.pinta-acoustic.de

poratec GmbH Dämmstoffsysteme (mineral foam)
www.poratec.de

Poraver (foamed glass)
www.poraver.de

Puren (PUR/PIR)
www.puren.com

Porextherm Dämmstoffe GmbH (VIP)
www.porextherm.de

ReadyTherm Maschinen-Dämmung GmbH (UF in situ foam)
Tel.: +49 (0)201 4500-20
Fax: +49 (0)201 4500-216

RECTICEL Dämmsysteme (PUR/PIR)
www.recticel-daemmsysteme.de

Rigips (EPS, XPS)
www.rigips.de

Rockwool (MW)
www.rockwool.de

Romonta Ceralith GmbH (cereal granulate)
www.ceralith.de

RYGOL DÄMMSTOFFE (EPS)
www.rygol.com

Schaum Chemie (UF, PUR)
www.schaum-chemie.de

SCHWENK Dämmtechnik (EPS, XPS, WF)
www.schwenk.de

Steico AG (WF, hemp)
www.steico.com

STEINBACHER Dämmstoffe (EPS)
www.steinbacher.at

swisspor AG (EPS, XPS, PUR, MW)
www.swisspor.ch

The Dow Chemical Company (XPS)
www.dow.com

Thermal Ceramics (ceramic fibres)
ww.thermalceramics.com

Thermo Hanf (hemp)
www.thermo-hanf.de

thermo-plastic Eiberger GmbH (EPS, PUR, MW, hemp)
www.thermo-plastic.de

UNIDEK Deutschland GmbH (EPS, PE)
www.unidek.de

URSA (MW, XPS)
www.ursa.de

va-Q-tec (VIP)
www.va-q-tec.com

VARIOTEC GmbH & CO. KG (VIP)
www.variotec.de

VWS-Ergotherm GmbH & Co (EPS)
www.caparol.de

WKI Isoliertechnik (EPS)
www.wki.de

Xella (mineral foam)
www.xella.de

Bibliography (selection)

Achtziger J., Zehendner H.: Wärmedämmstoffe. In: Bauphysik-Kalender 2001, pp. 189–222. Berlin, Ernst & Sohn, 2001.

EOTA – technical report 025: Determination of point thermal transmittance of plastic anchors for the anchorage of external thermal insulation composite systems (ETICS); TR025 final draft, Berlin, 6 Dec 2006.

Gellert, R.: Dämmen mit Hartschaumkunststoffen; Bauen mit Kunststoffen; yearbook 2002, Ernst & Sohn, 2001.

Hegger, R., et al.: Construction Materials Manual, Birkhäuser, 2006.

Merkel, H. Boy, E.: Langzeitverhalten von extrudierten Polystyrol-Hartschaumstoffen im Umkehrdach – Erfahrungen aus Praxisobjekten; Deutsches Architektenblatt, No. 9/1996.

Oswald, R.: Langzeitverhalten von Parkdecks mit Umkehrdach-Wärmedämmung – Floormate; report, June 1998, for DOW Deutschland Inc.

Spitzner M. H.: Dachsanierung von außen – Anforderungen und Hinweise. infodienst Holz, Nos. 11 & 12/2005.

Sprengard C.: Wärmebrückenkatalog der Wissensdatenbank zum Pilotprojekt "Niedrigenergiehaus im Bestand" der dena, Deutsche Energieagentur, Berlin, 2003; www.neh-im-bestand.de – Wissensdatenbank – Bauteile.

Steimle P.: Energieeffizientes Bauen – Wärmedämmung ist der erste Schritt – Dämmstoffe im Überblick. Ed. GDI Gesamtverband Dämmstoffindustrie. Frankfurt, 2004.

Zimmermann, G.: Gutachten über das Langzeitverhalten extrudierter Hartschaumplatten Floormate 500 in Umkehr-Parkdächern, Oct 1997, for DOW Deutschland Inc.

Index

Picture credits

The authors and publishers would like to express their sincere gratitude to all those who have assisted in the production of this book, be it through providing photos or artwork or granting permission to reproduce their documents or providing other information. All the drawings in this book were specially commissioned. Photographs not specifically credited were taken by the architects or are works photographs or were supplied from the archives of the magazine DETAIL. Despite intensive endeavours we were unable to establish copyright ownership in just a few cases; however, copyright is assured. Please notify us accordingly in such instances.

page 10, 47:
isofloc – Wärmedämmtechnik GmbH, Lohfelden

page 14, 33 centre, 48 left, 48 right:
Hock GmbH & Co. KG, Nördlingen

page 22, 24, 30, 34 left, 36, 38, 44, 46, 50 left, 57 left:
Frank Kaltenbach, Munich

page 26:
Dennert Poraver GmbH, Schlüsselfeld

page 27:
Caparol Farben & Lacke, Ober-Ramstadt

page 28 left, 29:
Silca GmbH, Mettmann

page 31 left, 31 right, 49, 100, 104:
Alexander Rudolphi, Berlin

page 32:
Liapor, Hallerndorf-Pautzfeld

page 33 left:
Erich Gormann, Stolberg

page 33 right:
Schlagmann GmbH & Co. KG, Zeilarn

page 35, 39, 56:
BASF AG, Ludwigshafen

page 40 left:
Elastogran GmbH, Lemförde

page 40 right, 81:
Industrieverband Polyurethan-Hartschaum e.V., Stuttgart

page 41:
Thermal Ceramics, Reinbek

page 62 right, 65, 70, 72:
FIW, Munich

page 45 left:
Holzabsatzfonds, Bonn

page 45 right:
Kazunori Hiruta, Tokyo, Japan

page 50 right, 52 right:
Kaufmann Massivholz GmbH, Oberstadion

page 52 left:
from: Willems, Schild, Dinter: Vieweg Handbuch Bauphysik Teil 1 – Wärme- und Feuchteschutz, Behaglichkeit, Lüftung. Vieweg Verlag, Wiesbaden, 2006

page 53:
Bau-Fritz GmbH, Erkheim

page 54:
Dirk Scharmer, Lüneburg

page 55 bottom:
MCA/Daniele Domenicali

page 57 centre, 57 right:
Carsten Grobe, Hannover

page 74 top left:
Güteschutzgemeinschaft Hartschaum e.V., Celle

page 74 top centre, 74 top right:
Bundesverband der Leichtbauindustrie e.V., Heidelberg

page 75 left, 102:
Deutsches Institut für Gütesicherung & Kennzeichnung e.V., Sankt Augustin

page 75 centre:
European Committee for Standardization, Brussels, Belgium

page 75 right:
Überwachungsgemeinschaft Polyurethan-Hartschaum e.V., Stuttgart

page 101:
ALAB, Berlin

page 103:
Deutsche Foamglas GmbH, Haan

Full-page plates
page 6:
Alexander Rudolphi, Berlin

page 16, 58:
BASF AG, Ludwigsburg

page 76:
Christian Richters, Münster

page 92:
Christian Schittich, Munich

page 106:
Frank Kaltenbach, Munich